A MATHEMATICAL dictionary for schools

Brian Bolt
David Hobbs
School of Education, University of Exeter

CAMBRIDGE
UNIVERSITY PRESS

PUBLISHED BY THE PRESS SYNDICATE OF THE UNIVERSITY OF CAMBRIDGE
The Pitt Building, Trumpington Street, Cambridge CB2 1RP, United Kingdom

CAMBRIDGE UNIVERSITY PRESS
The Edinburgh Building, Cambridge CB2 2RU, United Kingdom
40 West 20th Street, New York, NY 10011-4211, USA
10 Stamford Road, Oakleigh, Melbourne 3166, Australia

First published 1998

Printed in the United Kingdom at the University Press, Cambridge

Typeset in Times 10/12 pt.

A catalogue record for this book is available from the British Library

ISBN 0 521 55657 0 paperback

Designed by Marcus Askwith
Illustrations by Hardlines

To the reader

This book has been written to help you understand some of the words and phrases which you will come across in learning mathematics at school. We have tried to make the explanations easy to understand, by giving you the basic principles and including illustrations and examples rather than just bare definitions.

In the main you will probably use the book for reference to words you are unsure of or do not understand, but you will also find it useful for revision. You may well find new ideas to interest you which can be followed up with your teacher or in other books. Cross-referencing is done in two ways. Words in red have their own entries elsewhere in the book. Related words which you might also look up are given at the end of an explanation.

Brian Bolt and David Hobbs

School of Education, University of Exeter

Acceleration

Acceleration is the rate at which **speed** changes in a given direction:

$$\frac{\text{change of speed}}{\text{time taken}}$$

When speed is measured in metres per second and time in seconds, acceleration is in (metres per second) per second, usually written as

metres per second^2 or m/s^2 or m s^{-2}

For example, if the speed of a car travelling along a straight road increases steadily from 7 metres per second to 13 metres per second in 2 seconds, then the acceleration of the car in the direction of the road is

$$\frac{\text{change of speed}}{\text{time taken}} = \frac{13-7}{2} = 3 \text{ m s}^{-2}$$

When a heavy object falls under gravity, its speed increases by about 10 m s^{-1} every second, so it has an acceleration of 10 m s^{-2} downwards.

Acceleration, like **velocity**, is a **vector** quantity.

Accuracy of measurement

When a set of objects is being counted, the result is exact. But when something is being measured, the result is rarely exact. It depends on the scale of the instrument being used and the purpose of the measurement.

For example, international 100 m athletics races are timed to the nearest $\frac{1}{100}$th of a second.

If a pin is measured using a ruler and its length is given as 2.3 cm, then its length is not exactly 2.3 cm but will be between 2.25 cm and 2.35 cm (usually interpreted as 2.25 cm $\leq$ length $<$ 2.35 cm).

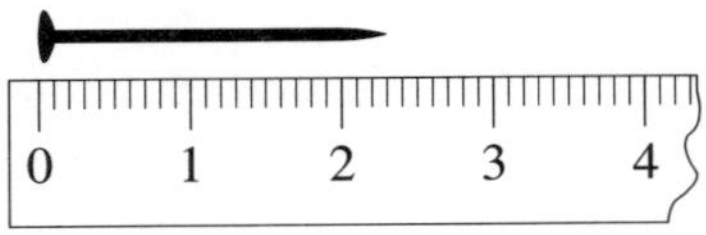

When a measurement is expressed using a given unit, the greatest possible *error* is half of that unit.

See **Approximation**, **Decimal places** and **Significant figures**.

Acre

An acre is a unit of **area** equal to 4840 square yards.

Acute angle

An acute angle is an **angle** whose size is between 0° and 90°.

Acute-angled triangle

This is a **triangle** whose angles are all **acute angles**.

Adjacent angles

Angles which have the same **vertex** and a line in common are called adjacent angles.

When two adjacent angles lie on a straight line, their sum is 180°.

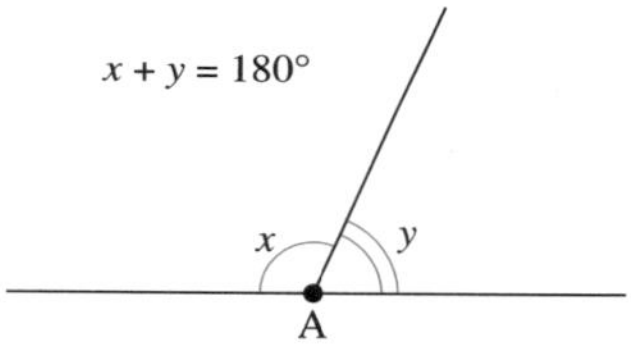

Adjacent sides

Two sides of a **polygon** which have a common **vertex**, such as BA and BC, are called adjacent.

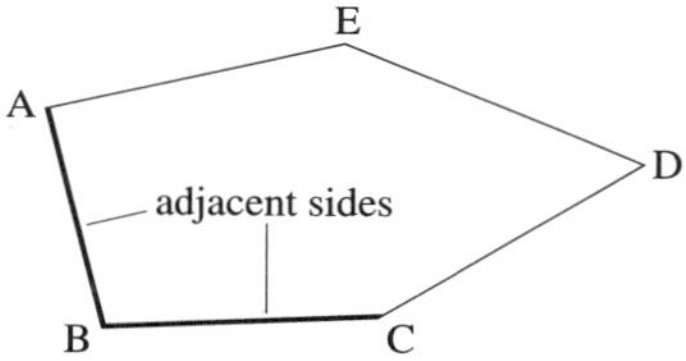

Algebra

Algebra is the branch of mathematics which uses letters and symbols to represent numbers or other mathematical objects, and the relationships between them. The word *algebra* comes from the Arabic words *al* (meaning 'the') and *jahr* (meaning 'joined together').

Algorithm

An algorithm is a systematic step-by-step process which leads to a conclusion. Here is an example.

To find the **highest common factor** of 24 and 60:

First express each as a product of **prime numbers**.

$24 = 2 \times 2 \times 2 \times 3$ $\quad$ $60 = 2 \times 2 \times 3 \times 5$

Next pick out the **prime factors** common to both.
Then multiply these common prime factors together.

$2 \times 2 \times 3 = 12$

Alternate angles

The alternate angles p and q are equal.

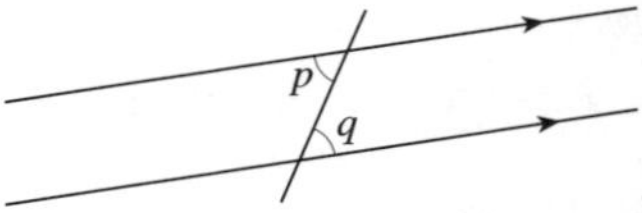

■ See **Parallel lines** and **Transversal**.

Altitude of a triangle

The line AN drawn from a **vertex** A of a **triangle** to meet the **opposite side** at **right angles** is called an altitude of the triangle.

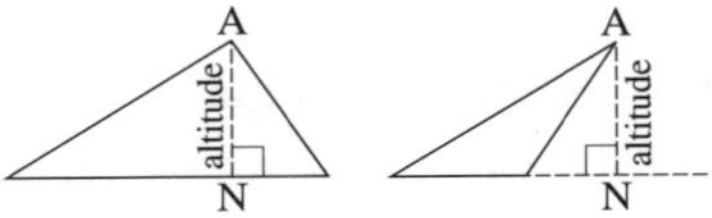

The three altitudes of a triangle meet each other at the same point, H, called the *orthocentre* of the triangle.

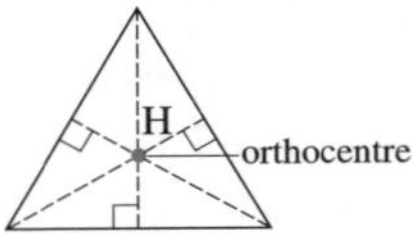

Angle

An angle is a measure of the amount of turning between two directions. For example, the minute hand of a clock turns through one-third of a revolution in 20 minutes; to turn from facing north to facing west you would turn through a quarter of a revolution **anti-clockwise**.

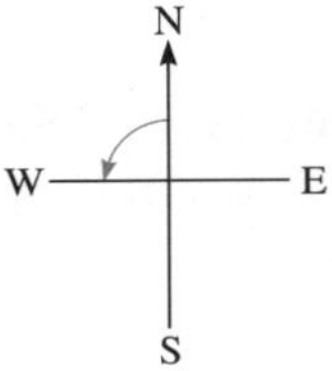

The angle between two lines is the amount of turn required to rotate one of the lines onto the other about their common point.

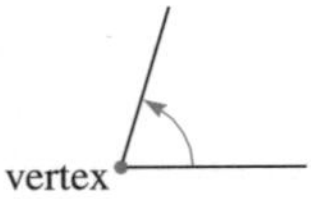

The term 'angle' is also used whenever two lines meet at a point, called the **vertex** of the angle. So, for example, a **triangle** has three angles. The angle at vertex A is referred to as ∠BAC, the angle at B as ∠ABC and the angle at C as ∠ACB.

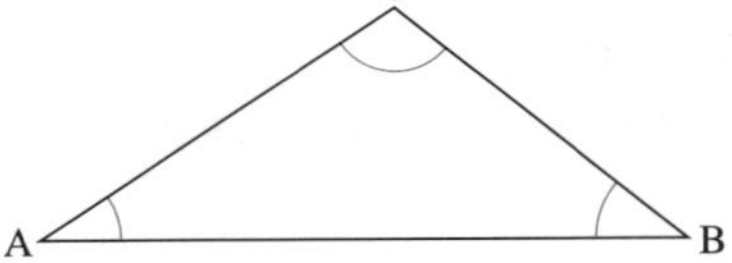

Angles are usually measured in **degrees** using a protractor or angle measurer. One complete turn is 360 degrees, usually written as 360°.

A quarter of a turn, known as a **right angle**, is equal to 90°.

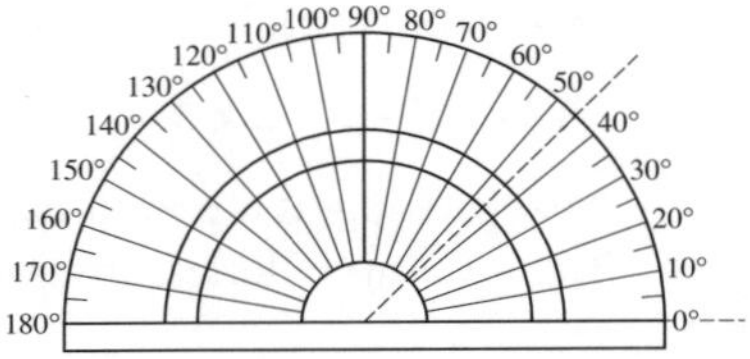

An acute angle is an angle whose size is between 0° and 90°.

An obtuse angle is an angle whose size is between 90° and 180°.

A reflex angle is an angle between 180° and 360°.

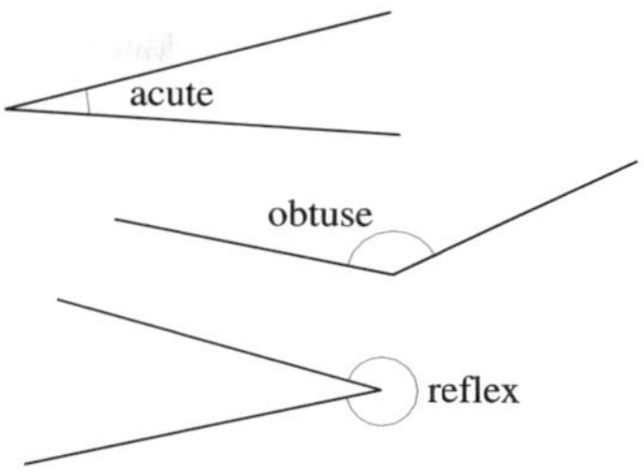

Angle bisector

See **Bisect** and **Construction**.

Angle of depression

The angle of depression of an object is the angle which the eye has to be lowered through from the horizontal in order to look at the object.

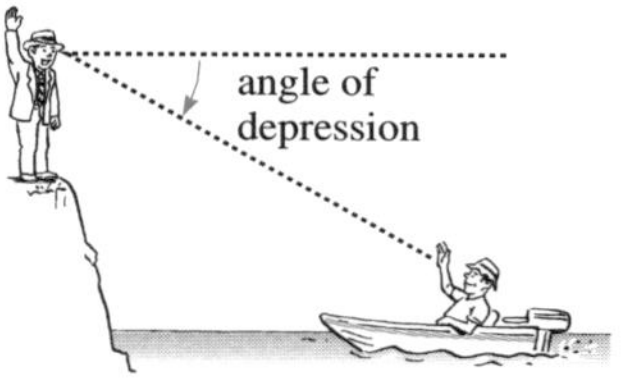

Angle of elevation

The angle of elevation of an object is the angle which the eye has to be raised through from the horizontal in order to look at the object.

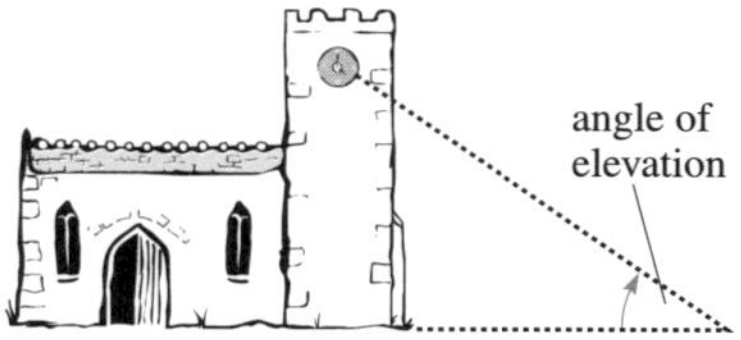

Anti-clockwise

The direction of a turn or rotation is said to be anti-clockwise if it is in the opposite direction to that in which the hands of a clock turn. An angle measured in this direction is considered to be positive.

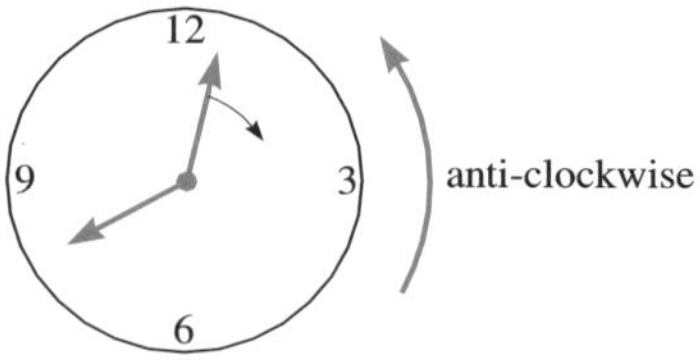

See **Clockwise**.

Apex

The apex is the tip or top of a figure or a building, labelled A in these diagrams.

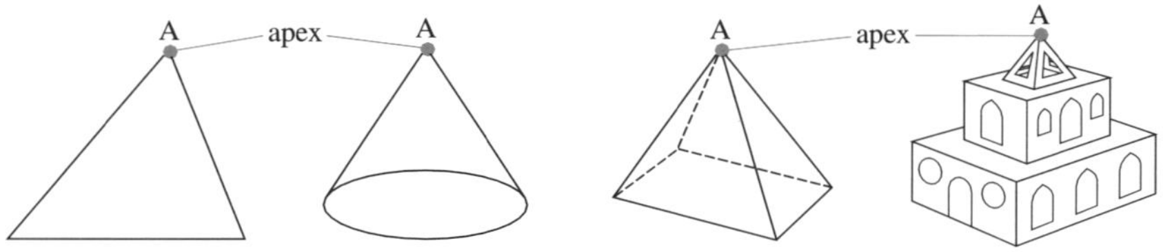

Approximation

Sometimes numbers and measurements are given approximately. For example, instead of giving the exact number of people (18 762) at a pop concert, a newspaper report may say that approximately 20 000 people were at the concert.

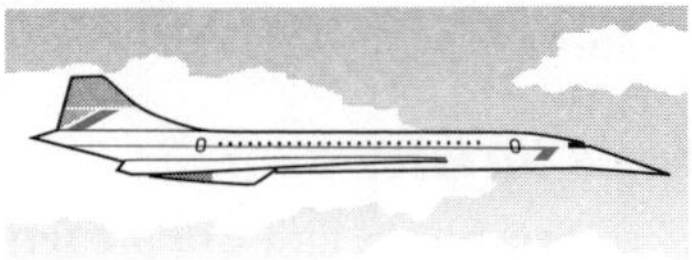

The average speed of a plane which travels 2073 miles in 3 hours is

$$\frac{2073}{3} = 691 \text{ mph}$$

For most purposes it would be sensible to give this as approximately 690 mph, or even 700 mph.

See also **Accuracy of measurement**, **Decimal places** and **Significant figures**.

Arc of a circle

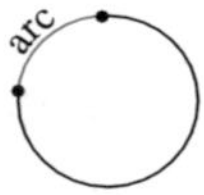

An arc of a circle is a part of its circumference.

See **Minor arc**.

Arc of a network

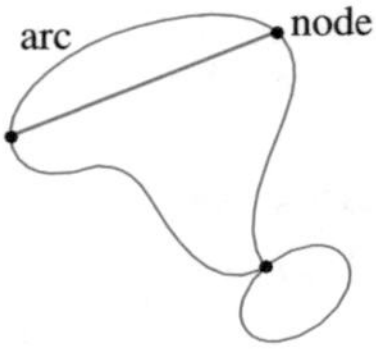

An arc of a network is any line (straight or curved) joining two nodes of the network. Exceptionally it may start and end at the same node. The network shown has 5 arcs and 3 nodes.

Area

The area of a region is the amount of space which it occupies. Area is normally measured using squares.

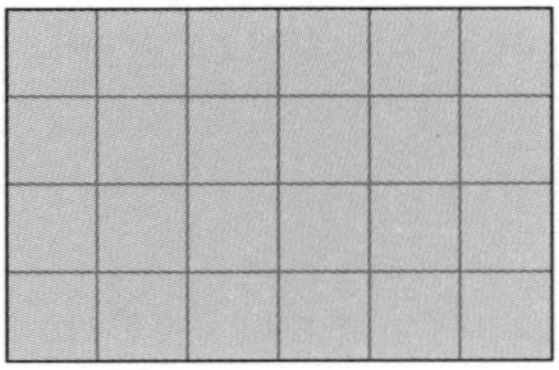

This rectangle has an area of 6 x 4 = 24 squares.

For small regions standard units of area are *square centimetres* and *square millimetres*.

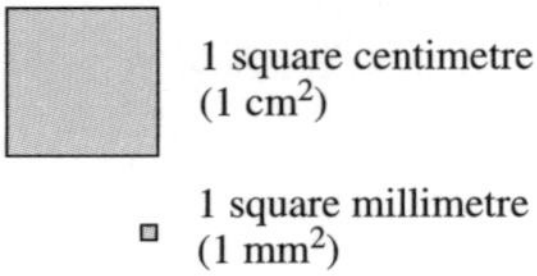

Large regions are measured in *square metres* (m^2) or *square kilometres* (km^2). Fields are usually measured in **hectares**, where 1 hectare equals 10 000 m^2, although the traditional unit was the *acre* equal to 4840 *square yards*, which is about half the area of a soccer pitch.

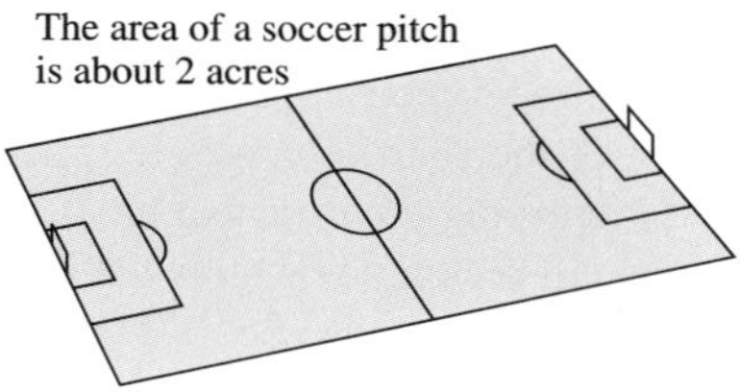

See **Centimetre**, **Kilometre**, **Metre**, **Millimetre** and **Yard**.

Area formulae

The area of a **rectangle** is calculated from the formula

length x breadth

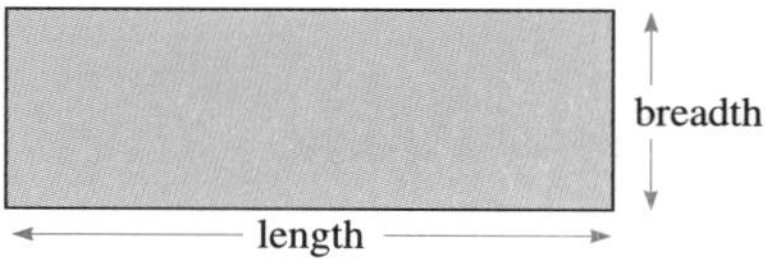

The area of a **parallelogram** is

base x perpendicular height

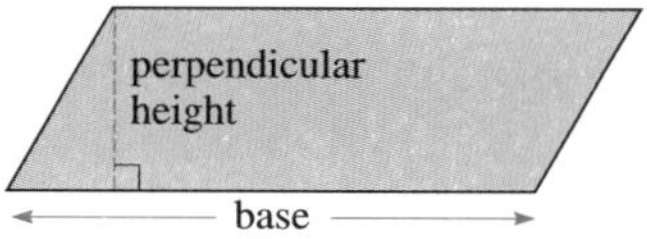

The area of a **triangle** is

$\frac{1}{2}$ (base x perpendicular height)

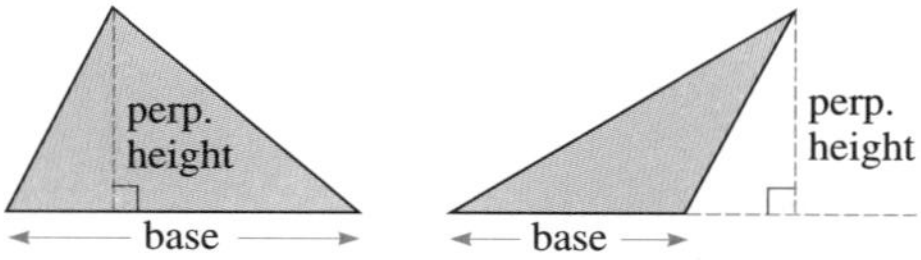

The area of a **trapezium** is

$\frac{1}{2}$ (sum of parallel sides x distance between parallel sides)

$= \frac{1}{2}(a + b)\,d$

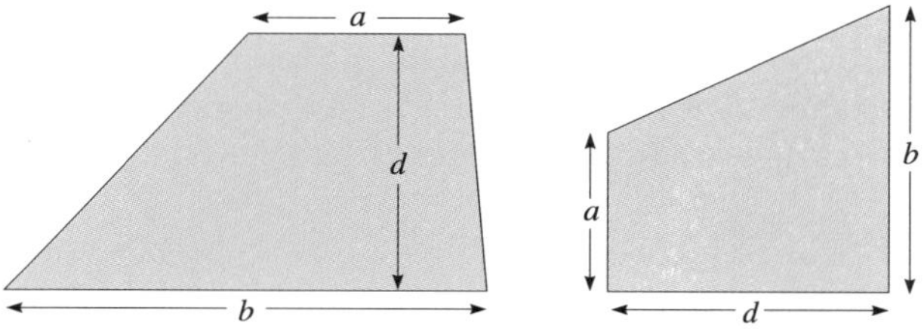

The area of a **circle** is

$\pi(\text{radius})^2 = \pi r^2$

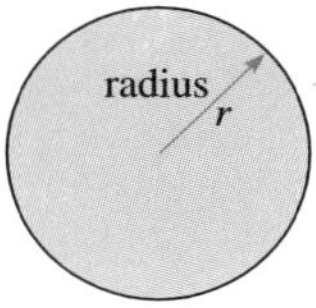

Area scale factor

When the dimensions of a shape are all enlarged by a linear scale factor k, the area of the shape changes by a scale factor of k^2. The example shows the effect of increasing the dimensions of a rectangle by factors of 2, 3 and 4. The number of small rectangles which can be fitted into the enlarged rectangles shows the area scale factors to be 4, 9 and 16.

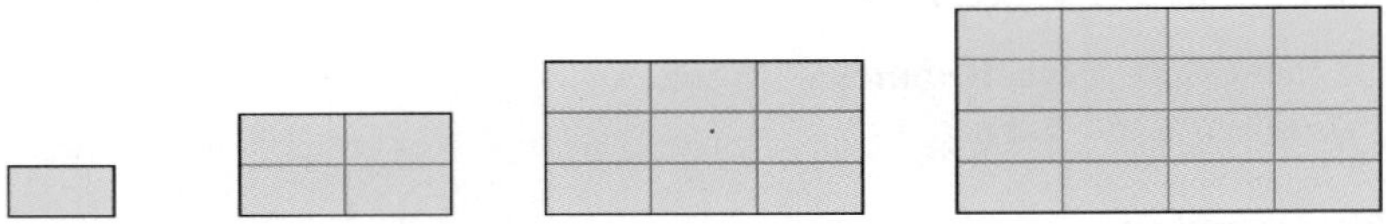

■ See **Enlargement** and **Volume scale factor**.

Area under a graph

The area from A to B below the graph and above the x-axis is called the area under the graph from A to B.

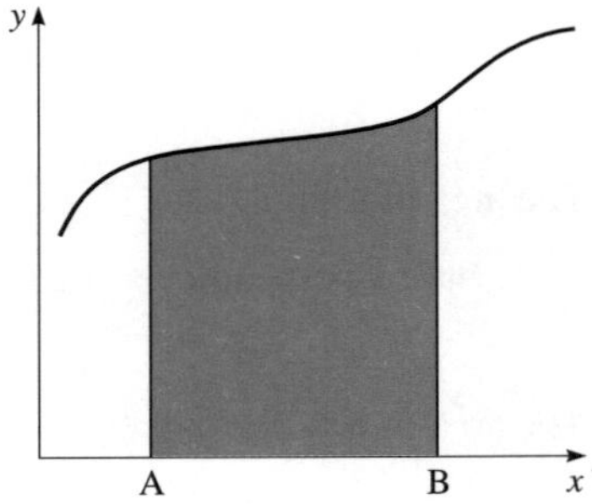

For a speed/time graph the area under the graph gives the distance travelled between the two times.

Arithmetic mean

■ See **Average**.

Arithmetic modulo *n*

■ See **Modulo arithmetic**.

Arrowhead

An arrowhead is a quadrilateral with two pairs of adjacent sides equal in length, and one of whose interior angles is a reflex angle. The diagonal through this angle is a line of symmetry for the shape.

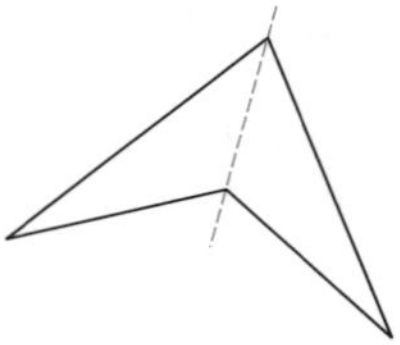

■ See **Kite**.

Associative

12 x 6 x 2 gives the same result 144, whether it is calculated as (12 x 6) x 2 or 12 x (6 x 2).

But 12 ÷ 6 ÷ 2 is not so straight forward, as (12 ÷ 6) ÷ 2 is 1, but 12 ÷ (6 ÷ 2) is 4.

An **operation** $*$ is associative if, when three elements are combined, it does not matter how the brackets are placed:

$$(a * b) * c \quad = \quad a * (b * c)$$

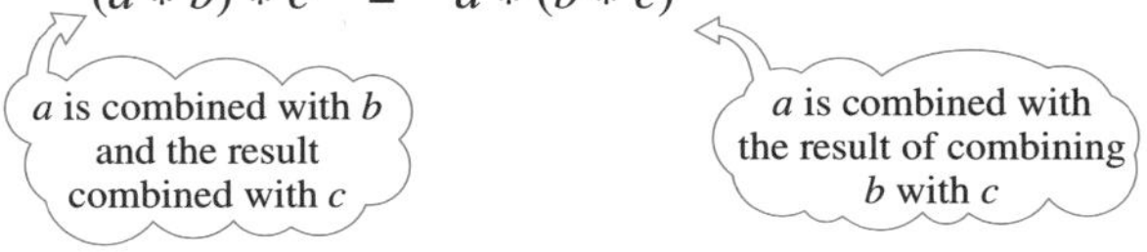
a is combined with b and the result combined with c
a is combined with the result of combining b with c

So multiplication is associative but division is not. Similarly the following examples illustrate that addition is associative but that subtraction is not.

$$(12 + 6) + 2 = 20 = 12 + (6 + 2)$$
$$(12 - 6) - 2 = 4 \quad \text{but} \quad 12 - (6 - 2) = 8$$

Average

An average is a single number which is used to represent a collection of numerical **data**.

There are various types of average. Three averages which are commonly used are the *mean* (or *arithmetic mean*), the *median*, and the *mode*. These are defined and illustrated using the following example.

In a skittles match Tina scored
6, 5, 8, 12, 3, 5, 7, 7, 5 in her nine goes.

The *mean* is obtained by dividing the sum of all the data by the number of data.

$$(6 + 5 + 8 + 12 + 3 + 5 + 7 + 7 + 5) \div 9$$

This gives the mean as 6.44 to 2 decimal places. Note that this number is not obtainable as a score, but it represents Tina's skill at skittles on the day.

The *median* is the middle score if the scores are put in order of size:

3 5 5 5 6 7 7 8 12

The middle score in this set of data is the 5th number along, namely 6, so 6 is the median score. If there were an even number of scores, the median would be taken as the mean of the middle two scores.

The *mode* is the number which occurs most often. In this example, 5 is the most frequently occurring score, so 5 is the mode.

Axis (pl. axes)

Positions in two dimensions can be given using **coordinates** referred to two lines, the x-axis and the y-axis. These lines are called the axes. The point P has x-coordinate 2 and y-coordinate 3, and is recorded as (2, 3).

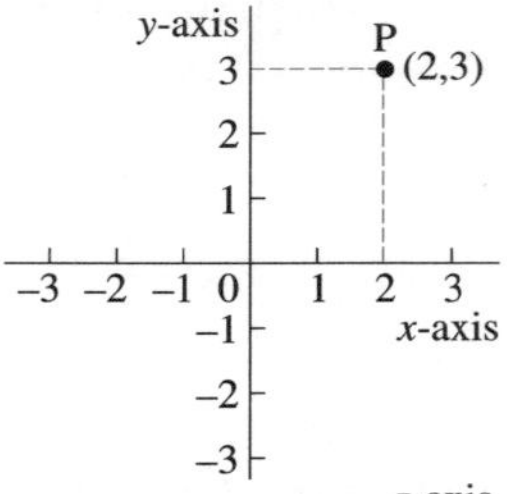

In three dimensions, three axes are required to specify the position of a point:
the x-axis, the y-axis, and the z-axis. The point Q has x-coordinate 3, y-coordinate 2, and z-coordinate 5, and is recorded as (3, 2, 5).

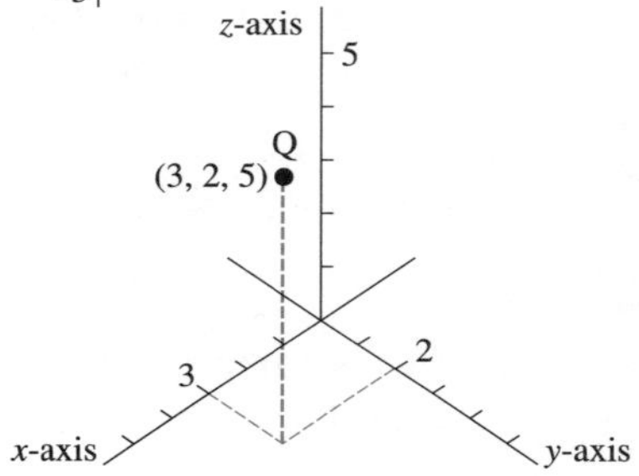

See **Coordinates**.

Axis of rotational symmetry

See **Rotational symmetry**.

Bar chart

A bar chart (or *block graph*) makes numerical information easy to see by showing it in a pictorial form.

In this bar chart, the height of each bar represents the average number of hours of sunshine per day for each month of the year in Athens.

Average number of hours of sunshine per day in Athens

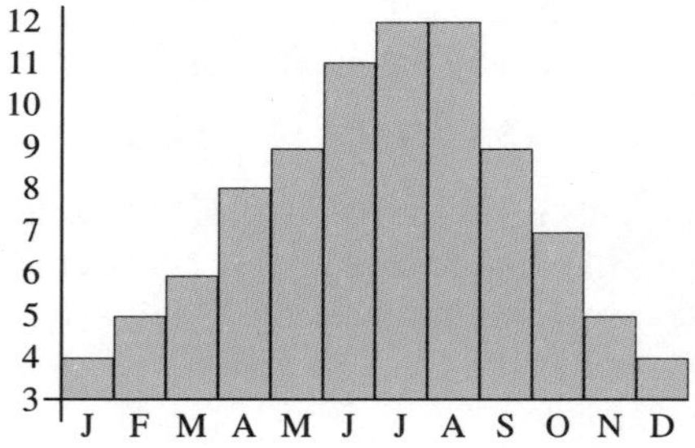

Base of a number

The numbers we use in everyday life are based on counting in tens. For example:

34 means 3 lots of ten and 4 ‘singles’ (units);

528 means 5 lots of a hundred (ten tens), 2 lots of ten and 8 units;

4916 means 4 lots of a thousand (ten hundreds), 9 lots of a hundred, 1 lot of ten and 6 units.

thousands	hundreds	tens	units
		3	4
	5	2	8
4	9	1	6

We count in base ten because we have ten fingers and thumbs. If we used only one hand we might count in groups of five (base five). Then this number of matchsticks could be written as 34_{five}, meaning 3 lots of five and 4 units.

412_{five} means 4 lots of twenty-five (five fives), 1 lot of five and 2 units.

In base five just the digits 0, 1, 2, 3, 4 are used.

34_{five} is the same as 19_{ten}. (In everyday life, when base ten is assumed, we normally write 19 rather than 19_{ten}.)

Counting could be done with groupings of any size. For example, computers work in base two.

See **Binary numbers**, **Duodecimal numbers** and **Hexadecimal numbers**.

Base of an object

The base of a three-dimensional object such as a pyramid or cone or cylinder is the face which it is resting on, normally its 'bottom' when it is the 'right way up'.

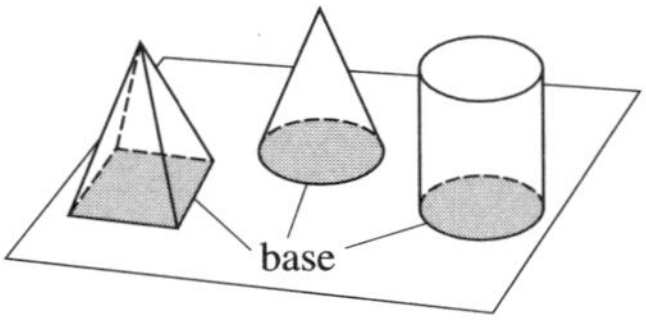

The base of a triangle is its bottom edge, AB in the diagram. But the triangle could be turned round to make BC or CA its bottom edge.

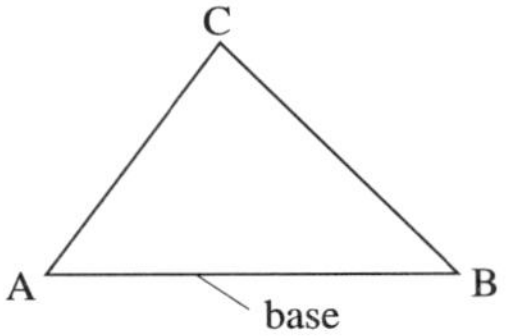

BASIC

BASIC is a computer language (Beginners All-purpose Symbolic Instruction Code). It was devised in the United States by J. G. Kemeny in 1964.

This program prints out triangle numbers.

```
10   INPUT N
20   T = 0
30   FOR C = 1 TO N
40   T = T + C
50   PRINT C, T
60   NEXT C
```

Bearing

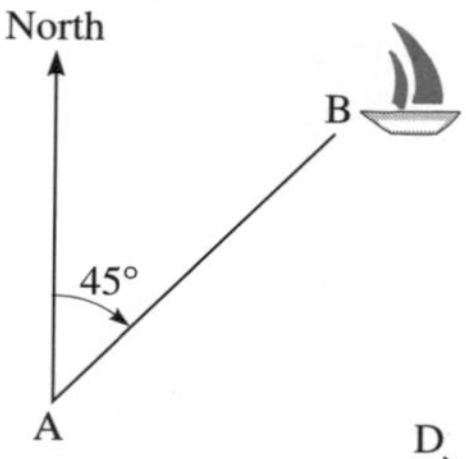

To find the bearing of an object B from a point A, imagine that you are standing at A facing north. Rotate **clockwise** until you are looking towards B. The angle through which you have rotated is the bearing of B from A.

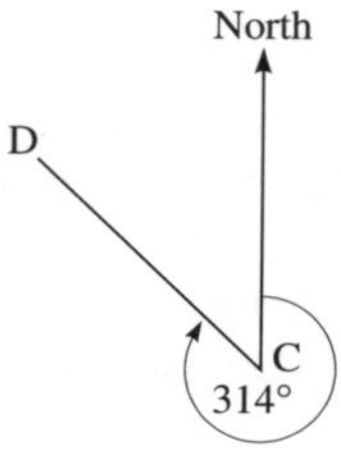

Bearings are always written with three digits. For example, in the first diagram, the bearing of B from A is 045°. The bearing of D from C is 314°.

Bilateral symmetry

See **Line symmetry** and **Symmetry**.

Billion

It is now usual for the word *billion* to mean a thousand **million** (1 000 000 000, often written 10^9). For example, the population of the world is about 5 billion. An older meaning of a billion is a million million (1 000 000 000 000 or 10^{12}).

Binary numbers

The word binary means 'composed of two'. Binary numbers are numbers in base two. They are written with two digits 0 and 1 using groupings of two, four (two twos), eight (two fours), etc. For example 1101_{two} stands for 1 eight, 1 four, 0 twos and 1 unit, which is 13 in base ten.

sixteens	eights	fours	twos	units
	1	1	0	1

Computers use binary numbers. In an electrical circuit, numbers can be represented by a current flowing (1) or not flowing (0).

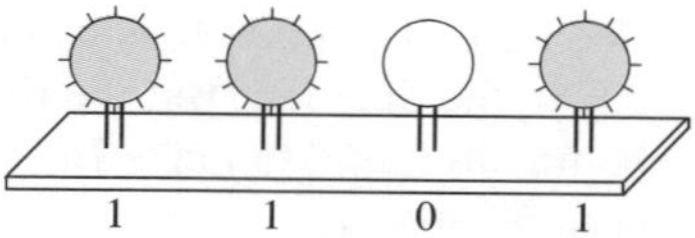

See **Base of a number**, **Duodecimal numbers** and **Hexadecimal numbers**.

Bisect, bisector

An **angle** is bisected when it is cut into two equal parts. For example, the angle AOB is bisected by the line OC. OC is called the *bisector*.

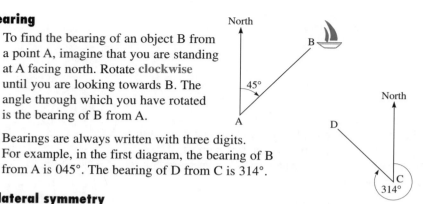

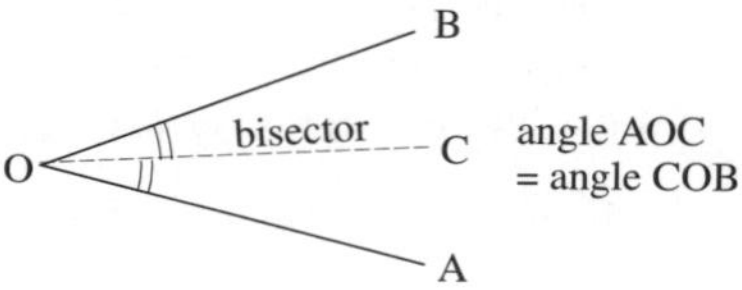

A line DE is bisected when it is cut into two equal parts. The line at **right angles** to DE through its mid-point M is called the *perpendicular bisector* of DE.

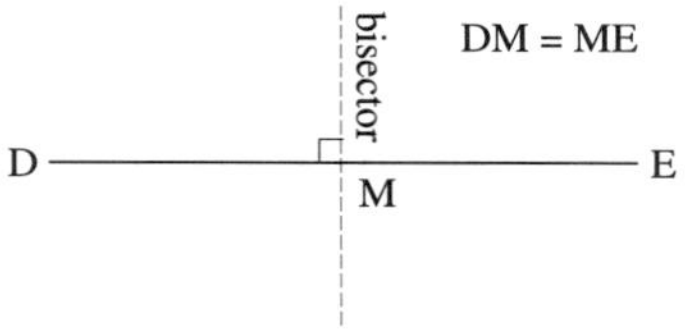

See **Construction** and **Perpendicular**.

Block graph

See **Bar chart**.

Brackets

Does 12 – 8 + 3 mean 4 + 3 which is 7, or 12 – 11 which is 1?
To avoid confusion brackets are used:

(12 – 8) + 3 means 4 + 3, which is 7;
12 – (8 + 3) means 12 – 11, which is 1.

The brackets show which numbers in a calculation are combined together. For example,

$$
\begin{aligned}
((4 \times 5) - 9) - (3 - 2) &= (20 - 9) - 1 \\
&= 11 - 1 \\
&= 10
\end{aligned}
$$

Brackets are used in algebra to group terms together. For example,

$$ax + bx + cx = (a + b + c)\,x$$

Cancel

The **fraction** $\frac{6}{8}$ can be cancelled down to give $\frac{3}{4}$ by dividing the top and bottom numbers by 2:

$$\frac{6}{8} \overset{\div 2}{=} \frac{3}{4} \quad (\text{top} \div 2,\ \text{bottom} \div 2)$$

$\frac{6}{8}$ and $\frac{3}{4}$ are said to be **equivalent fractions**.

The cancelling is often done like this:

$$\frac{\cancel{6}^{\,3}}{\cancel{8}_{\,4}}$$

Sometimes the cancelling is done in stages:

$$\frac{40}{100} \underset{\div 10}{\overset{\div 10}{=}} \frac{4}{10} \underset{\div 2}{\overset{\div 2}{=}} \frac{2}{5} \quad \text{or} \quad \frac{\cancel{40}\ \cancel{4}\ 2}{\cancel{100}\ \cancel{10}\ 5}$$

A **product** of fractions can be cancelled like this:

$$\frac{12}{35} \times \frac{14}{36} = \frac{\overset{1}{\cancel{12}}}{\underset{5}{\cancel{35}}} \times \frac{\overset{2}{\cancel{14}}}{\underset{3}{\cancel{36}}} = \frac{1 \times 2}{5 \times 3} = \frac{2}{15}$$

In the same way an algebraic fraction can be cancelled:

$$\frac{2a^2b}{6ab^3} = \frac{\overset{1}{\cancel{2}} \times \overset{1}{\cancel{a}} \times a \times \overset{1}{\cancel{b}}}{\underset{3}{\cancel{6}} \times \underset{1}{\cancel{a}} \times \underset{1}{\cancel{b}} \times b \times b} = \frac{a}{3b^2}$$

Capacity

The capac.ty of a container is its internal **volume**. For example, the capacity of a large carton of fruit juice is 1 **litre**. The capacity of the petrol tank in some small cars is about 50 litres.

Cardinal number

The set of sheep, the set of knots and the set of notches all have the same size: they can be tallied by a one-to-one correspondence. The number name *five* (5) is given to each of these sets. The cardinal number of the set is said to be 5.

When doing a statistical survey tally marks are often used. The cardinal numbers of each item can then be written down just by looking at the patterns of the tally marks.

Colour of car	Tally	Frequency
Red	~~////~~ //	7
White	///	3
Yellow	//	2

See **Ordinal number**.

Cartesian coordinates

■ See **Coordinates**.

Celsius

Temperature is usually measured in **degrees** Celsius (written °C). For example, water boils at 100°C and freezes at 0°C. The normal human body temperature is about 37°C.

Degrees Celsius were formerly referred to as degrees centigrade.

The Celsius temperature scale is named after a Swedish astronomer Anders Celsius (1701-1744).

Centimetre

A centimetre is a measure of length. One centimetre (1 cm) is one hundredth of a **metre**. This needle is just over 5 cm in length.

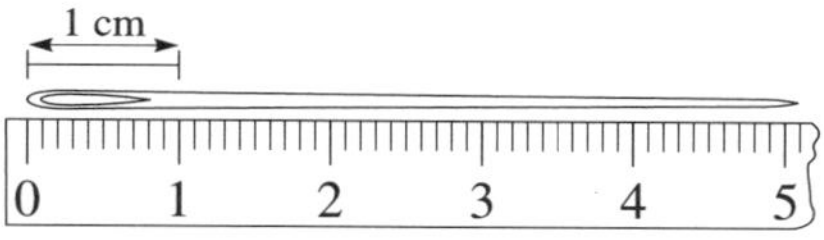

Centre of enlargement

■ See **Enlargement**.

Centre of rotational symmetry

■ See **Rotational symmetry.**

Chord

■ See **Circle**.

Circle

A circle can be drawn using compasses. All the points on the circle are the same distance, called the **radius**, from the centre.

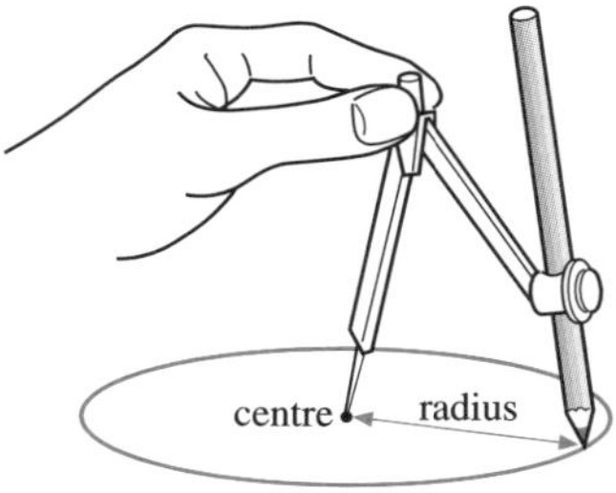

A line joining two points on a circle is called a *chord*. When the line passes through the centre, the chord is a **diameter**.

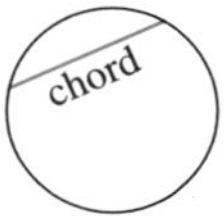

Circumcircle

See **Perpendicular bisector**.

Circumference of a circle

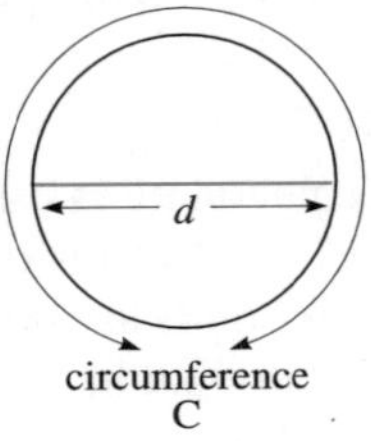

The circumference of a circle is the distance round the circle. It is about 3 times the length of the **diameter**:

$$C \approx 3 \times d$$

This symbol means 'is approximately equal to'

More accurately,

$$C = \pi \times d$$

where π ('pi') is 3.141 59…

For example, the circumference of a bicycle wheel of diameter 66 cm is about 3 x 66 cm, which is 198 cm. More accurately, it is approximately 3.142 x 66 cm which is 207 cm to the nearest cm.

The word 'circumference' is also used for the boundary of a circle as well as for the length of the boundary.

See **Pi**.

Class interval

When statistical data is being collected it is often convenient to group items together and record them in class intervals. For example, examination marks might be grouped in class intervals like this:

Mark	Tally	Frequency
40-49	//	2
50-59	///	3
60-69	~~////~~ /	6

Clockwise

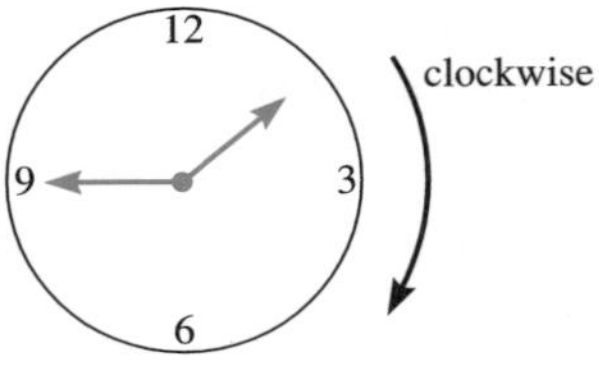

The direction of a turn or **rotation** is said to be clockwise if it is in the same direction as that in which the hands of a clock turn.

An angle measured in a clockwise direction is considered to be negative.

See **Anti-clockwise**.

Care needs to be taken when dealing with continuous data (i.e. data involving measurement). For example, the heights of some sixteen-year-old students were recorded to the nearest centimetre using class intervals 150–160, 160–170, etc. The first interval contained measurements up to 159.5 cm. Measurements from 159.5 cm to 160 cm were recorded as 160 cm and were included in the 160–170 interval.

Height (cm)	Tally	Frequency
150-160	//	2
160-170	///	3
170-180	~~////~~ /	6

See **Discrete**.

Coefficient

The coefficient of a symbol in an algebraic **expression** is the number which the symbol is multiplied by. For example, the coefficient of x in $3x + 11x^2 + 2y$ is 3. The coefficient of x^2 is 11 and the coefficient of y is 2.

Collinear

Three or more points are collinear when they are in a straight line.

The points A, C and D are collinear and the point E, C, F and G are collinear, but the points A, C and F are not collinear.

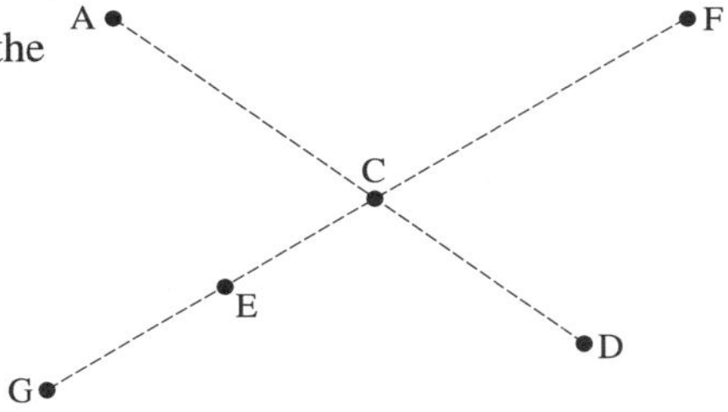

Columns

See **Rows and columns**.

Common denominator

In order to add $\frac{1}{4}$ and $\frac{2}{3}$ it is necessary to rewrite the **fractions** so that the bottom numbers (the **denominators**) are the same. In this case, since 12 is the smallest number which 4 and 3 divide into, the fractions can be rewritten as twelfths. 12 is the common denominator.

$$\frac{1}{4} \overset{\times 3}{=} \frac{3}{12} \qquad \frac{2}{3} \overset{\times 4}{=} \frac{8}{12}$$

Then $\frac{1}{4} + \frac{2}{3} = \frac{3}{12} + \frac{8}{12} = \frac{11}{12}$

See **Equivalent fractions**.

Common factor

The factors of a **whole number** are the whole numbers which divide into it exactly.

The factors of 20 are 1, 2, 4, 5, 10, and 20.
The factors of 30 are 1, 2, 3, 5, 6, 10, 15 and 30.

The common factors of 20 and 30 are the numbers which are in both lists:

1, 2, 5 and 10.

The *highest common factor* (HCF) is 10.

Common multiple

The multiples of 4 are 8 = 2 x 4, 12 = 3 x 4, 16 = 4 x 4, etc.
The multiples of 6 are 12 = 2 x 6, 18 = 3 x 6, 24 = 4 x 6, etc.

12 is a common multiple of 4 and 6 because it is in both lists (common to both lists). 24 is also a common multiple of 4 and 6, and so is 36, etc.

12 is the *lowest common multiple* (LCM) of 4 and 6.

Commutative

3 x 4 is the same as 4 x 3, and 3 + 4 is the same as 4 + 3. But 3 ÷ 4 is not the same as 4 ÷ 3, and 3 – 4 is not the same as 4 – 3. Multiplication and addition of numbers are said to be commutative. Division and subtraction of numbers are *not* commutative (non-commutative).

An **operation** $*$ on a set is commutative when it does not matter which way round two elements in the set are combined, i.e. when $a * b = b * a$ for all elements a and b in the set.

Complementary angles

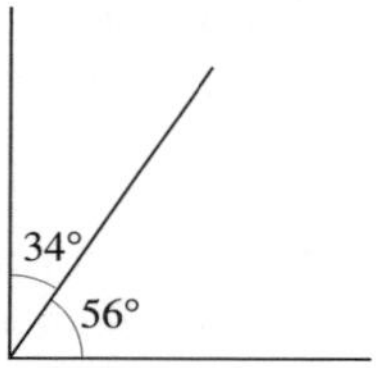

Angles such as 56° and 34° which add up to 90° are called complementary angles. 34° is the complement of 56° and 56° is the complement of 34°.

In a **triangle** with a **right angle**, the other two angles are complementary:

angle A + angle C = 90°

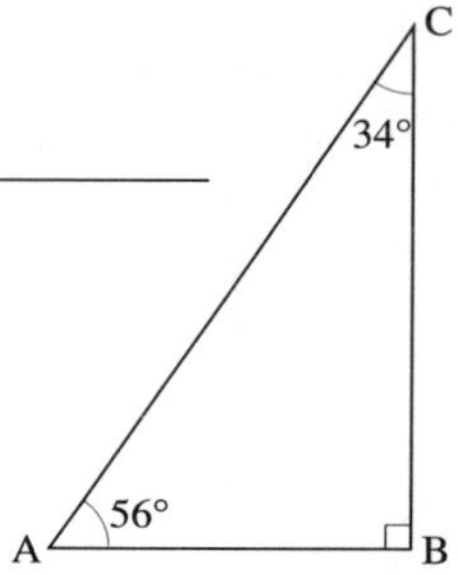

Completing the square

See **Quadratic equation**.

Component

The displacement shown in the diagram has a component of 3 in the x-direction and a component of 4 in the y-direction. It could be written as a column **vector**:

$$\begin{pmatrix} 3 \\ 4 \end{pmatrix}$$

3 and 4 are called the components of the vector.

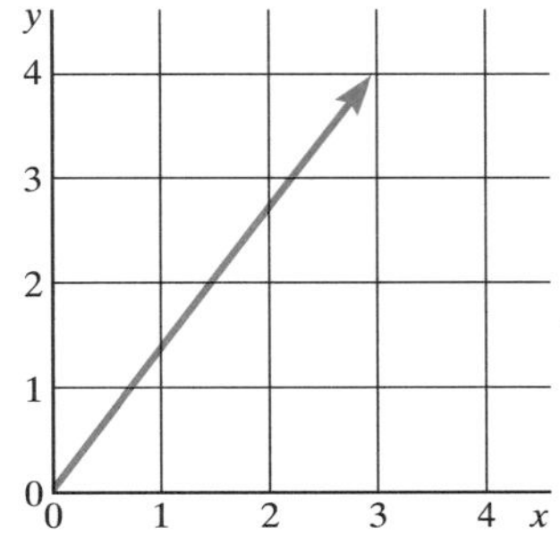

Composite function

A composite function is a **function** which is composed of (made up from) a sequence of simple functions.

For example, a composite function could be made up from the 'add 5' and the 'multiply by 3' functions. This can be represented by a 'machine chain'.

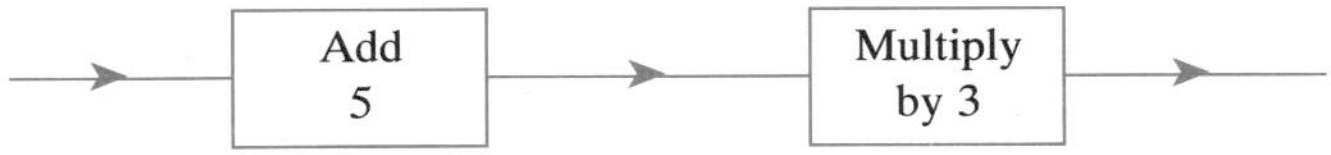

$f{:}x \mapsto x + 5$ $\quad$ $g{:}x \mapsto 3x$

An input of 4 would give an output of $f(4) = 4 + 5 = 9$ from the first machine and then $g(9) = 3 \times 9 = 27$ from the second machine.

In the same way an input of x gives an output of $f(x) = x + 5$ from the first 'machine' and then $g(f(x)) = g(x + 5) = 3(x + 5)$ from the second machine. The composite function is $x \mapsto 3(x + 5)$ and is symbolised by gf.

When the two functions are combined the other way round, the composite function is given by $f(g(x)) = f(3x) = 3x + 5$. This function $x \mapsto 3x + 5$ is symbolised by fg.

Note carefully the order: fg means first apply g, then apply f.

Composite number

A composite number is a **whole number** which can be composed (made up) by multiplying two other whole numbers together, neither of which is 1.

For example, 12 is a composite number because it can be written as 3 x 4 (or 2 x 6). 11 is not a composite number. It can be written only as 1 x 11 because it does not have factors other than 1 and 11.

Numbers which are not composite are called **prime numbers**.

A composite number can be shown as a rectangle of dots with more than one row. The dot patterns for prime numbers have one row only.

12
11

Compound interest

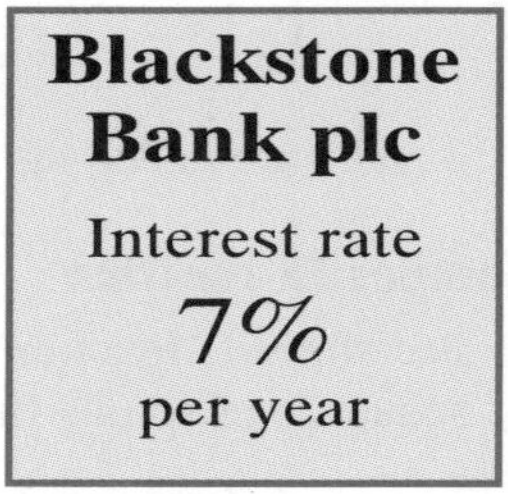
Blackstone
Bank plc
Interest rate
7%
per year

When £100 is invested in a bank or building society at 7% **interest** per year, it grows by £7 to £107 at the end of the first year. In the second year, interest is earned on the original £100 and on the £7 interest. So at the end of the second year the investment grows by £7 + £0.49 to £114.49. (This is more rapidly calculated as £107 x 1.07.) At the end of the third year it will have grown to £114.49 x 1.07 = £122.50 to the nearest penny.

When money grows in this way it is said to grow with compound interest.

An initial amount £P invested at r% per year grows to

$$£P\left(1+\frac{r}{100}\right)^n$$

at the end of n years.

See **Simple interest**.

Compound measure

A compound measure is made up of two (or more) other measures.

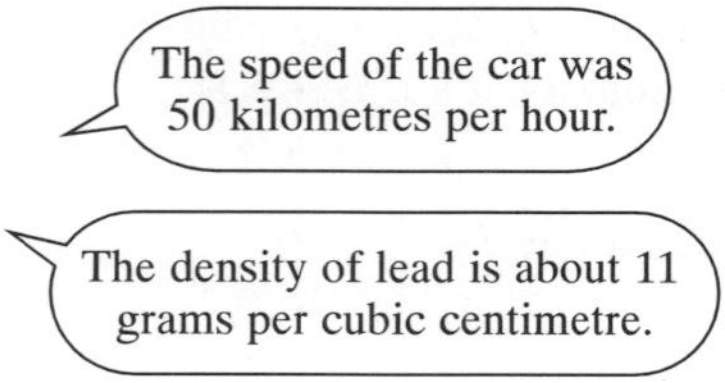
The speed of the car was 50 kilometres per hour.
The density of lead is about 11 grams per cubic centimetre.

Speed is a compound measure made up, in this case, from a measure of length (kilometres) and a measure of time (hours).

The compound measure density is made up, in this case, from a measure of **mass** (grams) and a measure of **volume** (cubic centimetres).

Concave polygon

A **polygon** is concave if part of it goes 'inwards'. One of its interior angles is then a reflex angle (that is, an angle between 180° and 360°). Concave polygons are sometimes called *re-entrant*.

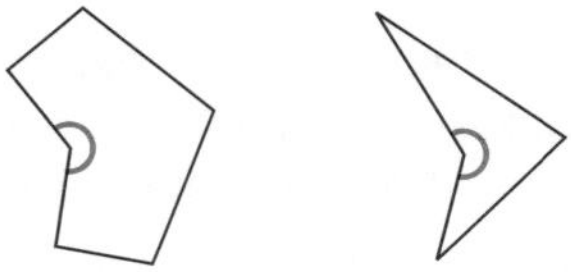

See **Convex polygon**.

Concentric circles

Concentric circles are **circles** with the same centre, like the ripples caused when a stone is dropped in a pond.

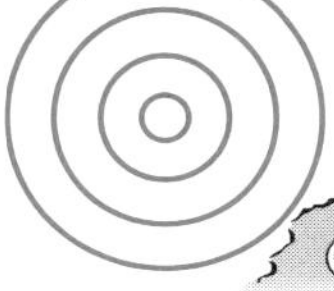

Concurrent

Lines which have a point in common are said to be concurrent.

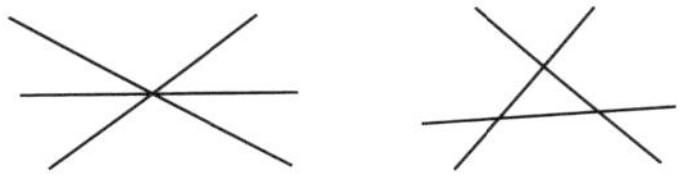

These lines are concurrent These lines are not concurrent

Conditional probability

Suppose a bag contains 3 red counters and 2 black counters. A counter is removed at random and then another one is removed at random. The **probability** that the second counter is red depends on (is conditional on) the colour of the first counter removed.

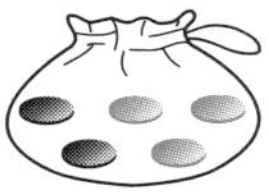

The conditional probability that the second counter is red, given that the first counter is red, is $\frac{2}{4}$.

The conditional probability that the second counter is red, given that the first counter is black, is $\frac{3}{4}$.

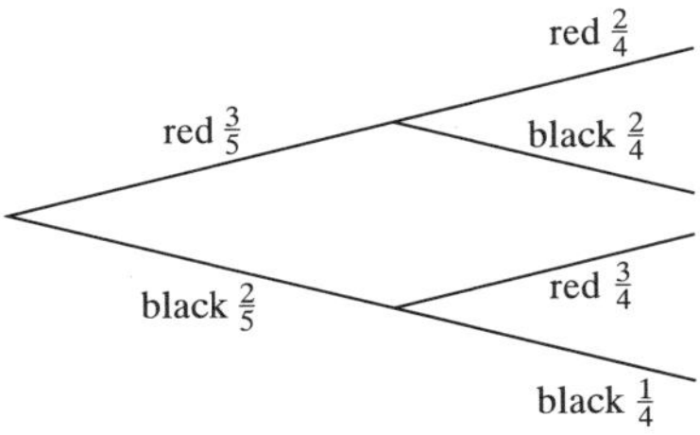

See **Tree diagram**.

Cone

A cone is a three-dimensional shape with a circular **base** tapering to a point (the **vertex**).

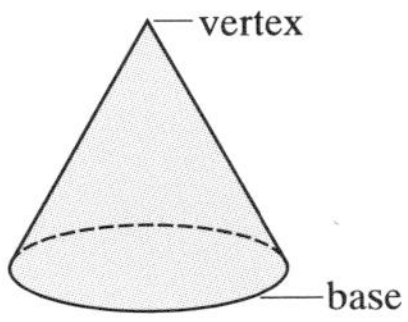

The **area** A of the curved surface of a cone is

π x radius x slant height

$A = \pi r l$

The *slant height* is the distance along the surface of the cone from the vertex to the base.

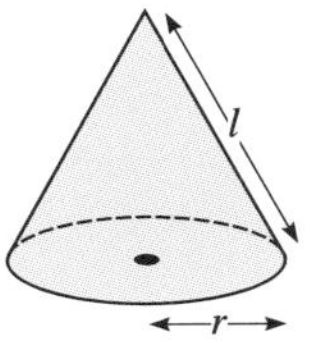

The **volume** ***V*** of a cone is

$\frac{1}{3}$ x base area x height

$V = \frac{1}{3}\pi r^2 h$

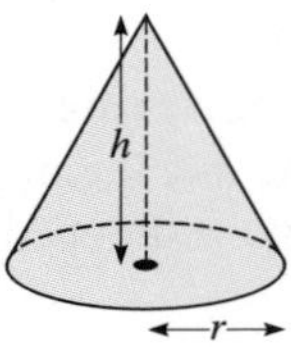

Congruent

Two objects are said to be congruent when they are the same size and shape.

For example, the two rectangles are congruent and the two triangles are congruent. In each case A could be moved to coincide with B.

The **transformations** of **translation**, **rotation** and **reflection** map shapes onto congruent shapes.

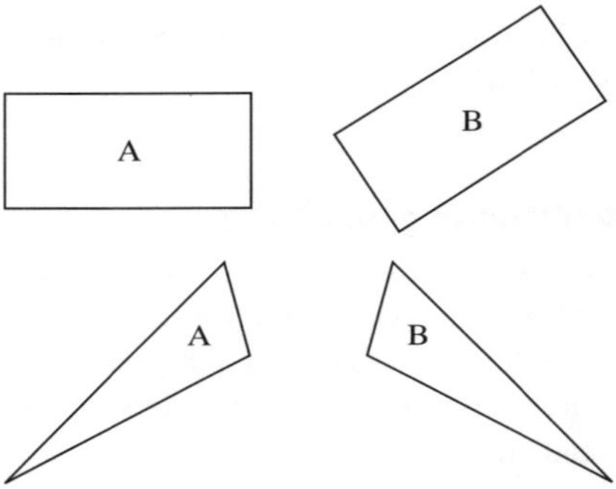

Conical

Any object in the shape of a **cone** is called conical.

Conic section

When a cone is intersected by a plane the resulting curve is called a conic section. The curve depends on the angle at which the plane intersects the cone.

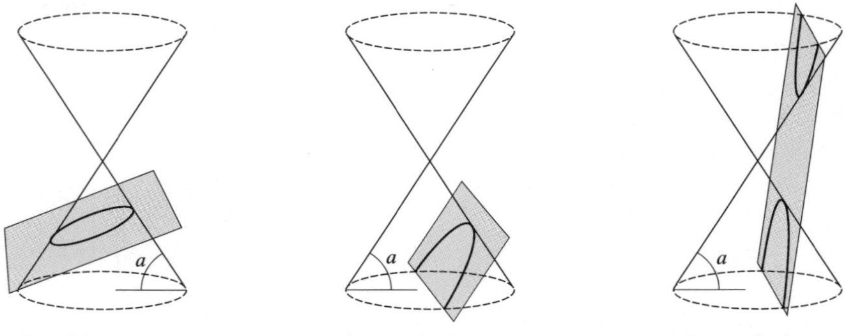

An **ellipse**
The angle of slope of the plane is less than angle *a*.

A **parabola**
The angle of slope of the plane is equal to angle *a*.

A **hyperbola**
The angle of slope of the plane is greater than angle *a*.

When the plane is **horizontal**, a **circle** is obtained (a special case of an ellipse).

Conjecture

A conjecture is a statement made by noticing a pattern based on some particular cases in the hope that it is true in all cases.

For example, by considering the numbers on the right you might make the conjecture that the sum of consecutive **odd numbers** is always a **square number**.

1	= 1	$= 1^2$
1 + 3	= 4	$= 2^2$
1 + 3 + 5	= 9	$= 3^2$
1 + 3 + 5 + 7	= 16	$= 4^2$

The next step would be to seek a general **proof** to show that the conjecture is correct or to find a **counter-example** to show that it is incorrect.

Constant

A constant is a fixed number, rather than a **variable** number.

In the equation

$$v = 10t + 15$$

the numbers 10 and 15 are constants. v and t can be given various values - they are variables.

Construction

Sometimes in geometrical drawing a construction is carried out using compasses and a straight edge.

For example, a line AB can be **bisected** (cut in half) by first drawing circular arcs with the same **radius** centred on A and B, and then joining up the intersections.

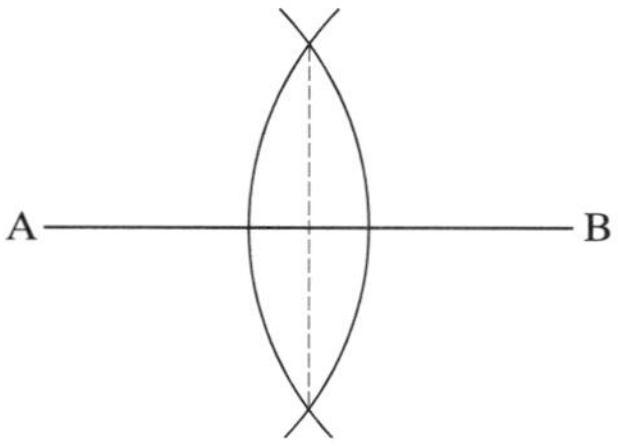

In the same way a construction can be carried out to bisect an angle. Draw a circular arc with centre A to cut the arms of the angle at B and C. Then draw arcs centred on B and C with the same radius, intersecting at D. Finally, join A to D.

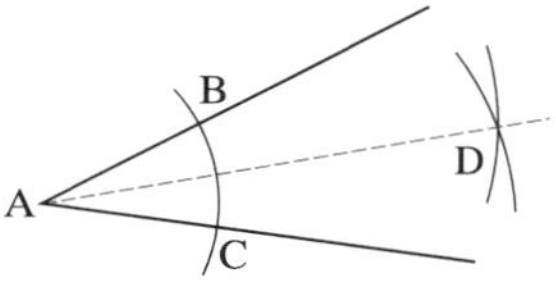

Continuous variable

When a **variable** can take any value in an **interval** it is said to be *continuous*. For example, the height of an adult person is a continuous variable (usually in the interval from 150 cm to 200 cm). Length, temperature and time are further examples of continuous variables.

See **Discrete variable**.

Converge

When the terms of a **sequence** get closer and closer to a number L so that the differences between them and L approach 0, the sequence is said to converge to L. The number L is called the **limit** of the sequence.

$2, 1\frac{1}{2}, 1\frac{1}{4}, 1\frac{1}{8}, 1\frac{1}{16},$ ... converges to 1.

$\frac{1}{2}, \frac{3}{4}, \frac{7}{8}, \frac{15}{16}, \frac{31}{32},$ ... converges to 1.

$\frac{1}{2}, -\frac{1}{4}, \frac{1}{8}, -\frac{1}{16}, \frac{1}{32},$ ... converges to 0.

See **Diverge**.

Conversion graph

A conversion graph is used to convert one set of numbers to another. For example, this graph can be used to convert **miles** to **kilometres** and vice versa.

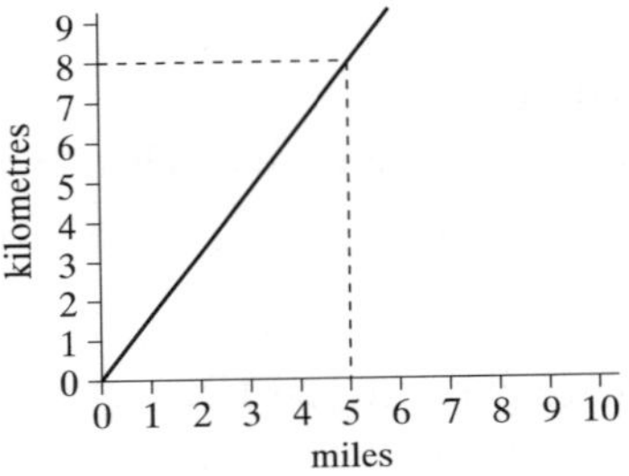

Convex polygon

A **polygon** is convex if all of its edges go 'outwards' rather than 'inwards'.

See **Concave polygon**.

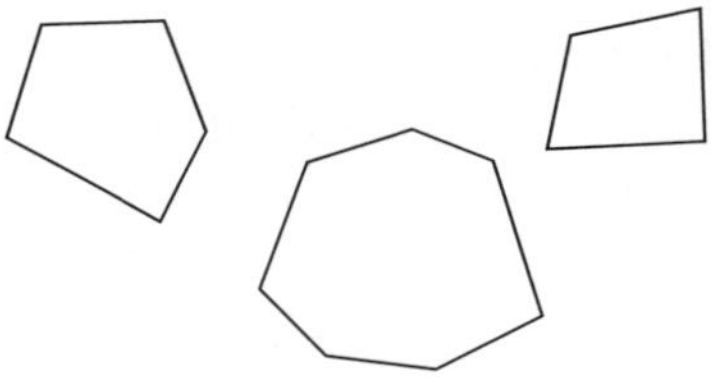

Coordinates

The position of a point on a grid can be given by a pair of numbers which are its distances from two lines called the x-axis and the y-axis.

A is the point (4, 3). The first number 4 is called the x-coordinate. The second number 3 is called the y-coordinate.

The coordinates must be given in the right order. The point (3, 4) is at B.

Coordinates given in this way are called Cartesian after the French Mathematician René Descartes 1596-1650.

See **Axes** and **Polar coordinates**.

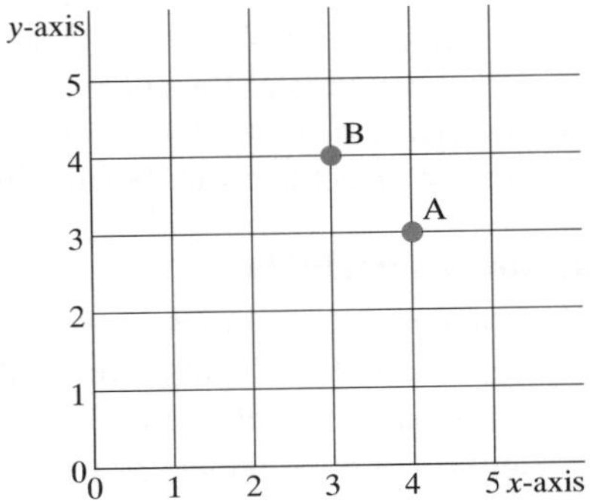

Coplanar

Points in three-dimensional space are coplanar when they are in the same **plane**.

For example, B, C, D and E are coplanar but A, B, C and D are not.

Any three points are coplanar. For example, A, B, and C are coplanar; A, E and C are coplanar; etc.

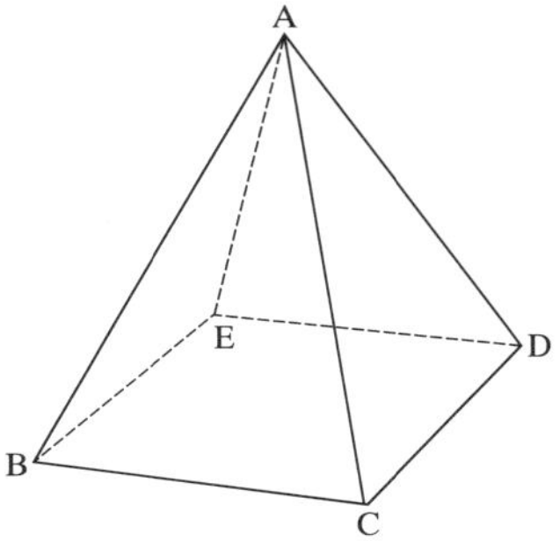

Correct to

When a number such as 14.376 is rounded to 2 **decimal places** it becomes 14.38 because it is nearer to 14.38 than to 14.37. So 14.376 is said to be 14.38 correct to 2 decimal places.

Correlation

Tall people usually have larger arm spans than shorter people. There is said to be a correlation between height and arm span, although there is no exact formula connecting them.

When two variables are such that as one changes the other changes in a related way, they are said to be correlated.

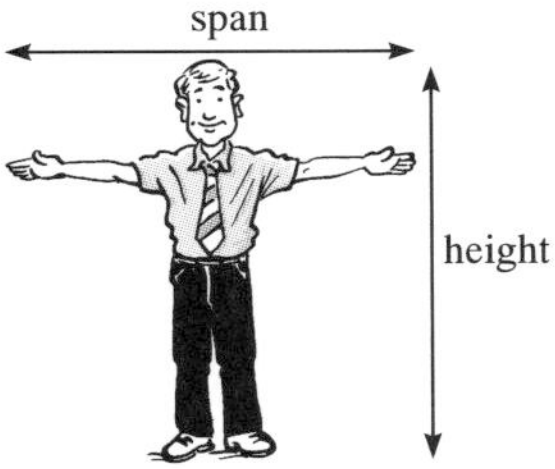

Corresponding angles

The corresponding angles x and y are equal.

See **Parallel lines** and **Transversal**.

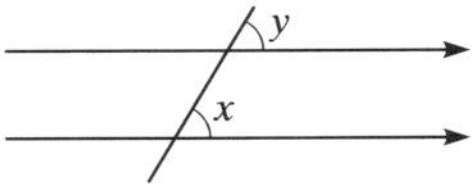

Corresponding points

In **transformations** such as **enlargements**, **reflections**, **rotations**, **translations**, etc. points which map onto each other are called corresponding points.

For example, in the rotation,

A and A′ are corresponding points,

B and B′ are corresponding points.

In the reflection, P and P′, and Q and Q′ are pairs of corresponding points.

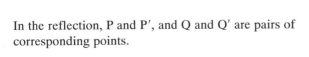

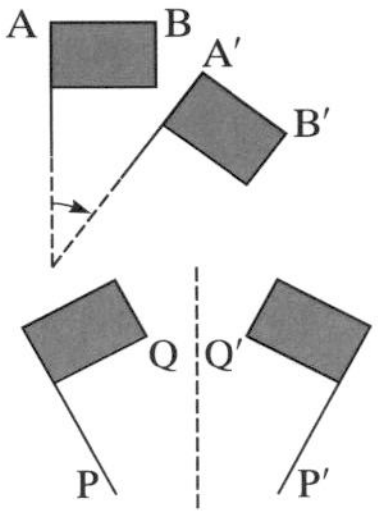

Cosine (cos) of an acute angle

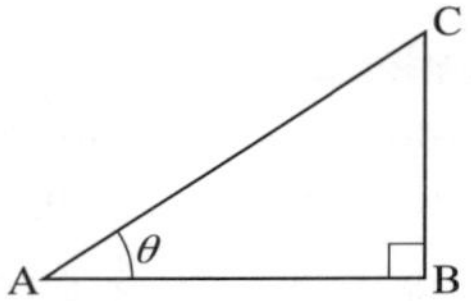

The cosine of an **angle** θ (cos θ as it is usually written) can be defined using a **right-angled triangle**, in which θ is one of the angles as shown, by

$$\cos\theta = \frac{AB}{AC} = \frac{\text{length of side adjacent to } \theta}{\text{length of hypotenuse}}$$

When AC = 1, then AB = cos θ, so,
by **enlargement**, if $A'C' = r$, then $A'B' = r\cos\theta$.

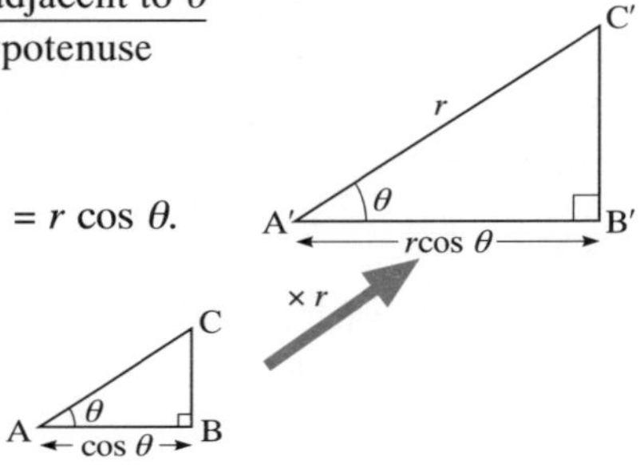

For example, if a ladder of length 5 metres leans against a wall at an angle to the **horizontal** of 65°, the distance d metres of the foot of the ladder from the wall is given by

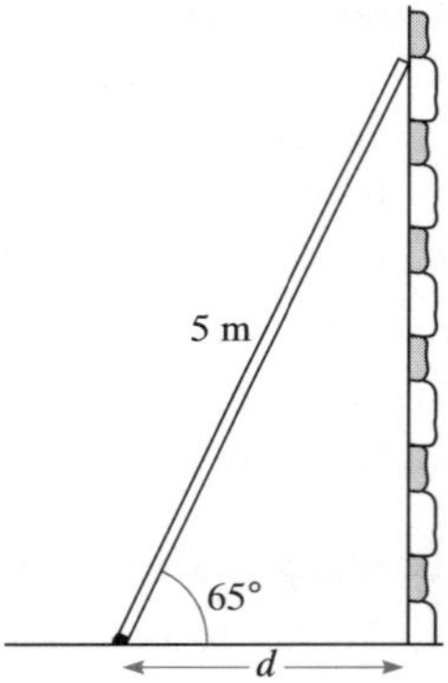

$$\frac{d}{5} = \cos 65°$$

so $\quad d = 5\cos 65°$

$= 5 \times 0.422\ 618\ 261$

$= 2.113\ 091\ 309$

(to full calculator accuracy)

The distance of the foot of the ladder from the wall is therefore about 2.11 metres.

Note: to find cos 65° using a scientific calculator, enter 65 and then press the cos key.

See **Sine** and **Tangent**.

Cosine of any angle

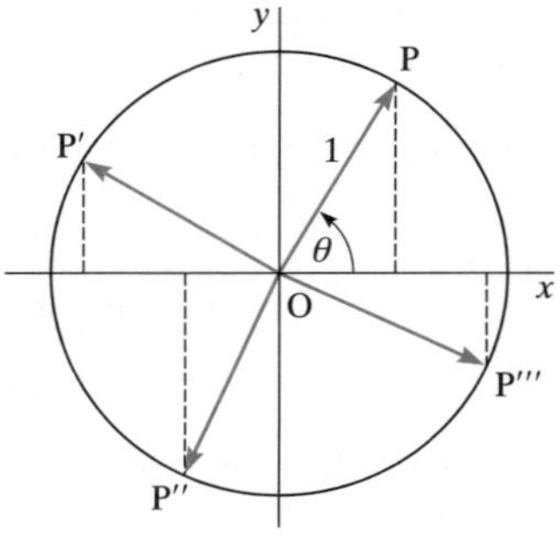

Consider a pointer OP of length 1 unit rotating about the origin. When it has turned through an **angle** θ from the x-axis as shown, the cosine of θ is defined as the x-coordinate of the end of the pointer. This is consistent with the definition above for angles up to 90° and extends it for angles of any size.

When P is at P′ and at P″, cos θ is negative. When P is at P‴, then cos θ is positive. The graph of cos θ plotted against θ gives a wave-like curve.

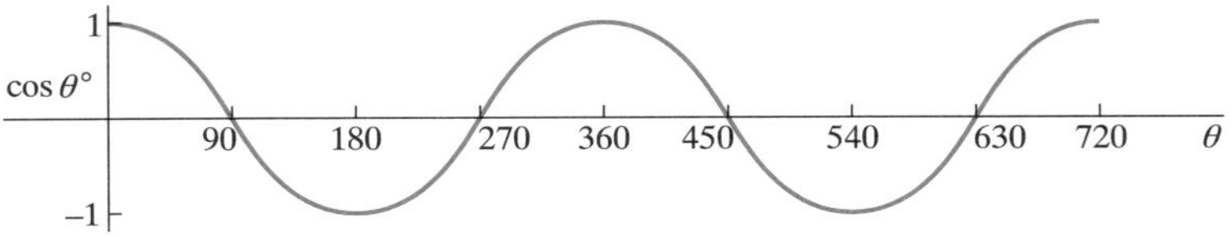

See **Sine** and **Tangent**.

Cosine rule

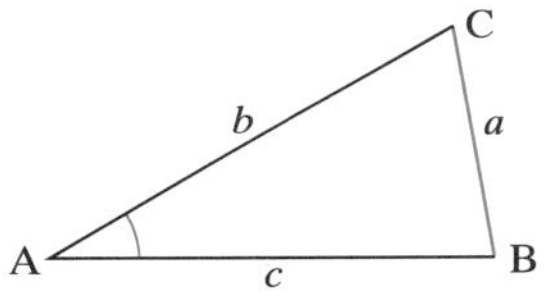

In the triangle ABC when the sides b and c and the angle A are known, the third side can be found using

$$a^2 = b^2 + c^2 - 2bc \cos A.$$

Alternatively, when the three sides are known, the angle A can be found.

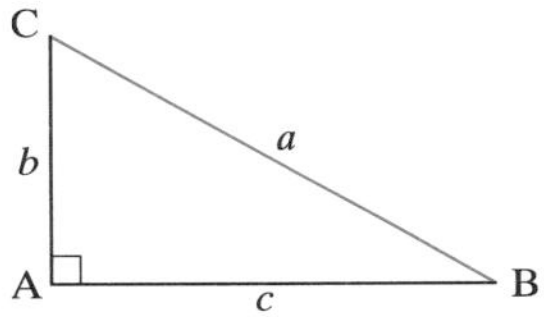

When angle A is 90° this reduces to

$$a^2 = b^2 + c^2$$

(since cos 90° = 0) which is **Pythagoras' theorem**.

Counter-example

A counter-example is a particular case which **disproves** a **conjecture**.

For example, the table on the right showing $n^2 - n + 11$ for n from 1 to 10 might lead you to make the conjecture that $n^2 - n + 11$ is always a **prime number**. However, when n is 11, $n^2 - n + 11$ is 121 (= 11 x 11) which is not a prime number. Taking n as 11 gives a counter-example.

n	$n^2 - n + 11$
1	11
2	13
3	17
4	23
5	31
6	41
7	53
8	67
9	83
10	101

See **Proof**.

Counting numbers

Counting numbers are the **whole numbers**

1, 2, 3, …

which we use for counting. Counting numbers are sometimes called **natural numbers**.

There are other types of numbers such as **directed numbers**, **rational numbers**, **irrational numbers**.

Critical path

A complicated job such as building a house is made up of smaller jobs - lay the foundations, build the walls, fit the window frames, etc.

Some jobs cannot be done until a previous job has been completed, while others might be independent of each other. The jobs can be shown diagrammatically using a **network** where the numbers on the **arcs** represent times to complete specific jobs. Then the best order for doing the jobs can be found by tracing routes on the network. The route from start to finish which takes the longest time is called the *critical path*. It is shown on the network here by the thick line. The total time the job will require is 20 weeks (4 + 8 + 2 + 3 + 3).

Job	Time (weeks)
Plaster the walls	3
Lay the foundations	4
Install the plumbing	2
Landscape the garden	3
Put on the roof	3
Build the walls	8
Paint and paper inside	3
Put in electric wiring	1

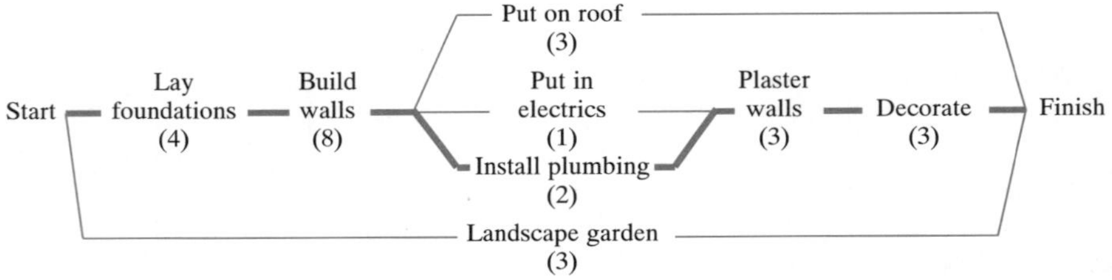

Cross-multiply

An **equation** such as

$$\frac{x}{3} = \frac{y}{2}$$

can be rewritten by multiplying both sides first by 2 and then by 3 to give $2x = 3y$. This process of multiplying is sometimes called cross-multiplying because the overall effect is to multiply across on both sides of the equation.

$$\frac{x}{3} = \frac{y}{2}$$

Cross-section

A slice through a three-dimensional shape usually **parallel** to its **base** or end is called a cross-section.

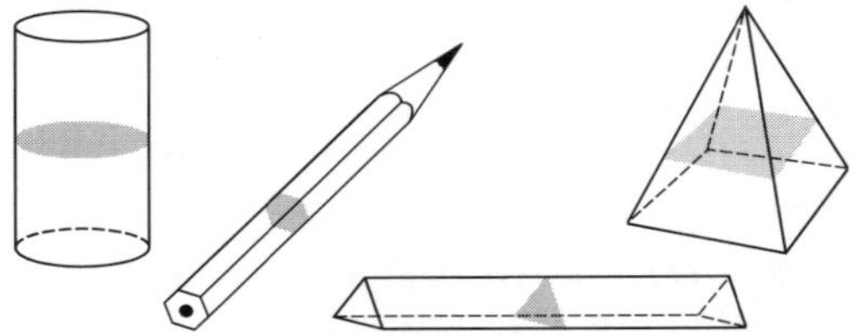

Cube

A cube is a three-dimensional shape with all its **faces square** and all its **edges** equal in length.

Cube of a number

A number 'cubed' is the number to the **power** of 3.
For example, 4 cubed is 4^3 which is 4 x 4 x 4 (= 64).
It is the **volume** of a **cube** measuring 4 by 4 by 4.

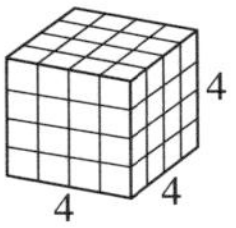

Cube root

4 is called the cube root of 64 because 4 x 4 x 4 is 64 ($4^3 = 64$, 'four cubed is sixty-four').

10 is called the cube root of 1000 because 10 x 10 x 10 is 1000 ($10^3 = 1000$, 'ten cubed is one thousand').

The number c such that $c^3 = N$ is called the cube root of N. The cube root of N is written $\sqrt[3]{N}$. The cube root of N is the side length of a **cube** whose **volume** is N.

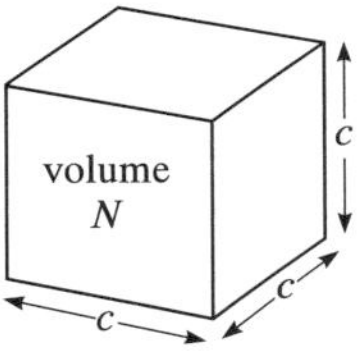

Cubic centimetre

A cubic centimetre is a unit for measuring **volume**.
A cube whose **edges** are all 1 cm long has a volume of 1 cubic centimetre (written 1 cm³).

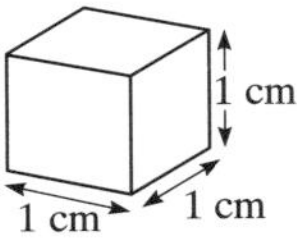

A **cuboid** measuring 1 cm by 2 cm by 0.5 cm also has a volume of 1 cm³.

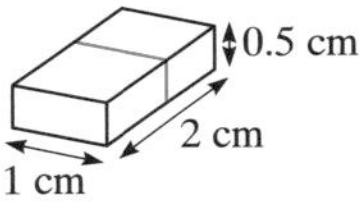

The volume of a cuboid measuring 2 cm by 3 cm by 5 cm is 2 x 3 x 5 cm³ which is 30 cm³.

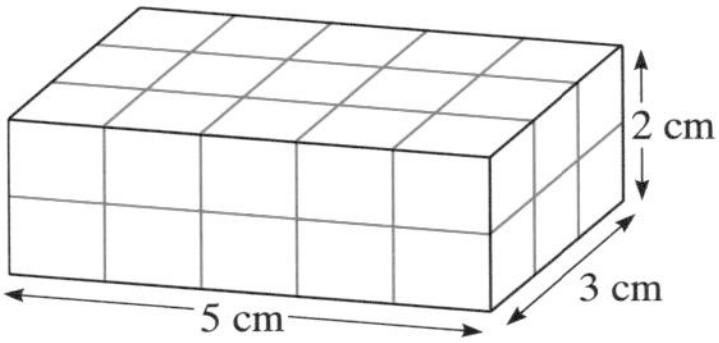

Cubic function

The simplest cubic function is of the form

$$x \mapsto x^3$$

A sketch of its graph is shown here.

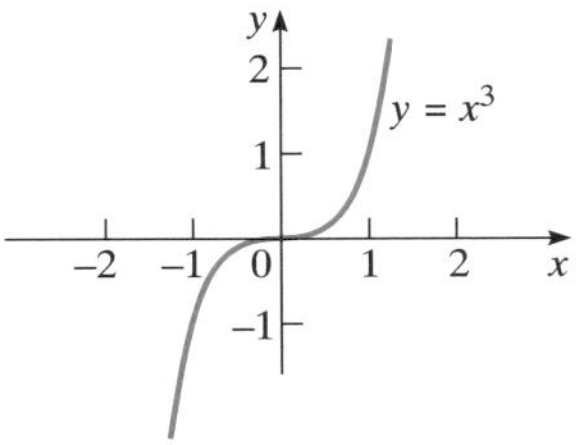

The most general form of a cubic function is

$$x \mapsto ax^3 + bx^2 + cx + d$$

where a, b, c and d are **constants** and $a \neq 0$.

A sketch of the graph of

$$x \mapsto 2x^3 - 7x^2 - 3x + 18$$

is shown on the right.

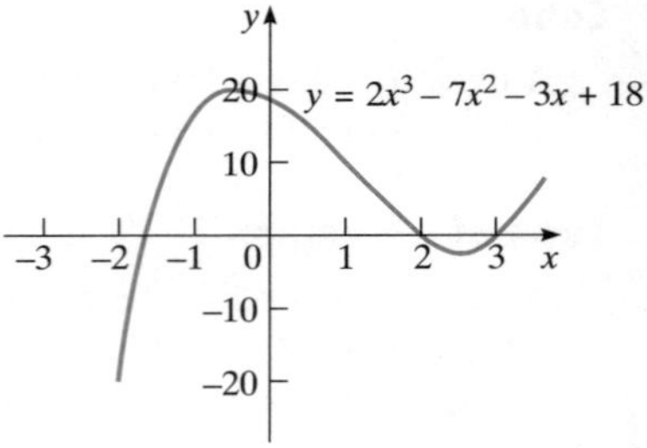

Cubic metre

A cubic metre is a unit for measuring **volume**.

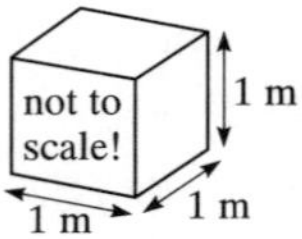

A **cube** whose **edges** are all 1 metre long has a volume of 1 cubic metre (written 1 m^3). Since 1 metre is 100 cm, the volume of such a cube is $100 \times 100 \times 100$ cm^3 which is 1 000 000 cm^3, a million **cubic centimetres** (often written 10^6 cm^3).

The volume of sand in the lorry is about $2 \times 4 \times 0.5$ cubic metres, which is 4 m^3.

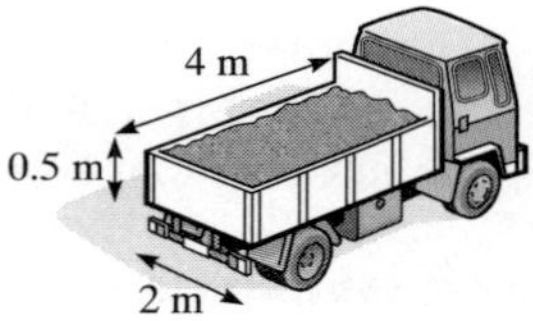

Cuboid

A cuboid is a three-dimensional shape whose **faces** are all **rectangles**. A **cube** is a special case of a cuboid in which the rectangular faces are all equal **squares**.

The **volume** V of a cuboid is

length x width x height

$$V = l \times w \times h$$

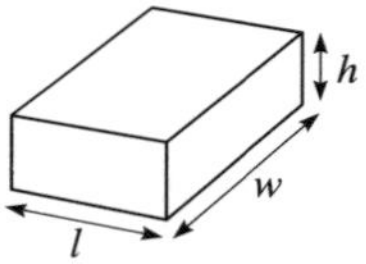

Cumulative frequency

In the table the second column shows the number of students scoring 0, 1, 2, …, 10 marks in a test. The third column has been obtained by adding up (accumulating) the **frequencies** in the second column. So, for example, 26 students had a mark of 7 or less. 26 is the cumulative frequency corresponding to 7 marks.

Mark	Frequency	Cumulative frequency
0	0	0
1	1	1
2	2	3
3	2	5
4	3	8
5	5	13
6	7	20
7	6	26
8	4	30
9	3	33
10	2	35

Cumulative frequencies can be shown graphically. This type of graph is sometimes called an *ogive*.

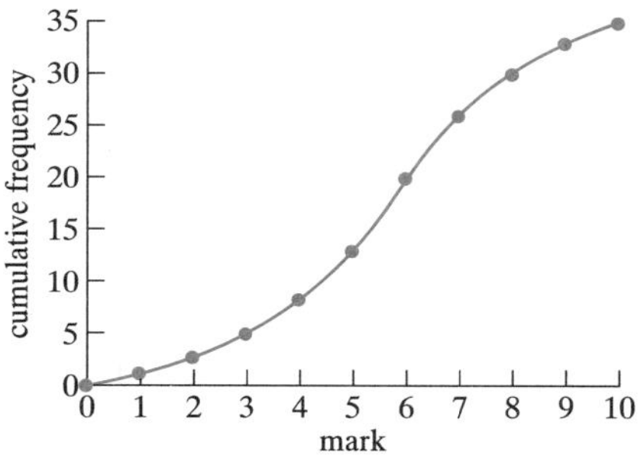

Curve of constant breadth

A circle has the obvious property that when it rolls along a flat surface the point at the top is always the same height above the surface.

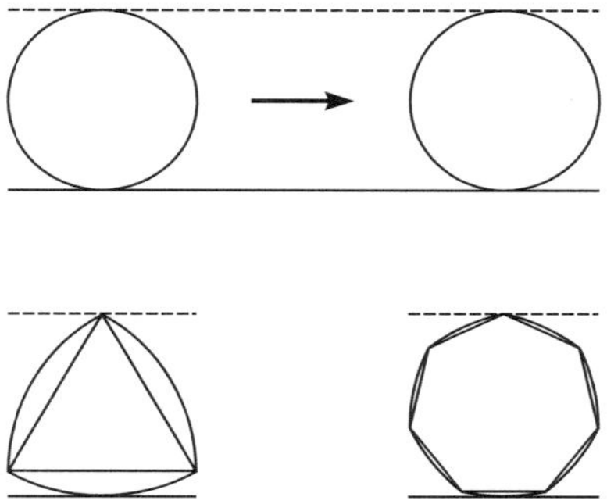

Surprisingly there are other curves with this property. Two examples are shown here. The curves consist of circular arcs and can be drawn with compasses. Twenty-pence and fifty-pence coins have the shape of the second example.

Curve of pursuit

When a dog chases a car it runs towards the current position of the car. Its path forms a curve called a curve of pursuit.

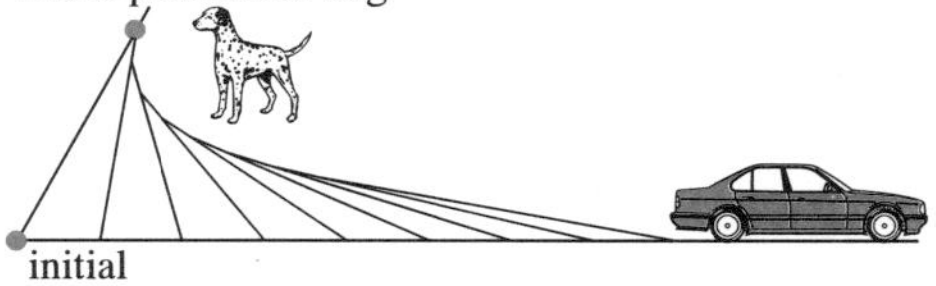

Cyclic quadrilateral

When a circle can be drawn through the four vertices of a quadrilateral, the quadrilateral is called cyclic.

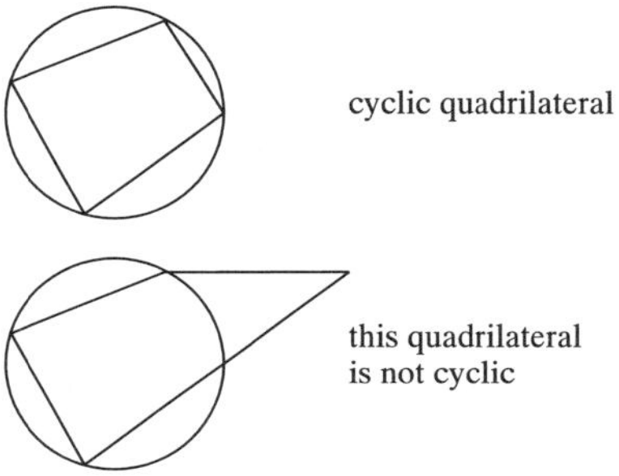

The second quadrilateral is not cyclic. Although it is possible to draw a circle through any three of its vertices, it is not possible to draw a circle through all four vertices.

Cycloid

A cycloid is the curve traced out by a point on the **perimeter** of a **circle** as the circle rolls along a straight line.

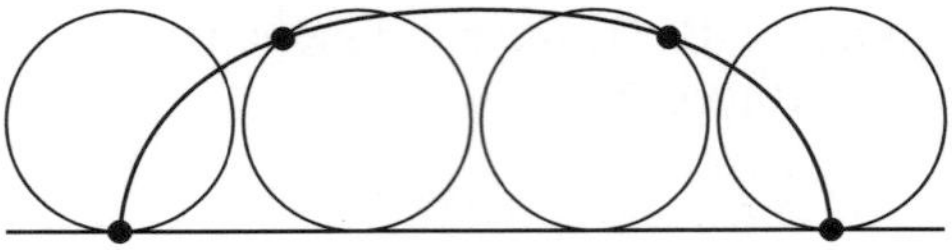

Cylinder

A cylinder is a three-dimensional shape whose **cross-sections** are all **circles** of the same **radius**. It could be solid like a stick of rock or hollow like a can.

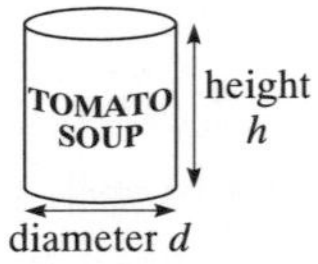

By opening out the label on the can of soup it can be seen that the **area** of the curved part of a cylinder is given by

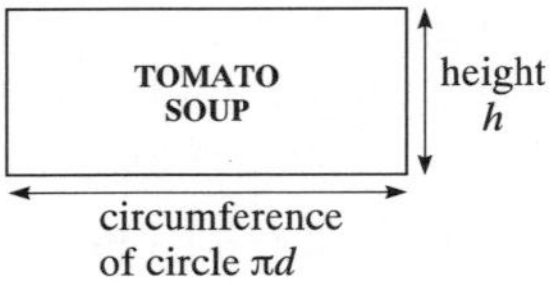

circumference x height

$= \pi d \times h = \pi d h$

The **volume** of a cylinder is

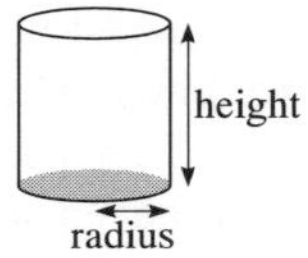

area of the circular base x height

$= \pi r^2 \times h = \pi r^2 h$

Data

This is the name given to a collection of numerical facts or information. Examples might be the scores of the players in a game of cricket, or the numbers of passengers carried by individual cars in a traffic survey.

Database

Often a large amount of information may be stored on a computer which can be processed in a variety of ways. For example, a supermarket will have information stored on all the products it has on the shelves. This data is being continually updated and processed to analyse sales and replenish stock. This large amount of stored data is an example of a database.

Decagon

A decagon is a **polygon** with 10 sides. When all of its sides and **angles** are equal, it is said to be regular.

Decay

A **function** is said to decay when its value decreases as the time increases. The graph shows a typical decay curve representing the value of a car as it decreases with time.

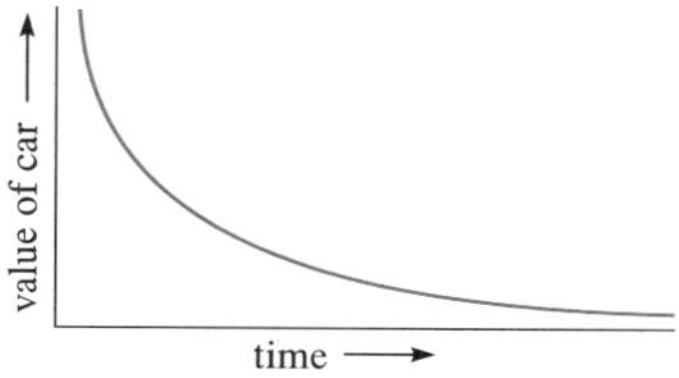

Decimal numbers

When a number is written in base ten notation it is referred to as a decimal number. The values of the places to the left of the decimal point (or comma in some countries) increase by a factor of ten, from units to tens, hundreds, thousands, tens of thousands, hundreds of thousands, thousands of thousands (**millions**) and so on. To the right of the decimal point the values of the places decrease by a factor of ten from tenths to hundredths to thousandths etc.

For example, 4 032.67, read as 'four thousand and thirty-two point six seven', is equivalent to

$$(4 \times 1000) + (0 \times 100) + (3 \times 10) + (2 \times 1) + (6 \times \tfrac{1}{10}) + (7 \times \tfrac{1}{100})$$

thousands	hundreds	tens	units		tenths	hundredths
4	0	3	2	•	6	7

See **Base of a number** and **Place value**.

Decimal places (d.p.)

In a calculation the numbers used are often approximate, as when they represent lengths measured to the nearest centimetre. When this is the case, the result of the calculation may be rounded off to an appropriate number of decimal places (d.p.), that is the number of figures to the right of the decimal point after the rounding process.

When rounding off, the last figure to be kept is increased by 1 or left as it stands depending on which the number is nearer to.

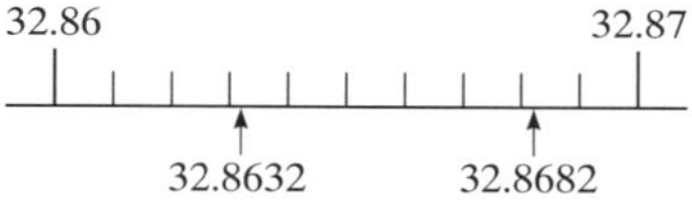

For example, 32.8632 is nearer to 32.86 than 32.87 so to 2 decimal places it is rounded to 32.86. But 32.8682 is nearer to 32.87 than 32.86 so it is rounded to 32.87 to 2 decimal places.

→

The size of the figure immediately to the right of the ones to be kept is critical. If it is 5 or more, then the remaining right-hand figure is increased by 1. If it is 4 or less, then all the remaining figures are unchanged.

The following examples illustrate what may happen:

4.9528 becomes 4.953 to 3 d.p.
4.95 to 2 d.p.
5.0 to 1 d.p.

See **Accuracy of measurement**, **Correct to ...**, and **Rounding off**.

Degree (angle measure)

A degree is the common unit used for giving the size of an angle. One complete turn is equivalent to 360°. So a right angle, which is a quarter of a turn, is 90°.

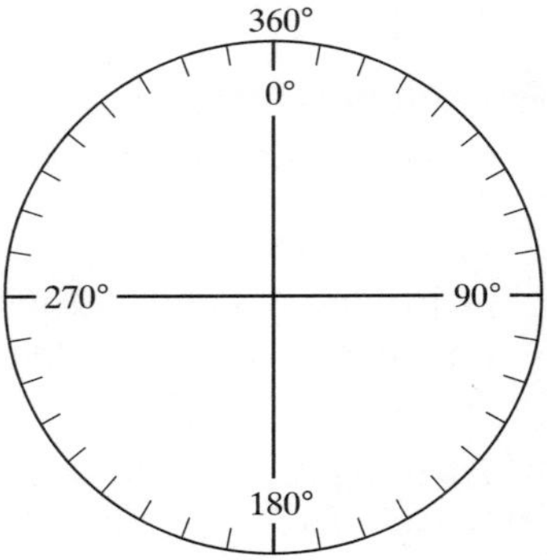

The degree is based on the system originally devised by the ancient Mesopotamians who divided a circle into 360 parts.

Bearings are measured in degrees.

Temperature is also given in units called degrees but this has no relation with angle measure.

Degree of a polynomial

This is the highest power of the variable occurring in a polynomial. For example,

$$2x^6 + 3x^4 - 5x^3 + x + 8$$

is a polynomial of degree 6.

Polynomials of degree 2 are called quadratic, and those of degree 3 are called cubic.

Denary

Denary is the name given to the base ten number system.

See **Decimal numbers**.

Denominator

Denominator is the name given to the bottom of a **fraction**. For example, 5, b and $(x + 2)$ are the denominators of the following fractions:

$$\frac{3}{5} \qquad \frac{a}{b} \qquad \frac{3x-4}{x+2}$$

See **Numerator** and **Common denominator**.

Dependent events

Two events are dependent when one depends on the other. For example, suppose a bag contains 4 red beads and 6 black beads. A bead is drawn out from the bag without looking. Then a second bead is drawn out without replacing the first bead. The chance of the second bead being red depends on the colour of the first bead removed.

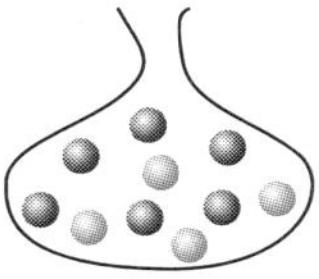

See **Conditional probability** and **Independent events**.

Dependent variable, independent variable

The graph shows the weight in kilograms of a baby from birth in the first 10 weeks. The weight of the baby depends on its age, so is said to be the *dependent* variable, while the baby's age is the *independent* variable.

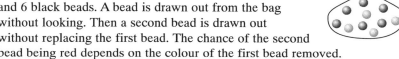

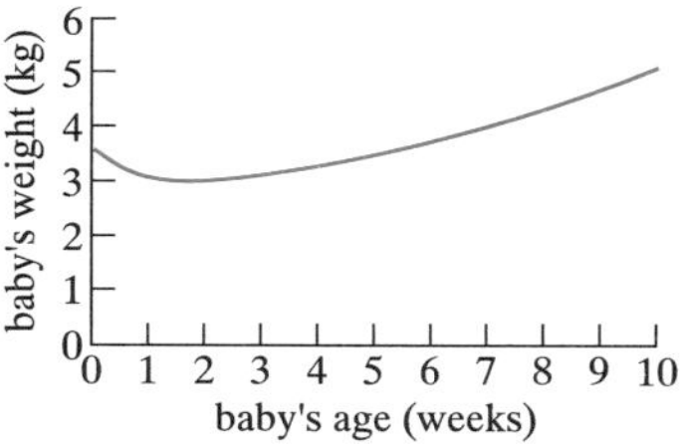

In the formula $V = \pi r^2 h$ for the volume of a cylinder, V is the dependent variable as it is calculated from r and h, which are both independent variables.

Depression

See **Angle of depression**.

Determinant

The determinant of a matrix

$$A = \begin{pmatrix} a & b \\ c & d \end{pmatrix}$$

is the number $ad - bc$.

It is denoted by $|A|$.

When the matrix represents a geometrical transformation, the value of its determinant gives the area scale factor of the transformation. For example, when

$$A = \begin{pmatrix} 4 & 2 \\ 7 & 5 \end{pmatrix} \qquad |A| = \begin{vmatrix} 4 & 2 \\ 7 & 5 \end{vmatrix} = (4 \times 5) - (2 \times 7) = 6$$

and any shape transformed using A would have its area multiplied by a factor of 6.

Diagonal

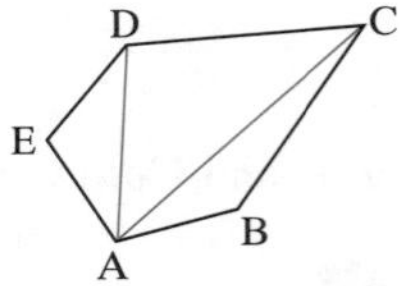

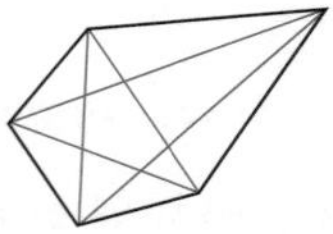

A diagonal is a straight line from a **vertex** of a **polygon** to any other vertex of the polygon not next to it. For example, there are two diagonals from A in the **pentagon**, namely AC and AD. The pentagon has a total of five diagonals.

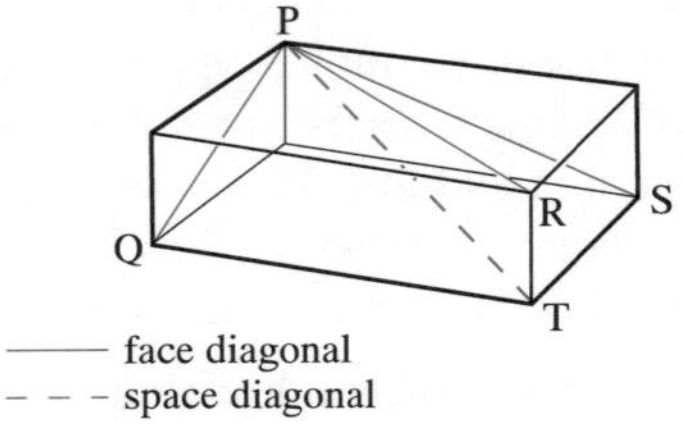

A **polyhedron** can have diagonals in its **faces** or space diagonals through its interior. The **cuboid** has three face diagonals from P, (PQ, PR and PS), and one space diagonal PT.

Diameter

A diameter of a **circle** is a straight line through its centre which joins two points on its circumference, such as A and B. Its length is twice that of the **radius**. Each diameter is a **line of symmetry** for the circle and cuts it into two **semi-circles**.

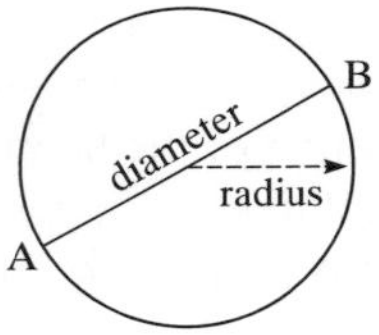

Difference

The difference between two numbers is the size of the gap between them, and is found by subtracting the smaller from the larger. The difference, for example, between 2 and 7 is $7 - 2 = 5$, while the difference between –3 and 7 is $7 - (-3) = 10$, as seen clearly on the **number line**.

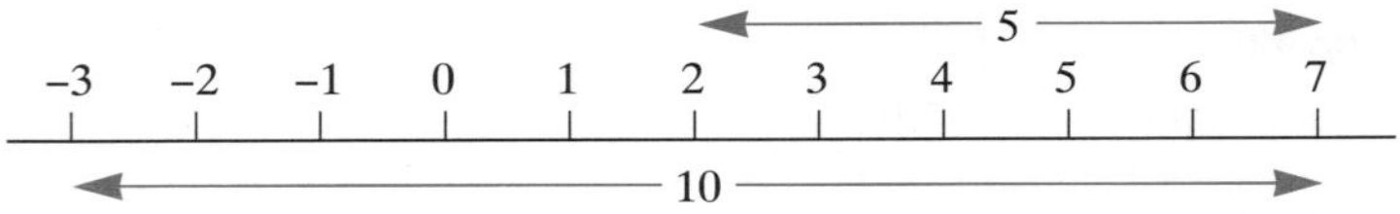

Digit

This is the name given to any one of the symbols 0, 1, 2, 3, 4, 5, 6, 7, 8 and 9 used in our **base** ten number system.

Sometimes the size of a **whole number** is referred to by giving the number of digits needed to write it, so a number like 5628 is called a four-digit number.

Digit sum

The sum of the digits forming a number is called its *digit sum*. For example, the digit sum of 3687 is

$$3 + 6 + 8 + 7 = 24$$

Dimension

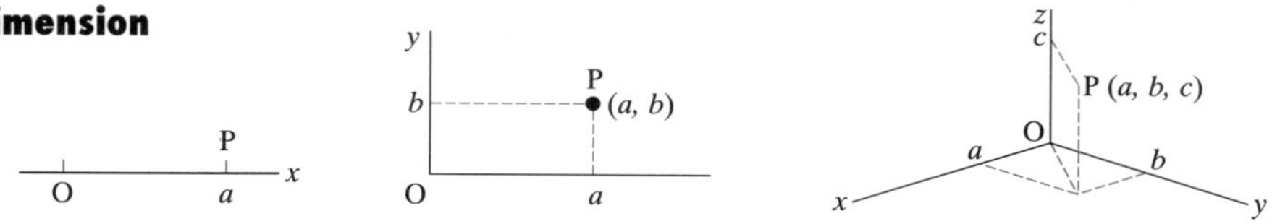

The dimension of a space is the number of **coordinates** needed to fix the position of a point P in it. A line is one-dimensional, a **plane** is two-dimensional, and the space we live in is three-dimensional.

A shape drawn in a plane is said to be two-dimensional, but a solid such as a **sphere** or a **pyramid** needs a third dimension to exist, so is called three-dimensional.

Directed number

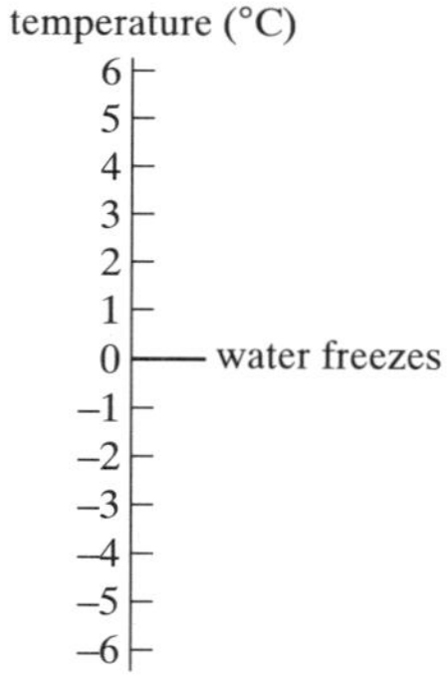

Positive and **negative numbers** such as +3 and –5 are called directed numbers because when represented on a number line the direction in which they are measured from the **origin** has to be taken into account.

Directed numbers are met in everyday life as temperatures. 0°C is the origin: it is the freezing point of water. Negative numbers such as –8 are used to indicate temperatures below freezing, and positive numbers (usually with the + sign omitted) indicate temperatures above freezing.

Direct isometry

See **Isometry**.

Direct proportion, directly proportional to

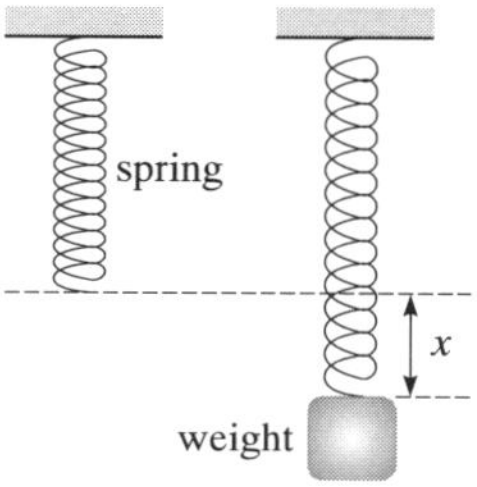

When different weights are attached to one end of a spring whose other end is fixed, the extension of the spring is proportional to the weight on its end. If the weight is doubled, the extension doubles; if the weight is trebled, the extension trebles and so on. Because of this, the extension x of the spring is said to be directly proportional to the weight w on its end. This is expressed as

$$x \propto w \text{ or } x = kw$$

where k is a **constant**.

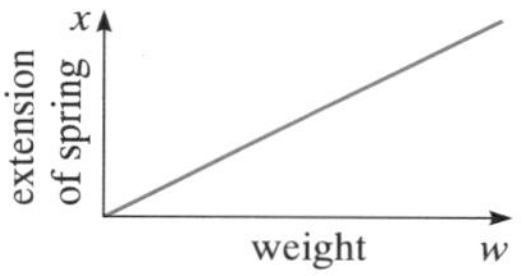

Whenever one **variable** is equal to a constant times another variable in this way they are directly proportional, and a **graph** representing them will be a straight line through the **origin**.

■ See **Inverse proportion** and **Varies directly as.**

Discrete variable

A **variable** is said to be *discrete* if it can take just **whole-number** values. For example, the number of children in a family can only be a whole number such as 1, 2, 3, etc. and not a number such as 1.6 or $\sqrt{3}$.

■ See **Continuous variable**.

Displacement

To displace an object is to translate it. The change in its position is called its displacement. This is a **vector** quantity.

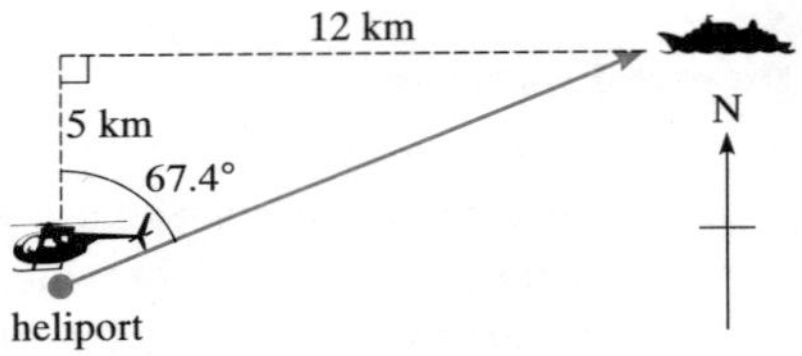

Consider, for example, the displacement of a helicopter on a rescue mission from its heliport to a ship at sea. Its displacement can be given as 12 km east and 5 km north, which can be represented by the vector $\begin{pmatrix}12\\5\end{pmatrix}$, or as 13 km on a **bearing** of 067.4°.

■ See **Translation.**

Disprove

To disprove a statement is to show that it cannot be true.

■ See **Proof, prove**.

Distance

In space the shortest distance between two points is via the straight line between the points. On a **network** the distances will depend on the lengths of the **arcs**. On the surface of a sphere, the shortest distance is along a **great circle**.

Distributive

$$6 \times (7 + 3) = (6 \times 7) + (6 \times 3)$$

$$6 \times (7 - 3) = (6 \times 7) - (6 \times 3)$$

In the examples above, the 6 has been distributed to both numbers inside the bracket by multiplication. This would have been true whatever numbers had been used. So it is said that multiplication is distributive over addition and subtraction.

In general, if two **operations** ∇ and $\square$ are such that

$$a \nabla (b \square c) = (a \nabla b) \square (a \nabla c)$$

then the operation ∇ is said to be distributive over $\square$.

See **Brackets** and **Expand**.

Diverge

When the terms of a **sequence** of numbers grow so that there is no upper bound to their size, the sequence is said to diverge.

For example, 1, 2, 4, 8, 16, 32, … diverges. However

$$\frac{1}{2}, \frac{3}{4}, \frac{7}{8}, \frac{15}{16}, \frac{31}{32}, \ldots \text{ does not diverge.}$$

Its terms, although increasing, never exceed 1. This sequence is said to **converge** to 1.

Dividend, divisor

In the division 73 294 ÷ 48, the number being divided (73 294) is called the *dividend*. The number doing the dividing (48) is called the *divisor*.

Divisibility

17 divides into 51 exactly 3 times, so it is said that 51 is *divisible* by 17. It also follows that 51 is divisible by 3.

The property of being divisible by a number is known as divisibility. There are many tests for divisibility, such as:

- any **whole number** ending in the **digits** 0 or 5 is always divisible by 5;
- any whole number whose **digit sum** is divisible by 3 or 9 is itself divisible by 3 or 9.

For example, the number 234 675 ends in 5 and its digit sum is $2 + 3 + 4 + 6 + 7 + 5 = 27$ which is divisible by 9, so 234 675 is divisible by 5 and by 9.

Dodecagon

'Dodeca' means 12 and the ending 'gon' suggests a **polygon**. So a dodecagon is a 12-sided polygon.

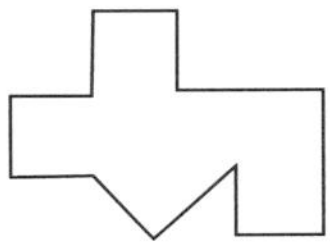

Dodecahedron

A dodecahedron is a **polyhedron** with 12 faces. The diagram shows a regular dodecahedron which has 12 regular **pentagons** meeting 3 at a time at each of its 20 **vertices**.

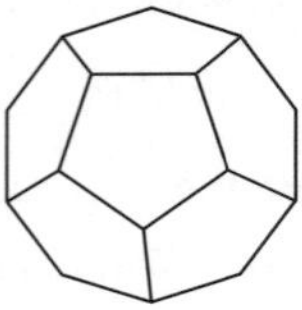

Domain

The domain of a function is the set of elements on which the function operates. In the example illustrated it is the set {–3, –2, –1, 0, 1, 2, 3} and the function is $x \mapsto x^2 - 4$

See **Range**.

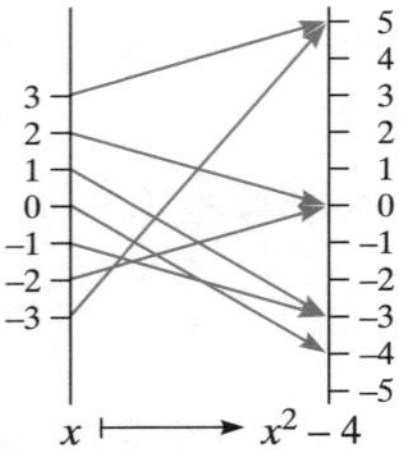

Duodecimal numbers

These are numbers in **base** twelve. They are expressed using groupings of units, twelves, $(\text{twelve})^2$, $(\text{twelve})^3$ and so on. In addition to the digits 0, 1, 2, …, 9, two further symbols are required for ten and eleven, usually taken as T and E. Then, for example,

$$32E_{\text{twelve}} = (3 \times 144_{\text{ten}}) + (2 \times 12_{\text{ten}}) + 11_{\text{ten}} = 467_{\text{ten}}$$

Edge

The edges of a **polyhedron** are the lines where two **faces** meet.

A **tetrahedron** has 6 edges, a triangular **prism** 9, and a **cube** 12.

See **Euler's formula**.

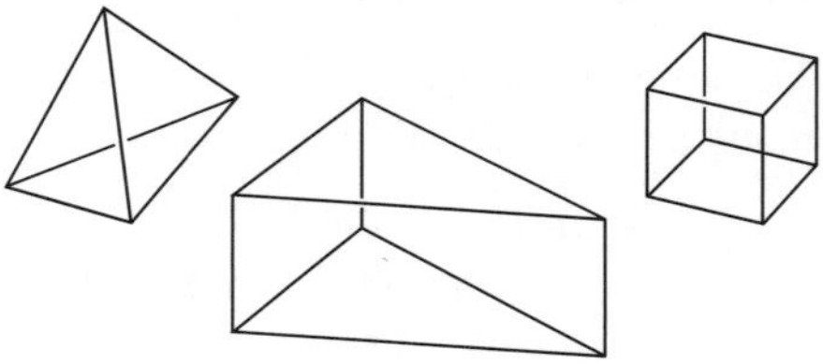

Element of a set

The individual members of a **set** are called its elements.

For example, for the set A = {days of the week}, the elements of A are

Sunday, Monday, Tuesday, Wednesday, Thursday, Friday, Saturday

For the set B = {prime numbers less than 16}, the elements of B are

2, 3, 5, 7, 11, 13

The symbol $\in$ is used to indicate that an object is an element of a set, so 'Monday $\in A$' means 'Monday is an element of A'.

The letter n before a set denotes the number of elements in the set, so $n(A) = 7$ and $n(B) = 6$.

Elevation of a building

An elevation of a building is a view of the building as seen from the front as at A, or the side as at B.

See **Plan view**.

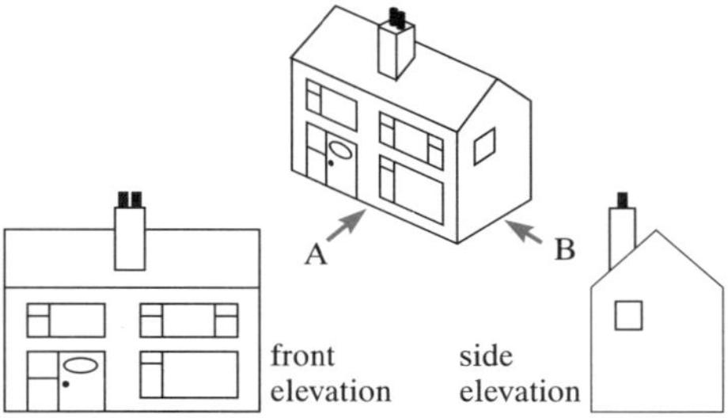

Ellipse

An ellipse is the shape of the **cross-section** when a circular **cylinder** is cut at an angle, or a **circle** is stretched in opposite directions.

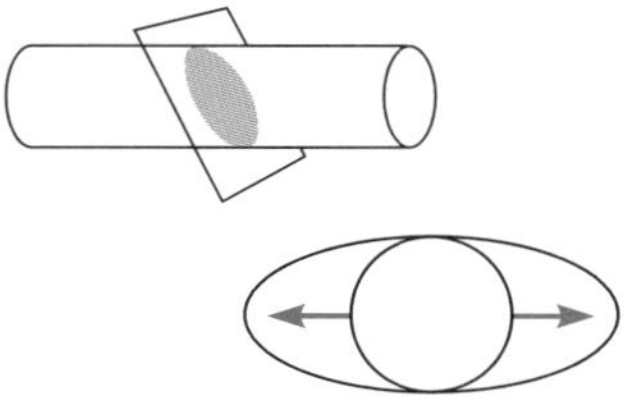

Whenever a circular object, such as the rim of a cup or saucer, is viewed from an angle the shape seen is an ellipse, and an artist will draw it as such. It is also the shape of the orbit of a satellite around the Earth.

See **Conic section**.

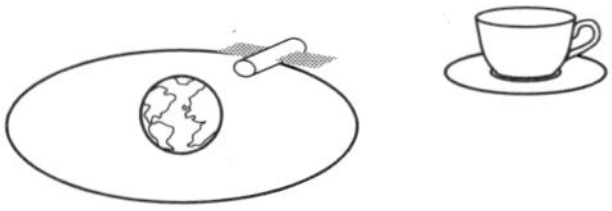

Empty set, null set

An empty set (or null set) is a **set** which has no **elements** in it. For example, the set A = {letters common to SARAH and BETTY} has no elements. Empty sets are symbolised by { } or ∅.

Enlargement

An enlargement is a **transformation** which changes the size of an object without changing its shape, rather as a projector enlarges the details of a photographic slide onto a screen.

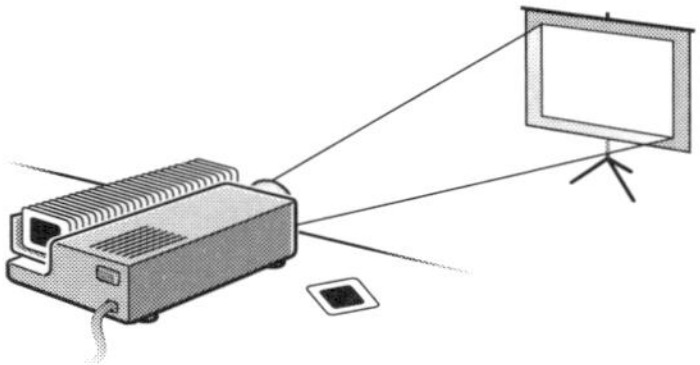

An enlargement of a diagram can be constructed by first drawing lines from a point O, the *centre of enlargement*, through points of the figure such as A, B and C, then marking off the image points A′, B′ and C′ so that OA′ = kOA, OB′ = kOB and OC′ = kOC, where k is

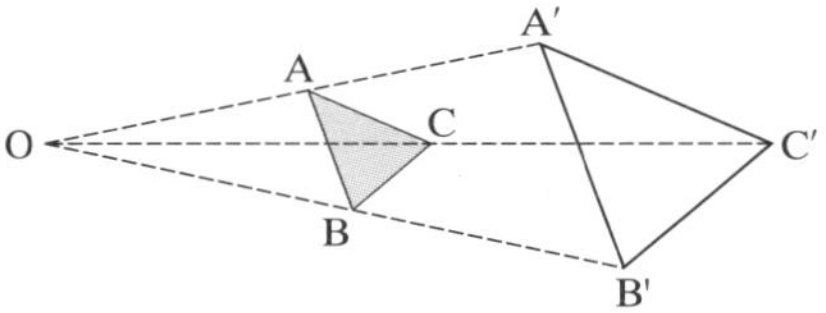

the scale factor of the enlargement. In the example shown, triangle ABC has been enlarged with scale factor $k = 2$. (k is sometimes known as the linear scale factor.)

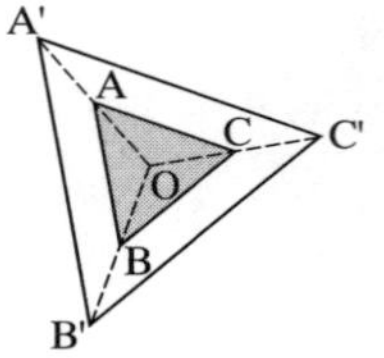

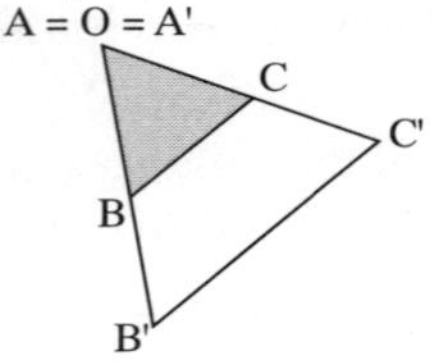

The centre of the enlargement may be a point outside the object, inside it, or on its boundary. Also, the scale factor can be negative. In this case it is still true that for every point P its image point P′ is given by OP′ = kOP, but now OP′ is measured from O in the opposite direction to OP. The example shows the effect of $k = -\frac{3}{2}$. It is equivalent to an enlargement with $k = \frac{3}{2}$ followed by a half-turn rotation about O.

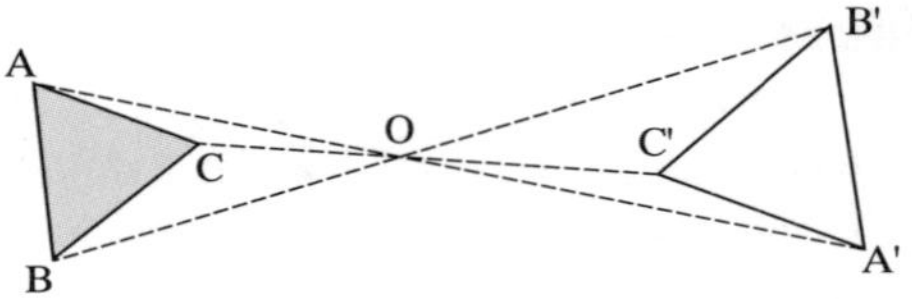

■ See **Area scale factor** and **Volume scale factor**.

Enlargement matrix

Any matrix of the form

$$\begin{pmatrix} k & 0 \\ 0 & k \end{pmatrix}$$

will produce an enlargement with a linear scale factor k when used for a geometrical transformation.

Envelope

Consider the pattern produced by drawing the lines from the points on the x-axis to those on the y-axis where the sum of the x-coordinate and the y-coordinate is always 12. All the lines appear to touch a curve. This curve is called the *envelope* of the lines, and in this example it is a parabola.

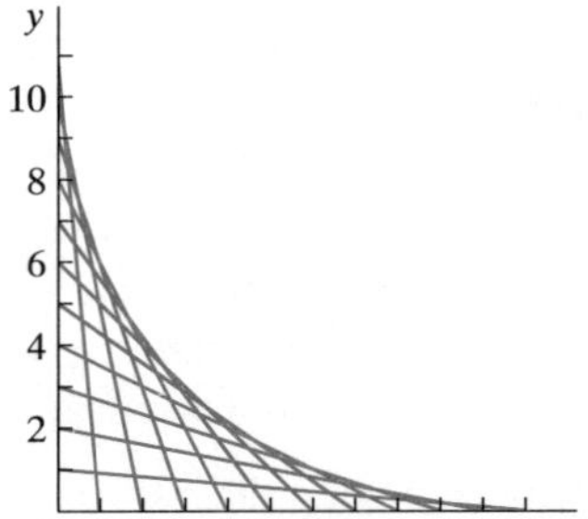

There are many curves formed from families of lines in this way.

Equally likely

When the chances of two things happening are the same, they are said to be equally likely. For example, when an unbiased coin is tossed it is as likely to land heads up as tails up, while an ordinary dice has an equal chance of landing with any one of 1, 2, 3, 4, 5, or 6 on top.

Equation

An equation is a mathematical statement involving an '=' sign. For example,

$$3x - 2 = 4 \qquad x^2 - 3x + 2 = 0 \qquad x + y = 8$$

Any value of the **variable** which makes the equation true is called a **solution** of the equation. In the examples given, 2 is a solution of the first two equations because $(3 \times 2) - 2 = 4$ and $2^2 - (3 \times 2) + 2 = 0$. The second equation also has 1 as a solution. The third equation has two variables, x and y, and its solution requires values for each of them. Any pair of numbers such as $x = 3$ and $y = 5$ or $x = -2.5$ and $y = 10.5$ whose sum is 8 is a solution in this case.

See **Equation of a line**, **Linear equation** and **Quadratic equation**.

Equation of a line

When pairs of numbers such as (4, 0), (5, 1) and (6, 2) satisfying $y = x - 4$ are plotted as points on a **graph**, they all lie on a straight line, and $y = x - 4$ is called its equation.

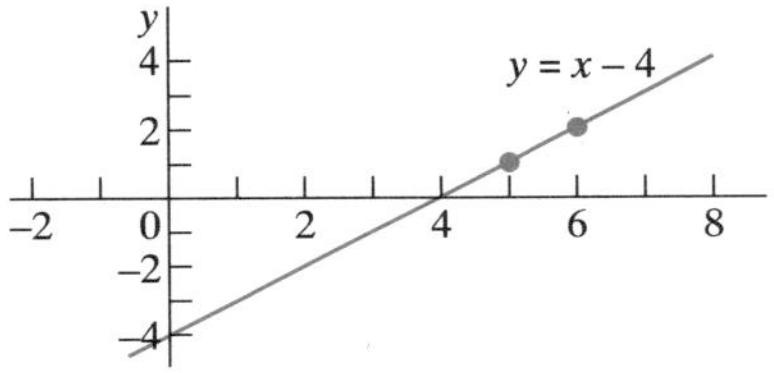

Almost all straight lines in the plane can be represented by an equation of the form $y = mx + c$, where the number c gives the value of the y-coordinate where the line crosses the y-axis, and the number m is the **gradient** of the line.

The second example shows the line with equation $y = 3x + 2$, which cuts the y-axis where $y = 2$, and has a gradient of 3.

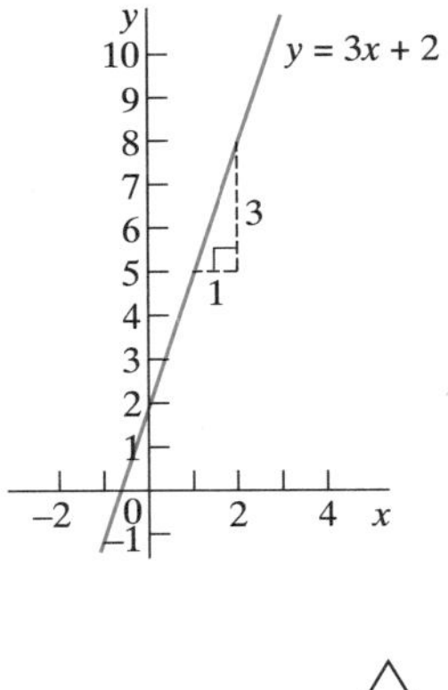

See **Intercept**.

Equilateral triangle

An equilateral triangle is a **triangle** whose sides are all of equal length. Its angles are all 60°.

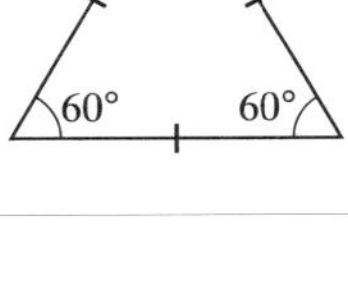

Equivalent fractions

$$\frac{2}{3}, \quad \frac{4}{6}, \quad \frac{6}{9}, \quad \frac{10}{15}, \quad \frac{14}{21}, \quad \ldots, \quad \frac{2a}{3a}$$

are **fractions** which all **cancel** down to $\frac{2}{3}$ in their *simplest form*, so they are all equal in value. Such fractions are said to be equivalent to each other.

See **Reduce to simplest form**.

Equivalent ratios

Two **ratios** such as 8 : 20 and 6 : 15 are equivalent when they can be reduced to the same numbers by division or multiplication by a **common factor**. In this case dividing the numbers in the first ratio by 4 and the second by 3 reduces them both to 2 : 5.

See **Equivalent fractions**.

Error

See **Accuracy of measurement**.

Estimate

To estimate is to give an approximate answer. This may be to give a rough idea of the result of a numerical calculation, for example, by first giving the numbers to 1 **significant figure**:

$$\frac{3.124 \times 98.76}{18.34} \approx \frac{3 \times 100}{20} = 15$$

Areas may be estimated by approximating a shape by a simple **polygon** whose area is easy to find.

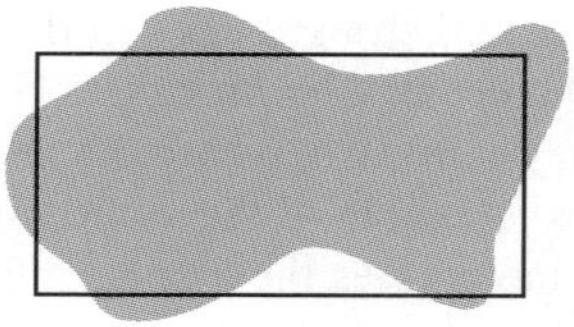

Euler's formula

The Swiss mathematician Leonard Euler (1707-83) showed that the numbers of **vertices** (V), **edges** (E) and **faces** (F) of a **polyhedron** satisfy the formula

$$V - E + F = 2.$$

For example, for a **cube** $V = 8$, $E = 12$ and $F = 6$, while for a triangular **prism** $V = 6$, $E = 9$ and $F = 5$.

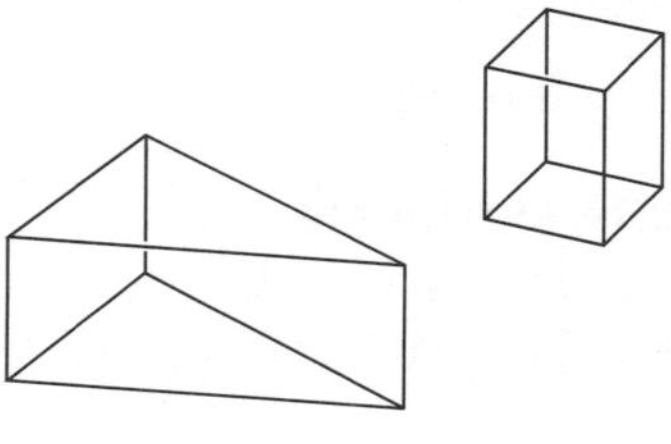

A similar formula applies to networks:

$$N - A + R = 2$$

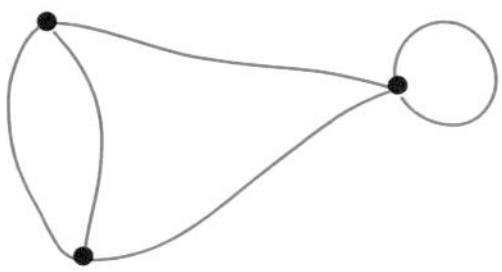

where N is the number of **nodes**, A the number of **arcs**, and R the number of **regions** into which a **network** divides the **plane**, including the region 'outside' the network. In the example shown, $N = 3$, $A = 5$ and $R = 4$.

Evaluate

To evaluate means to find the value of. Evaluating $\sqrt{a^2 + b^2}$, for example, when $a = 5$ and $b = 12$, requires that the numbers are substituted for the letters and the resulting calculation carried out:

$$\sqrt{5^2 + 12^2} = \sqrt{25 + 144} = \sqrt{169} = 13$$

Even numbers

These are the numbers, 2, 4, 6, 8, 10, …, the **multiples** of 2. Any number which has 2 as a factor is even. Every number which ends in 0, 2, 4, 6 or 8 is an even number. For example, 3678 and 24 790 are even but 24 683 is odd.

See **Odd numbers**.

Evens

When a coin is tossed there is an equal chance of it landing head or tail uppermost. This is sometimes described as an *even chance*. Evens is the name given to the **probability** of any **event** which has a 50% chance of happening.

Event

'Event' is a term used in statistics for a happening whose **probability** is being sought. For example, the event may be drawing the name of a person from a hat. If there are five names in the hat the probability of drawing the name of a particular person is $\frac{1}{5}$.

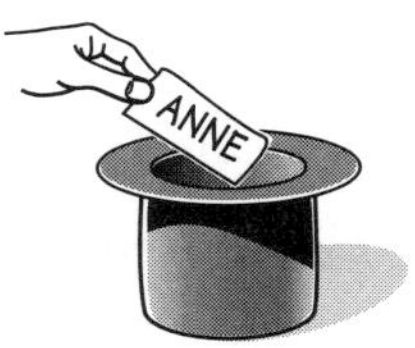

Exchange rates

When travelling abroad it is necessary to exchange British money for the currency of the country being visited: dollars in the USA, francs in France, marks in Germany, yen in Japan, and so on. The rate at which you can buy the foreign currency is known as the exchange rate. For example, when the exchange rate for the US dollar was quoted as \$1.54 to £1, a traveller could exchange £250 for 250 x \$1.54 = \$385. Or an American coming to England with \$462 could buy £(462 ÷ 1.54) = £300.

Exclusive events

Two **events** A and B are exclusive if they cannot occur together. For example, if A is the event 'getting a total of 6 when throwing two dice' and B is 'getting a total of 9 when throwing two dice' then A and B are exclusive, for they cannot both happen at the same time. However, if C is the event 'getting a double when throwing two dice' A and C are not exclusive as both are possible with a throw of two 3s.

When three or more events are such that no two of them can occur at the same time, they are said to be *mutually exclusive*.

Expand

An algebraic expression is expanded by multiplying out **brackets**. For example, $a(b + c)$ becomes $ab + bc$, while

$$\begin{aligned}(2x + 3)(x - 1) &= 2x(x - 1) + 3(x - 1)\\ &= 2x^2 - 2x + 3x - 3\\ &= 2x^2 + x - 3\end{aligned}$$

■ See **Distributive law**.

Exponent

$$32 = 2^5 \qquad 27 = 3^3 \qquad 5 = 25^{\frac{1}{2}}$$

When one number is expressed as a **power** of another number, the power to which the second number has been raised is called its exponent. In the above examples the exponents are 5, 3, and $\frac{1}{2}$.

Many calculators have an exponential key labelled x^y for raising numbers to a power. For example, to calculate 2^9 using a calculator press the keys

[2] [x^y] [9] [=].

Exponential function

Suppose a population of bacteria doubles in size every hour. If its population was 100 when first seen, then the population P after t hours will be given by

$$P = 100 \times 2^t$$

Any **function** like this which involves a **power** is called an exponential function.

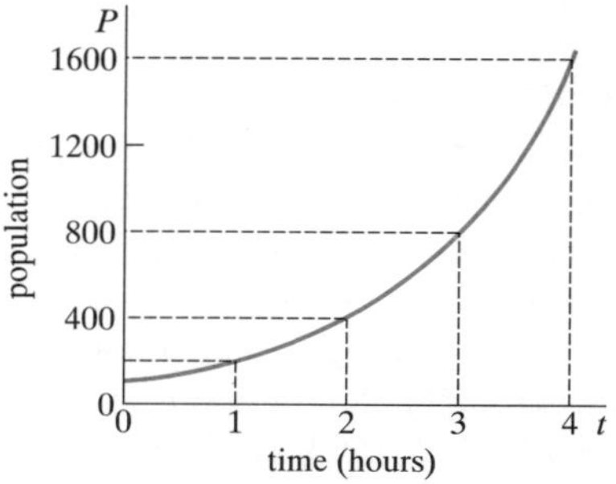

Another example is the amount £A accumulated after n years from investing £500 at 6% **compound interest**:

$$A = 500 \times 1.06^n$$

Expression

An expression is a set of connected mathematical symbols such as

$5xy^2$ $\quad$ $3 \sin x + 2 \cos x$ $\quad$ $\sqrt{a^2 + b^2}$

See **Formula**.

Exterior angle

When a side of a **polygon** is extended beyond the **vertex**, as at A, then the **angle** between the extended side and the **adjacent side** is called the exterior angle of the polygon at A.

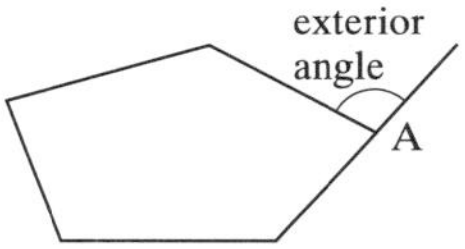

The sum of all the exterior angles of any polygon is 360°, as can be seen by an imaginary walk around the **perimeter** of the polygon and noting the angles turned through.

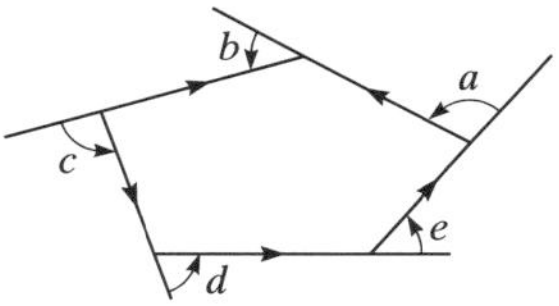

$$a + b + c + d + e = 360°$$

See **Interior angle**.

Extrapolate

Town planners use the evidence of population numbers up to the present to predict the likely population in the years ahead. When they do this they are said to be extrapolating from the known **data** into the unknown beyond. To extrapolate is to use known data to predict data outside the range of the known data.

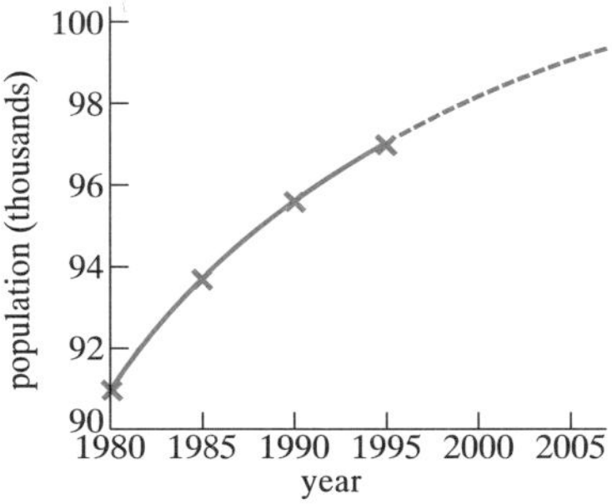

See **Interpolate**.

Face

The flat sides of a **polyhedron** are called its faces.

A **cube** has 6 faces.

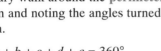

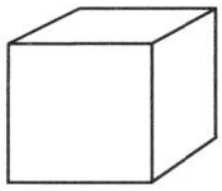

The **prism** shown here has 5 faces (3 of them are rectangular and 2 of them are triangular).

The **pyramid** shown has 5 faces (4 of them are triangular and 1 is square).

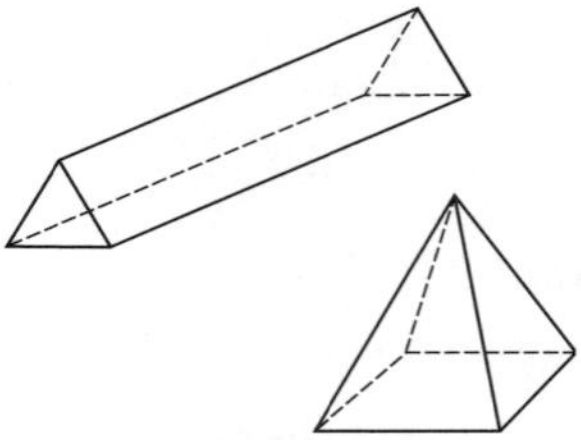

■ See **Euler's formula**.

Factorise

To factorise a number means to write it as a **product** of its factors. For example, 10 can be written as 1 x 10 or 2 x 5, while 12 can be written as 1 x 12 or 2 x 6 or 3 x 4.

In the same way an algebraic **expression** can be factorised by writing it as a product of its factors. For example, $2x + 2y$ can be factorised as $2 \times (x + y)$, usually written $2(x + y)$. Similarly,

$$pq + ps = p(q + s)$$
$$a^2 - b^2 = (a - b)(a + b)$$
$$3x^2 - 5x - 2 = (3x + 1)(x - 2)$$

■ See **Distributive law**.

Factors

The factors of a **whole number** are the whole numbers which divide into it exactly. For example, the factors of 18 are 1, 2, 3, 6, 9 and 18.

A **prime number** has only two factors, 1 and the number itself. For example, the factors of the prime number 7 are 1 and 7, the factors of the prime number 19 are 1 and 19.

A whole number can be written as a product of its **prime factors**. For example,

$$18 = 2 \times 3 \times 3 = 2 \times 3^2$$
$$60 = 2^2 \times 3 \times 5$$

■ See **Common factor**.

Fibonacci sequence

The Fibonacci **sequence** is the set of numbers

1, 1, 2, 3, 5, 8, 13, 21,…

in which each number from the third onwards is obtained by adding the previous two. For example,

$5 = 2 + 3$

$21 = 8 + 13$

Any sequence which obeys this rule is a Fibonacci sequence, no matter what the first two numbers are. For example,

4, 7, 11, 18, 29, 47, …

Fibonacci (1180-1250) was an Italian mathematician who is said to have introduced the sequence in connection with a problem about the growth in the number of rabbits.

Finite

A set of numbers which does not go on and on for ever is said to be finite. For example, the set consisting of 1, 3, 5, 7, 9, 11 is a finite set containing 6 numbers. By contrast, the set of all **odd numbers** is not finite - it is said to be **infinite**.

Flow chart, flow diagram

A flow diagram (or chart) is used to show a set of instructions.

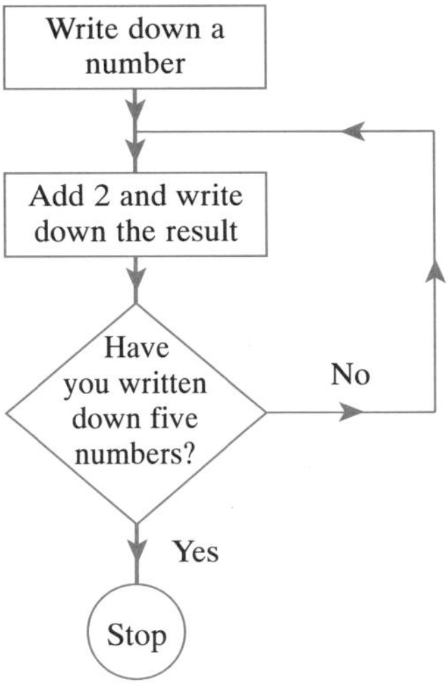

An **equation** such as $2x + 7 = 19$ can be written as a flow diagram:

The equation can be solved by putting the flow diagram into 'reverse':

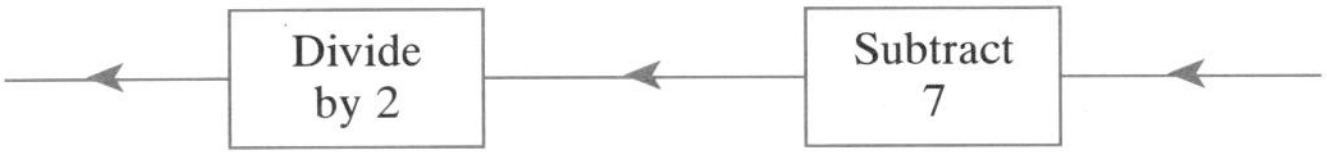

Focus

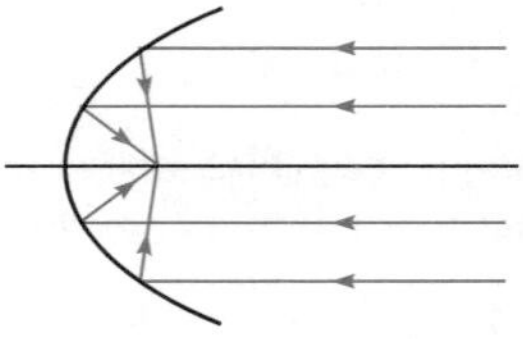

The curve called a **parabola** has the property that when rays of light (or heat) **parallel** to the axis of the parabola are reflected by the curve, they all pass through a single point. This point is called the focus of the parabola.

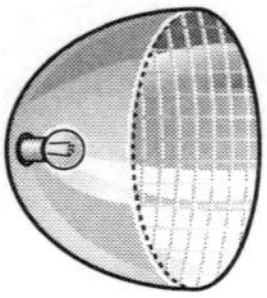

The principle is used the other way round in a car headlight: the cross-section of a headlight is a parabola, and the bulb is at the focus. The reflected rays of light then form a parallel beam.

Foot (*pl.* feet)

A foot is a unit of length, roughly corresponding to the length of an average person's foot. It is about 30 centimetres.

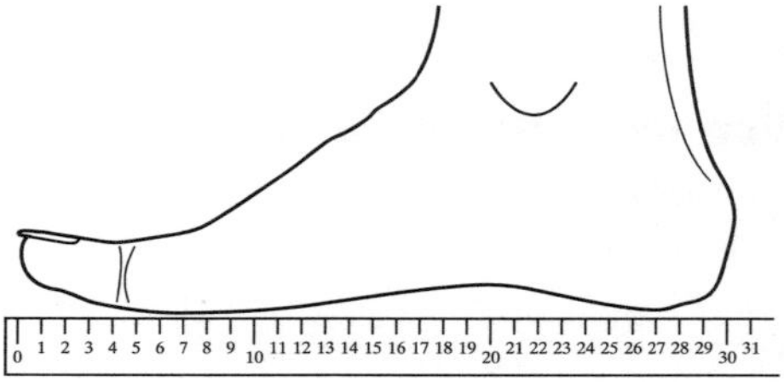

A tall person is about 6 feet high. 6 feet is sometimes written 6′.

A foot is subdivided into 12 inches.

There are 5280 feet in a mile.

See **Imperial units**.

Foot of the perpendicular

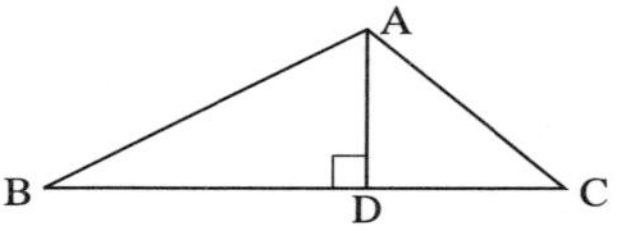

In the diagram D is called the foot of the **perpendicular** from A to BC.

Formula (*pl.* formulae)

A formula is a general rule usually expressed algebraically.

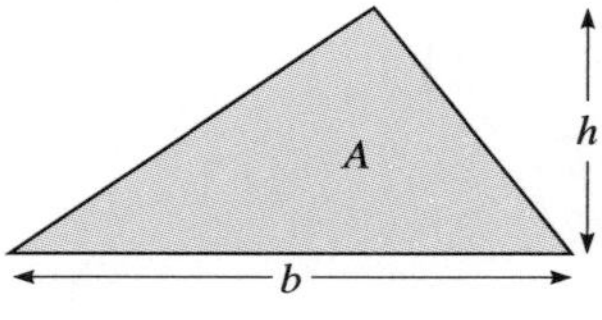

For example, the **area** A of a **triangle** can be found by multiplying the base by the height and dividing by 2. This can be written as a formula $A = (b \times h) \div 2$ or more usually

$$A = \frac{1}{2} bh$$

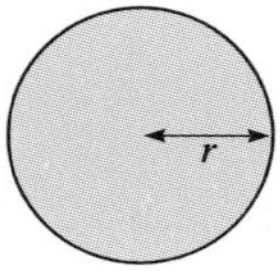

The area A of a **circle** of **radius** r can be found by squaring the radius and multiplying by π (about 3.14). This can be written as $A = r^2 \times \pi$ or more usually

$$A = \pi r^2$$

When a heavy object is dropped, an approximate formula for the distance d metres fallen in t seconds is

$$d = 5t^2$$

The approximate time T seconds for a pendulum of length l metres to complete one swing is given by

$$T = 2\pi\sqrt{\frac{l}{10}}$$

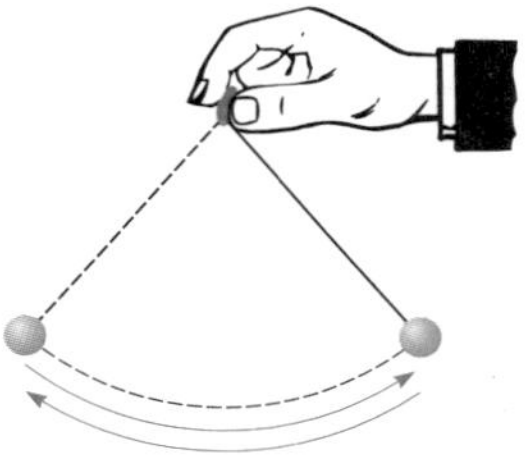

Fractal

A fractal is a curve which has the same degree of regularity no matter at what distance or magnification it is viewed. One of the simplest such curves is the Koch snowflake curve, named after the Swedish mathematician Helge von Koch who first described it in 1904. To see how it is formed, start with an equilateral triangle, then construct equilateral triangles on the middle third of each side, as shown, to form a six-pointed star. Now construct equilateral triangles on the middle third of each side of the star, and continue the process indefinitely.

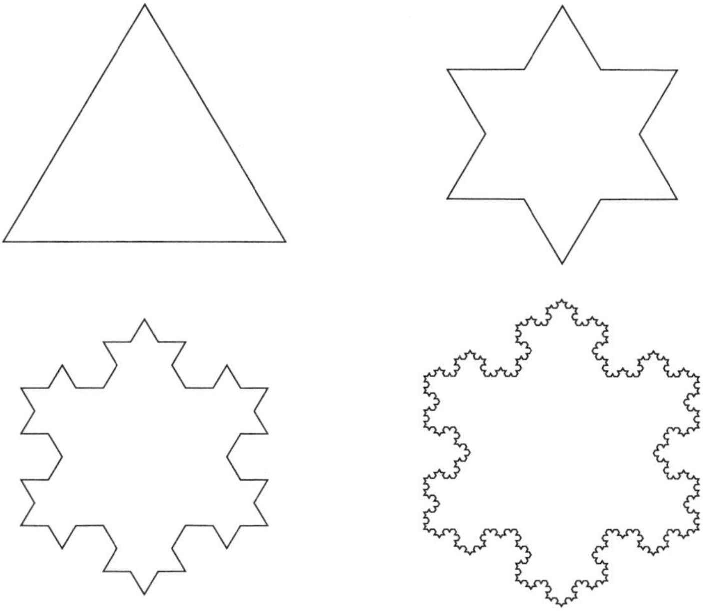

Fractals are commonly used in computer-generated graphics.

Fractional change

Which is of more significance, an increase in price from £100 to £110, or an increase from £20 to £30? In both cases the actual change is £10, but in the first one the fractional change is $\frac{10}{100}$, which is $\frac{1}{10}$, and in the second one the fractional change is $\frac{10}{20}$, which is $\frac{1}{2}$. Although the actual change is the same in both cases, the fractional change is larger in the second case.

The fractional change is

$$\frac{\text{actual change}}{\text{original value}}$$

■ See **Percentage change**.

Fractions

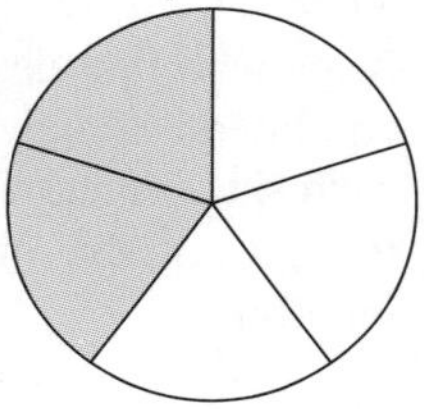

A fraction is part of a whole. For example, the circle on the right has been split into 5 equal parts. Each is called a fifth, written $\frac{1}{5}$. The fraction of the whole circle which has been shaded is

$$\frac{\text{the number of shaded parts}}{\text{the number of parts altogether}} = \frac{2}{5} \text{ (two fifths)}$$

The top number of a fraction is called the **numerator** and the bottom number is the **denominator**.

■ See **Decimal numbers**, **Equivalent fractions**, **Improper fraction** and **Percentage**.

Frequency

When collecting **data** the number of times a particular item occurs is called its frequency. For example, suppose the shoe sizes of the 25 people in a class were recorded and the shoe size 7 occurred 9 times. Then the frequency of shoe size 7 was 9.

Shoe size	Frequency
5	2
6	5
7	9
8	6
9	3
Total	25

The table is called a *frequency table*.

The information in the table can be illustrated using a frequency diagram (a **bar chart**). The mid-points of the tops of the bars can be joined to form a frequency polygon.

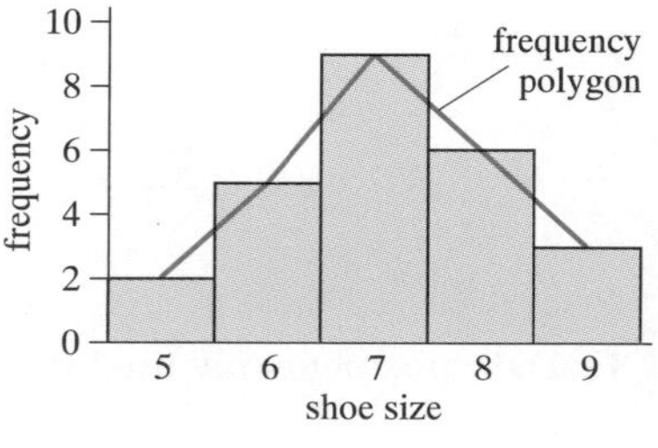

Function

A function is a rule connecting two sets such that for each item in the first set there is just one item which it is related to in the second set.

It can be thought of as a 'machine' with an input and an output. For example,

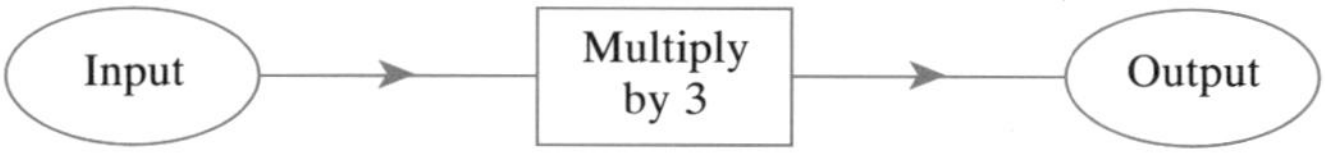

This can be written algebraically as $x \mapsto 3x$.

Strictly, to specify a function the input set (the **domain**) and the output set (the **range**) should be stated. Usually they are sets of numbers such as the **real numbers**.

Functions can be represented on **number lines** or by using the input and output numbers as **coordinates** to obtain a **graph**

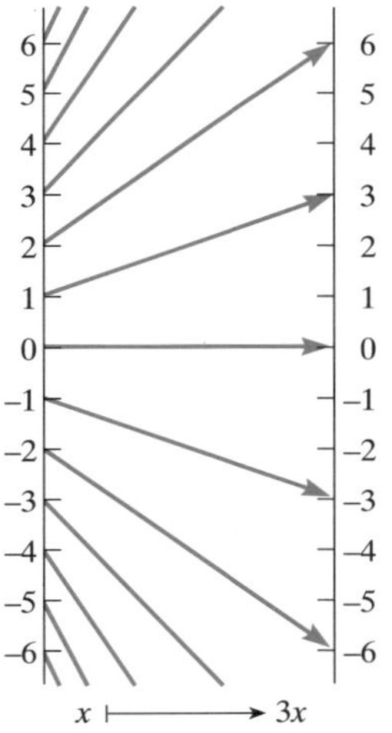

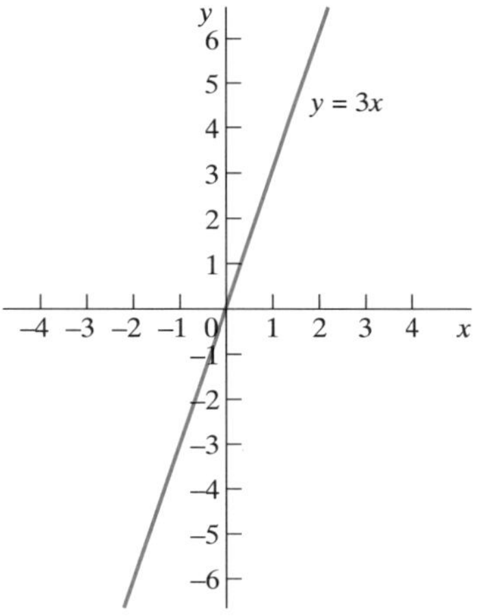

A function is often represented by a letter. For example, the 'multiply by 3' function could be represented by *f*. Then the function is written

$$f{:}x \mapsto 3x$$

which is read as '*f* is the function such that *x* goes to 3*x*'.

The output corresponding to an input of *x* is written $f(x)$ (read as '*f* of *x*'). For example, for the 'multiply by 3' function $f(x) = 3x$.

See **Composite function**.

Gallon

A gallon is a measure of **capacity** (**volume**) in the imperial system of measures. One gallon is about 4.55 **litres**. A petrol tank in a small car might hold about 8 gallons.

1 gallon = 8 **pints** = 4 quarts

See **Imperial units**.

Generalise

To generalise means to make a statement which holds in *all* cases, not just in some particular cases. A generalisation is often expressed algebraically.

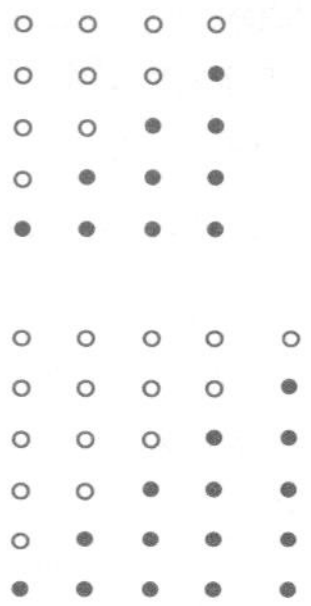

For example, the diagram on the right shows that the 4th **triangle number** is (4 x 5) ÷ 2 (because two lots of the 4th triangle number make a '4 by 5' rectangle).

In the same way the 5th triangle number is (5 x 6) ÷ 2.

The method can be generalised:
the *n*th triangle number is $n(n + 1) \div 2$.

Geometry

Geometry is the study of properties of shapes and of space. The word 'geometry' comes from the Greek words *geo*, meaning 'earth' (as in 'geography') and *metry*, meaning 'measurement'.

Glide reflection

A glide reflection is a **transformation** involving a **translation** and a **reflection** in a line **parallel** to the translation.

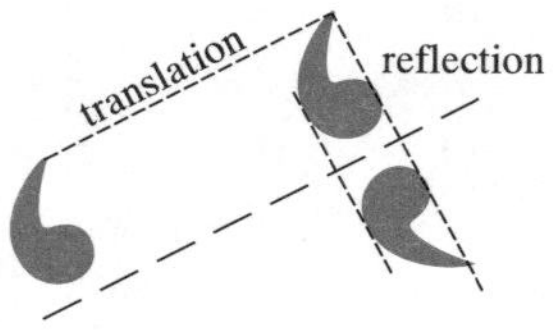

Some strip patterns (on belts or wallpaper borders) are based on glide reflections.

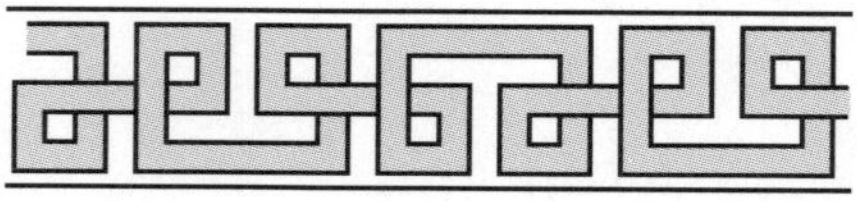

Gradient

The gradient, or slope, of a line can be obtained by taking any two points, A and B, on it and dividing the distance up from A to B by the distance across:

$$\text{gradient} = \frac{\text{distance up}}{\text{distance across}}$$

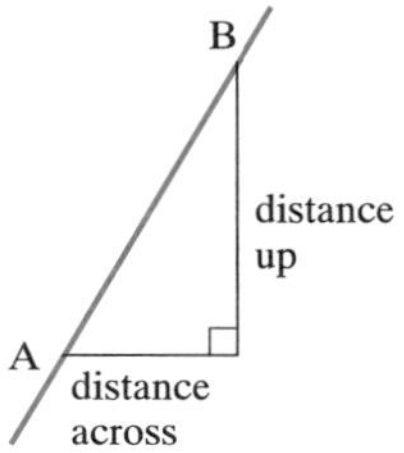

This tells you how far you go up for each unit step across.

The gradient of the line with equation $y = 2x + 1$ is 2.

The gradient of the line with equation $y = -2x + 1$ is -2.

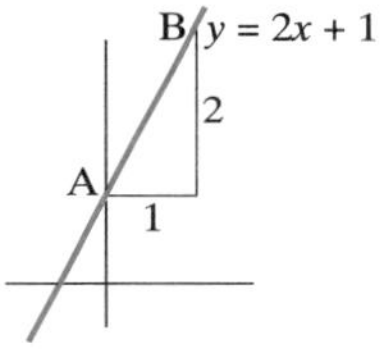

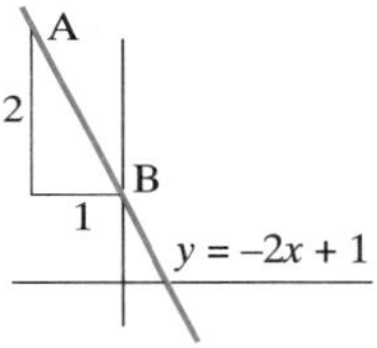

Gram

A gram is a measure of **mass**. It is roughly the mass of a **cubic centimetre** of water at 4°C.

A packet of crisps has a mass of about 25 grams, written 25 g.

There are 1000 grams in 1 **kilogram**.

Graph

A graph is a way of showing a relationship pictorially. For example, the diagram on the right shows how the distance travelled by a car on a motorway changes when it goes at 70 mph for 30 minutes and then at 40 mph for 15 minutes.

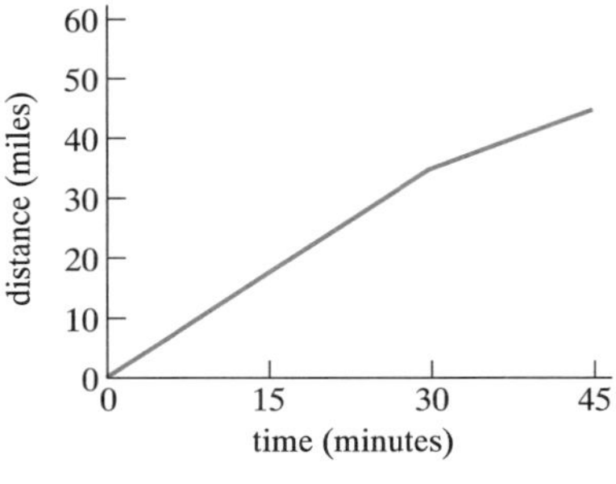

The diagrams below show graphs of sets of points whose **coordinates** are connected by algebraic **relationships**.

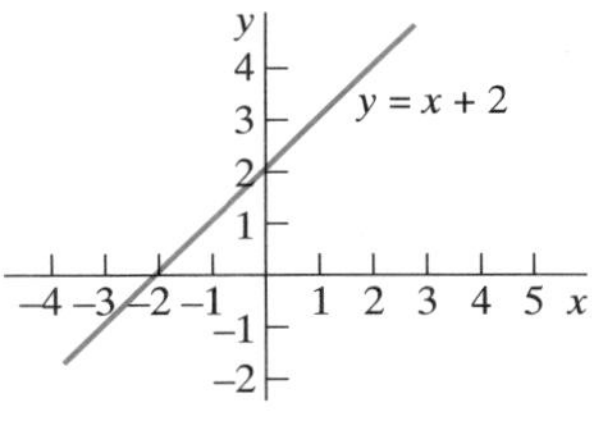

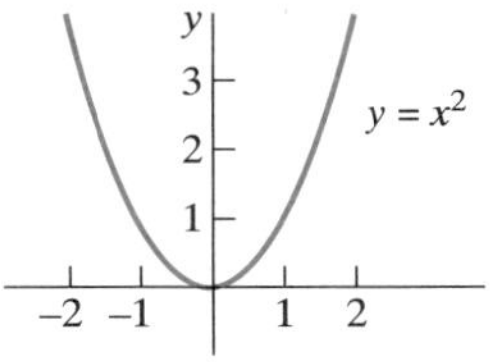

Great circle

A **plane** which passes through the centre of a **sphere** intersects the sphere in a great circle.

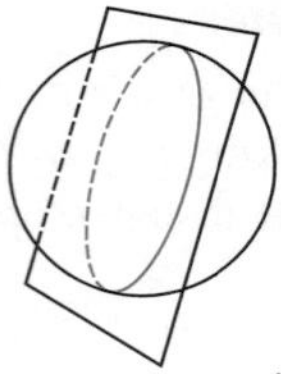

For example, circles of **longitude** on a globe are great circles, but circles of **latitude** are not great circles (except for the equator). Great circles are the largest circles which can be drawn on a sphere. Circles of latitude, apart from the equator, are not as large.

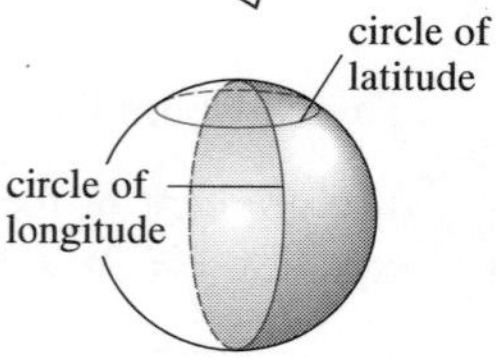

The shortest distance between two points on a sphere is along the great circle passing through the points.

Greater than

See **Inequality**.

Grouped data

When **data** is being collected it is sometimes convenient to record it in groups or **class intervals**. For example, the percentage marks in an examination might be recorded in groups as shown in the table.

Mark	Tally	Frequency
41-50	//	2
51-60	~~////~~ /	6
61-70	~~////~~ ~~////~~	10
71-80	~~////~~ ~~////~~ /	11
81-90	////	4
91-100	///	3
		36

With continuous data (i.e. involving measurement), such as heights, a decision has to be taken in advance as to whether a measurement which appears to be on a boundary is counted 'up' or 'down'.

See **Frequency** and **Histogram**.

Half-line

A line extends indefinitely in two directions, for example to the left and to the right. This is indicated by the dashes at each end.

A half line has one end point and extends indefinitely in one direction.

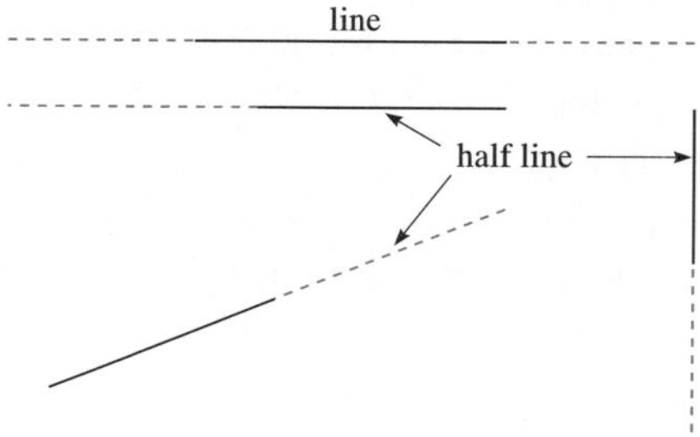

Half turn

A half turn is a **rotation** through 180° (half of a full turn).

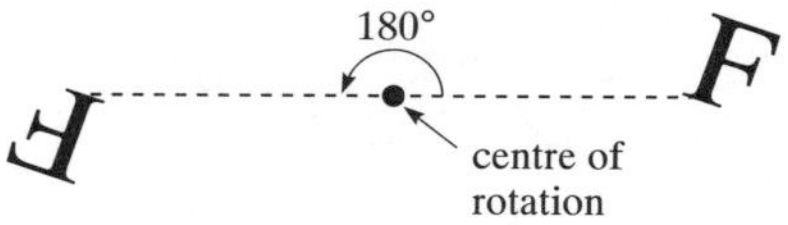

Hectare

A hectare is a measure of **area**. One hectare is 10 000 square **metres**, equivalent to the area of a square 100 metres by 100 metres. A hectare is approximately $2\frac{1}{2}$ **acres**, about the size of a rugby pitch.

Helix

A helix is a **spiral** in three dimensions.

Hemisphere

A hemisphere is half of a **sphere**. The **volume** of a hemisphere of **radius** r is $\frac{2}{3}\pi r^3$.

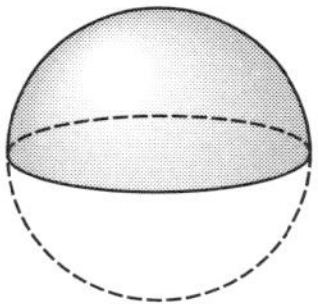

Heptagon

A heptagon is a **polygon** with 7 sides. A regular heptagon has all its sides equal in length and all its **interior angles** equal to $128\frac{4}{7}°$.

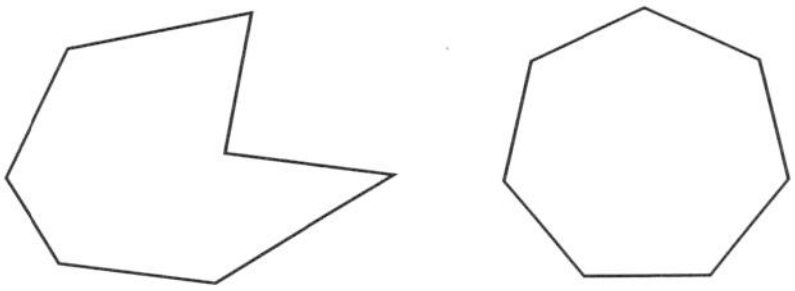

Hexadecimal numbers

Hexadecimal numbers are numbers in **base** sixteen. They are expressed using groupings of units, sixteens, $(\text{sixteens})^2$, $(\text{sixteens})^3$ and so on. In addition to the **digits** 0, 1, 2, …, 9, the letters A, B, C, D, E and F are used to represent the numbers ten to fifteen. For example, the hexadecimal number 23D stands for $2 \times 256 + 3 \times 16 + 13$ in base ten which is 573.

Hexadecimal numbers are used in electronics and information technology (for example, in specifying background and text colours on Internet Web pages). They are more compact than **binary numbers** since they use fewer digits but they can easily be converted into binary numbers, and vice versa. For example, to express 47_{sixteen} as a binary number, write each digit as a binary number with four columns and then delete any zeros on the left:

$$47_{\text{sixteen}} = 0100_{\text{two}} | 0111_{\text{two}} = 1000111_{\text{two}}$$

Hexagon

A hexagon is a polygon with 6 sides. A regular hexagon has all its sides equal in length and all its interior angles equal to 120°.

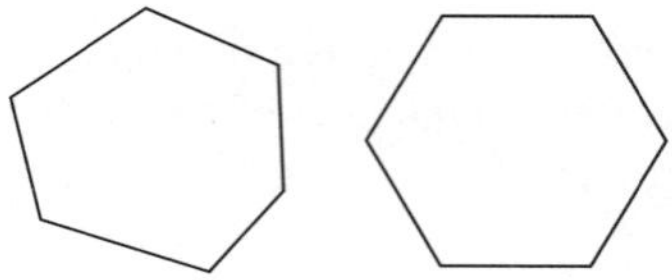

Highest common factor (HCF)

See **Common factor**.

Histogram

A histogram is a frequency diagram (bar chart) in which the area of each bar, rather than the height of each bar, gives the frequency. It is particularly useful when the class intervals are unequal.

For example, a student recorded the time gaps between vehicles passing along a road, obtaining the results and frequency diagram shown.

Time (seconds)	Frequency
0–5	26
5–10	20
10–15	16
15–30	12
30–50	4

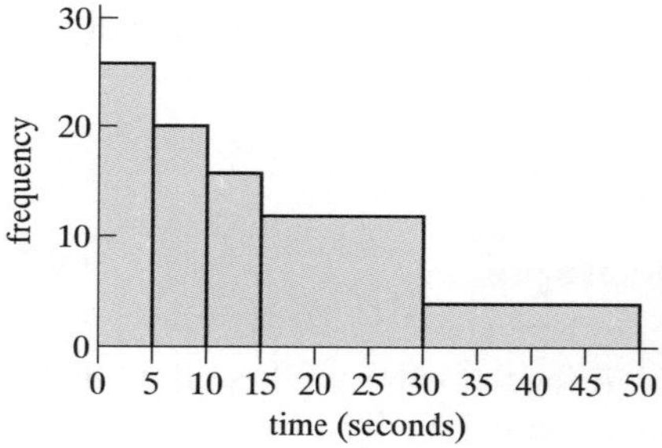

On the frequency diagram the large blocks for 15–30 and 30–50 give a misleading impression. It is more sensible to make the area of each bar, rather than the height, represent the frequency. Then the axis up the page is labelled 'frequency per 5 seconds'. Such a diagram is called a histogram.

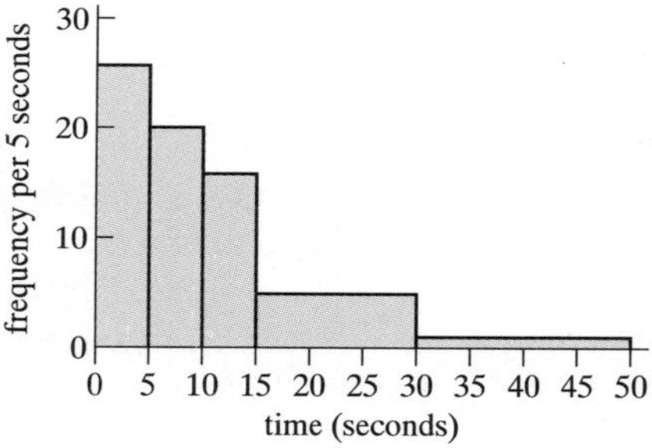

Horizontal

Horizontal means parallel to the horizon.

We appear to live on a flat surface and we think of the horizon as a straight line.

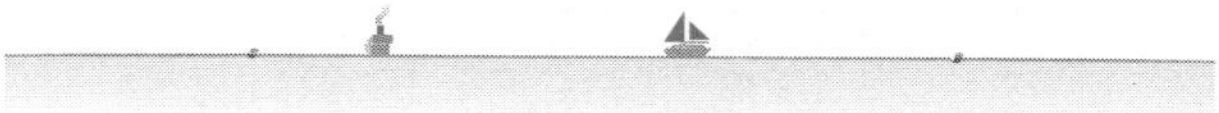

Lines on this flat surface are said to be horizontal. For example, any line across the floor of a room is horizontal. Any line on a level table is horizontal.

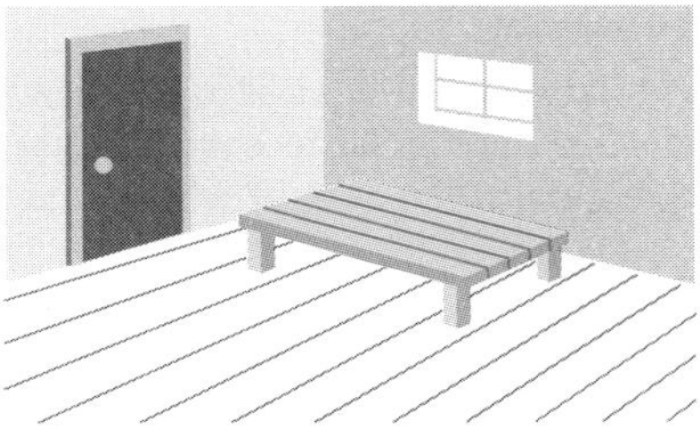

See **Vertical**.

Hyperbola

The graph shows the **relationship** between the lengths x cm and y cm of the sides of rectangles of area 24 cm². The **equation** of the graph is

$$xy = 24 \quad \text{or, equivalently,}$$

$$y = \frac{24}{x}$$

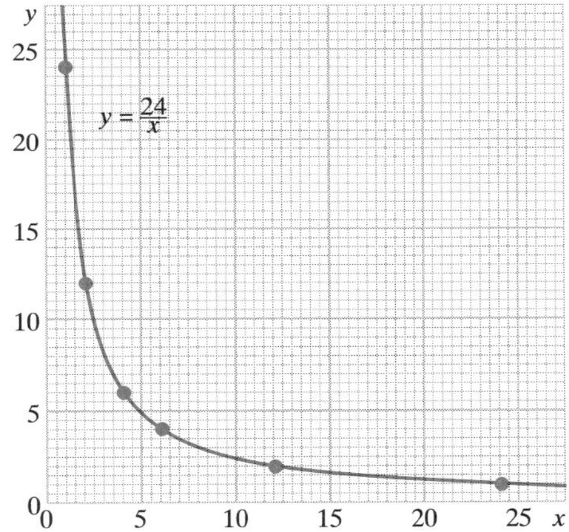

The curve formed by the graph is called a hyperbola.

More generally, the graph of any equation of the form

$$y = \frac{c}{x}$$

where c is a constant, is a hyperbola. (When x and y are allowed to be negative, the graph of such an equation is in two parts, one in the positive quadrant, as shown here, and the other, related to it by a half turn about the origin, in the negative quadrant.)

A hyperbola also arises as a section of a **cone**.

See **Conic section** and **Varies inversely as**.

Hypotenuse

The longest side of a **right-angled triangle** is called the hypotenuse of the triangle.

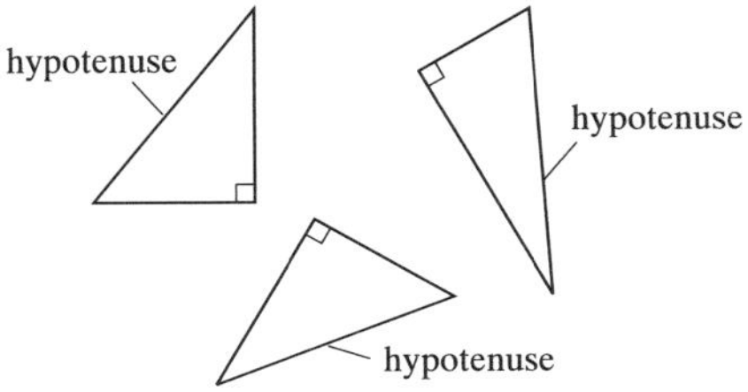

See **Pythagoras' theorem**.

Icosahedron

An icosahedron is a **polyhedron** with 20 **faces**. A regular icosahedron has triangular faces each of which is an **equilateral triangle**. The word *icos* comes from the Greek for 'twenty'.

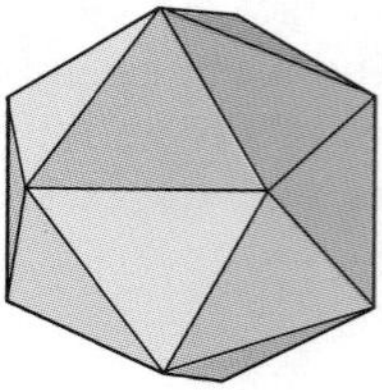

Identity element

An identity element is an **element** which when combined with another element does not change it. For example, 0 is the identity element for addition of numbers because, when a is any number, $0 + a = a$ and $a + 0 = a$; 1 is the identity element for multiplication of numbers because $1 \times a = a$ and $a \times 1 = a$; the **matrix** $\begin{pmatrix}1 & 0\\0 & 1\end{pmatrix}$ is the identity element for multiplication of 2 by 2 matrices because

$$\begin{pmatrix}1 & 0\\0 & 1\end{pmatrix}\begin{pmatrix}p & q\\r & s\end{pmatrix} = \begin{pmatrix}p & q\\r & s\end{pmatrix} \quad \text{and} \quad \begin{pmatrix}p & q\\r & s\end{pmatrix}\begin{pmatrix}1 & 0\\0 & 1\end{pmatrix} = \begin{pmatrix}p & q\\r & s\end{pmatrix}$$

for any 2 by 2 matrix $\begin{pmatrix}p & q\\r & s\end{pmatrix}$

Image

The image of an object (such as a shape or a number) is the result after it has been transformed. Here are some examples.

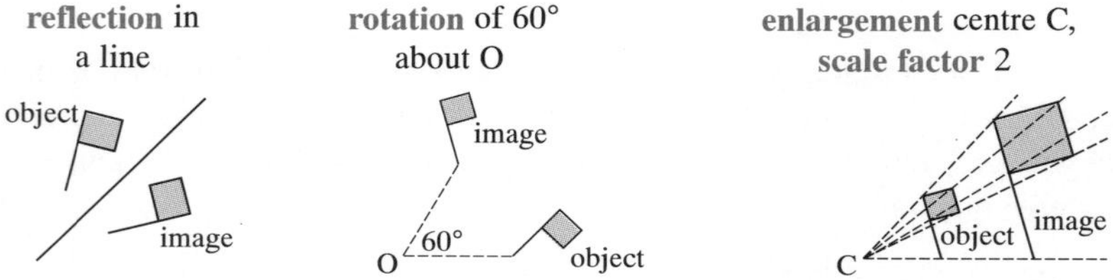

For the **function** $x \mapsto 3x$, the image of 2 is 6.

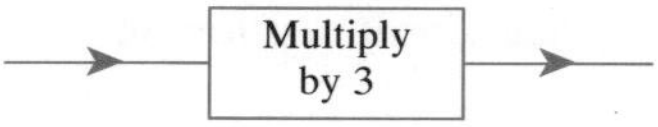

The set of numbers {0, 1, 2} is transformed to the set {0, 3, 6}. The set {0, 3, 6} is called the *image set*.

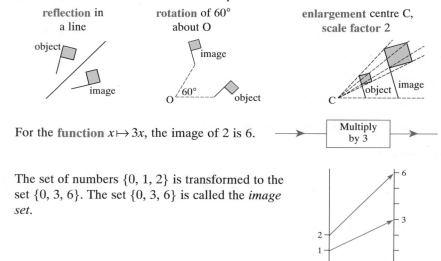

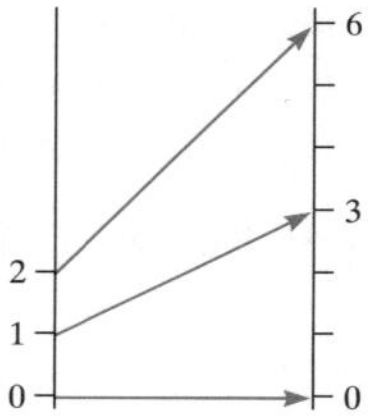

Imperial units

Imperial units are the traditional units of measurement. In many countries they have now been replaced by **metric units**.

In imperial units length is measured in **inches**, **feet**, **yards**, **miles**; **mass** is measured in **ounces**, **pounds**, stones, hundredweights, **tons**; **capacity** is measured in **pints**, quarts, **gallons**.

Improper fraction

An improper fraction is a fraction in which the top number (the **numerator**) is larger than the bottom number (the **denominator**). For example, $\frac{5}{4}, \frac{17}{10}, \frac{123}{100}$ are improper fractions.

See **Proper fraction**.

Incentre, incircle

The three lines which **bisect** the angles of a triangle all meet at a point inside the triangle. This point is the same distance from each side of the triangle and so a **circle** can be drawn with its centre at this point touching the sides of the triangle. This point is called the *incentre* and the circle is called the *incircle*.

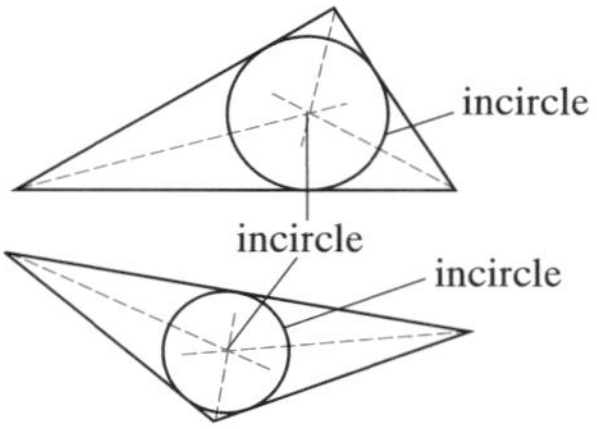

Inch

An inch is a unit of measurement in the **imperial system**. It is exactly 2.54 **centimetres**. The width of a man's thumb is about 1 inch. 1 inch is sometimes written 1″.

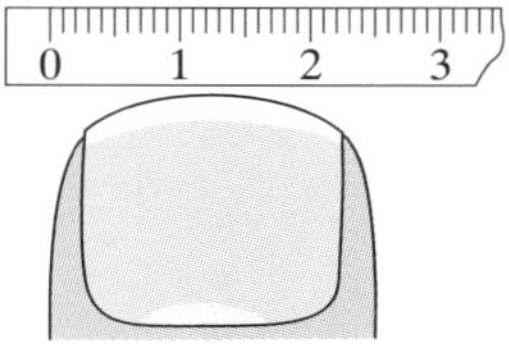

Independent events

Two **events** are independent when one does not depend on the other. For example, when a die and a coin are thrown together, the events 'The die shows a three' and 'The coin shows tails' are independent because the result on the coin does not depend upon the result on the die (and vice versa).

See **Dependent events**.

Independent variable

See **Dependent variable**.

Index (*pl.* indices)

When a number is raised to a power, for example 2^4 (meaning 2 x 2 x 2 x 2), the power is called the index, 4 in this case.

The pattern

$$\begin{array}{cccc} \rightarrow & \text{multiply by 2} & & \rightarrow \\ 2 & 4 & 8 & 16 \\ 2^1 & 2^2 & 2^3 & 2^4 \\ \rightarrow & \text{add 1 to the index} & & \rightarrow \end{array}$$

can be put into reverse and extended to the left

$$\begin{array}{ccccccccccc} & & & & & & \leftarrow & \text{divide by 2} & \leftarrow & & \\ \dots & \frac{1}{8} & \frac{1}{4} & \frac{1}{2} & 1 & 2 & 4 & 8 & 16 & \dots \\ \dots & 2^{-3} & 2^{-2} & 2^{-1} & 2^0 & 2^1 & 2^2 & 2^3 & 2^4 & \dots \\ & & & & \leftarrow & \text{subtract 1 from the index} & & & \leftarrow & \end{array}$$

This leads to the suggestion that

$$2^0 = 1 \qquad 2^{-1} = \frac{1}{2^1} \qquad 2^{-2} = \frac{1}{2^2} \qquad 2^{-3} = \frac{1}{2^3} \quad \text{etc.}$$

More generally, for any number a

$$a^0 = 1 \qquad a^{-n} = \frac{1}{a^n}$$

Particular examples such as

$$2^3 \times 2^4 = 2 \times 2 \times 2 \times 2 \times 2 \times 2 \times 2 = 2^7 \text{ and } (2^3)^4 = 2^{12}$$

suggest the general laws of indices (for integral powers)

$$a^m \times a^n = a^{m+n} \qquad a^p \div a^q = a^{p-q} \qquad (a^s)^t = a^{st}$$

These laws are also valid when m and n are not integers and can be used to give a meaning to a^x when x is any real number. For example, taking m and n as $\frac{1}{2}$ gives $a^{\frac{1}{2}} \times a^{\frac{1}{2}} = a^1$ and hence $a^{\frac{1}{2}}$ is the square root of a.

More generally, $a^{\frac{1}{q}}$ is the qth root of a, and $a^{\frac{p}{q}}$ is the qth root of a^p or the pth power of $a^{\frac{1}{q}}$.

Inequality

An inequality is a statement involving 'less than' (<) or 'greater than' (>) or 'less than or equal to' (≤) or 'greater than or equal to' (≥) or 'not equal to' (≠). For example,

$a < b$ means 'a is less than b';
$a > b$ means 'a is greater than b';
$a \leq b$ means 'a is less than or equal to b';
$a \geq b$ means 'a is greater than or equal to b'.

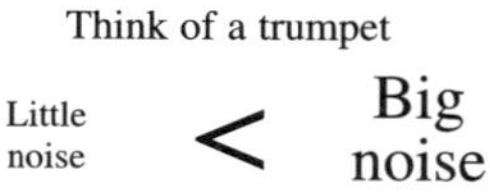

Inequalities between numbers can be pictured on a **number line**:

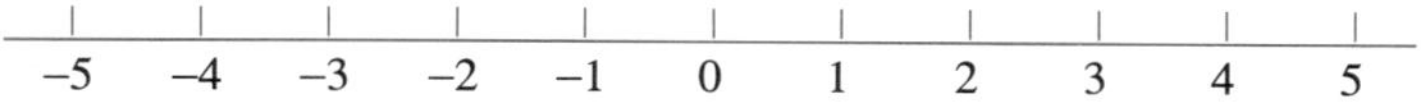

The numbers increase going from left to right. For example,

$-3 < -1$ $\quad -2 < 3$ $\quad 1 < 4$

$4 > 2$ $\quad 1 > -1$ $\quad -1 > -4$

Infinite

An infinite set of numbers is one which goes on and on without ending. For example,

2 4 8 16 32 … (powers of 2)

The dots at the end mean 'going on and on'.

■ See **Finite**.

Inscribe

Inscribe means to draw inside. When one shape fits inside another it is said to be inscribed. For example, a **circle** can be inscribed in a **triangle** to touch the sides, and a **square** can be inscribed in a circle so that its vertices are on the circle.

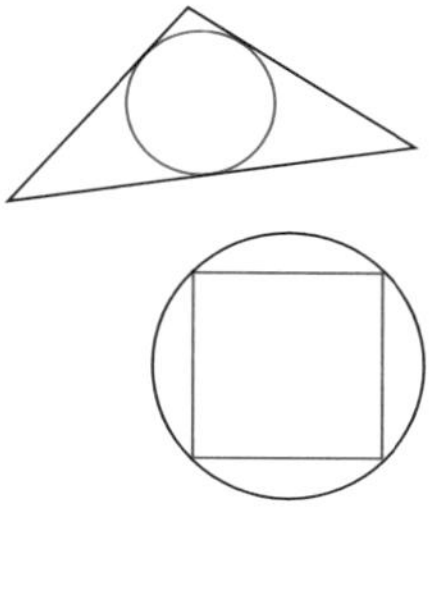

Integers

The set of integers is the set of numbers

… −5 −4 −3 −2 −1 0 1 2 3 4 5 …

They can be thought of as positions on a **number line**:

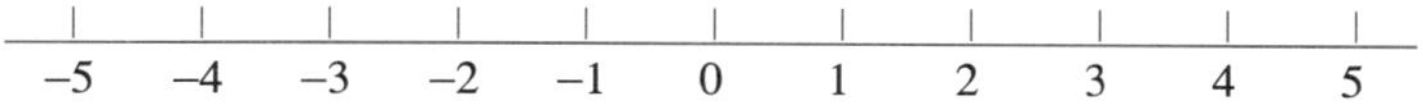

or as changes of position:

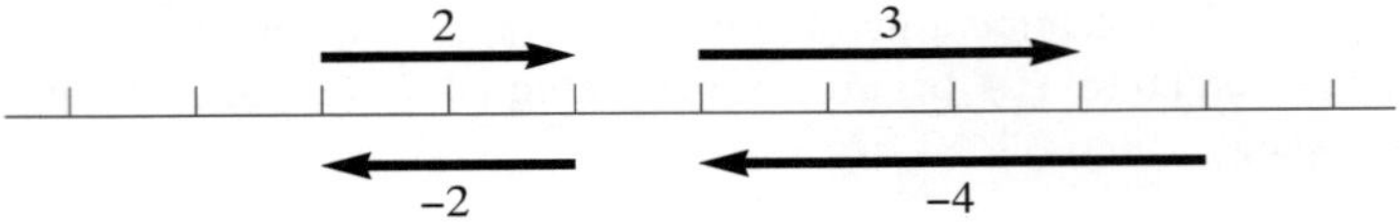

Intercept

The line whose **equation** is $3x + 2y = 12$ cuts the x-axis at 4 and the y-axis at 6. It is said to have an x-intercept of 4 and a y-intercept of 6.

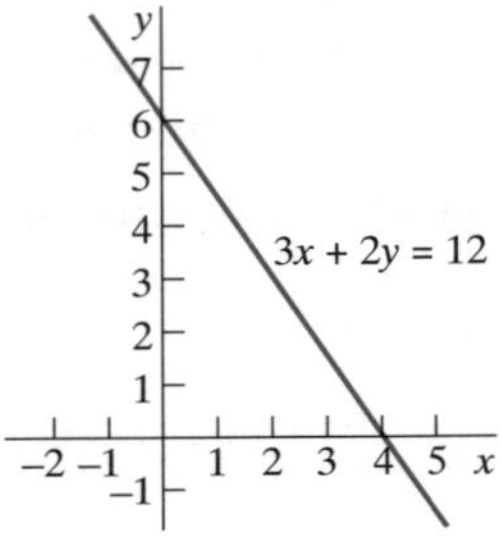

Interest

The amount gained when money is invested (in a building society, for example) is called interest. An interest rate of 7% per year means that every £100 invested gains £7 interest at the end of a year.

■ See **Compound interest** and **Simple interest**.

Interior angle

The interior angles of a **polygon** are the **angles** inside it at the **vertices**.

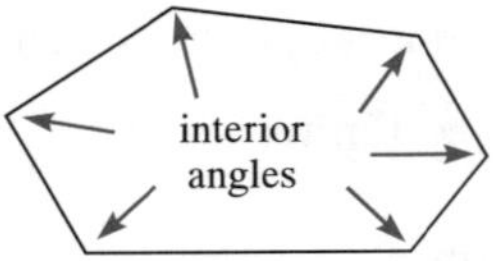

The interior angles of a polygon with n sides add up to

$$(n - 2) \times 180°$$

(since $n - 2$ **triangles** are formed by drawing **diagonals** from one vertex).

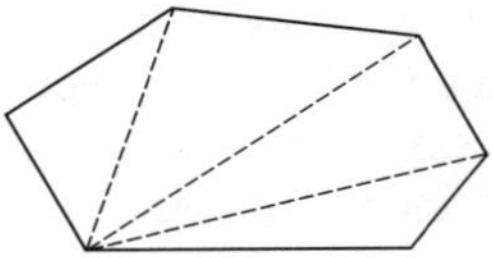

For a regular polygon the interior angles are all equal. In a regular **hexagon** each angle is

$$(6 - 2) \times 180° \div 6 = 120°.$$

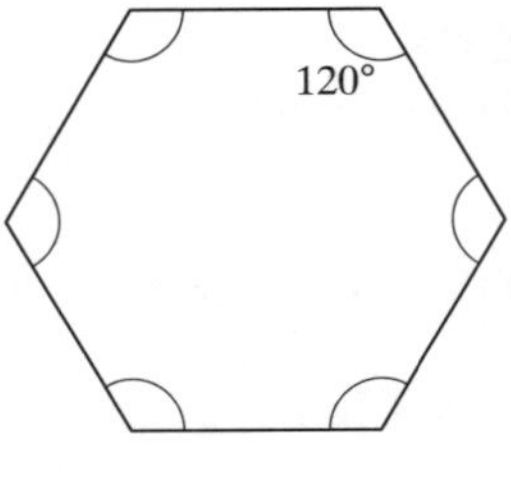

■ See **Exterior angle**.

Interpolate

To interpolate means to **estimate** between two known numbers. For example, suppose a girl's height was 152 cm on 1st January last year and 156 cm on 1st January this year. A reasonable estimate of her height on 1st July halfway through last year is 154 cm.

■ See **Extrapolate**.

Interquartile range

This is a measure of **spread** of a set of statistical data. It is the difference between the lower **quartile** and the upper quartile.

Intersect

When two (or more) lines or curves cross they are said to intersect.

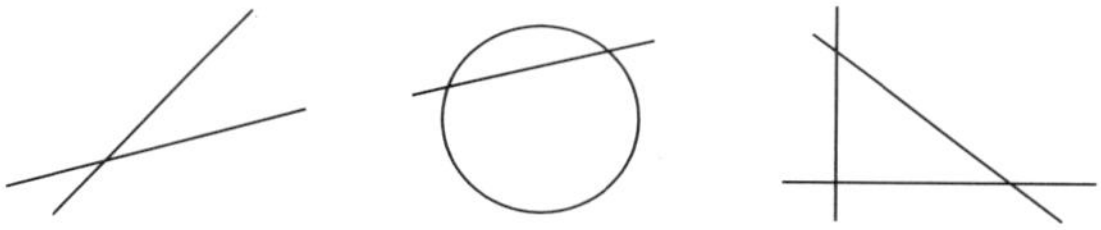

Intersection of sets

The intersection of two **sets** is the set of elements which are in both of the sets. For example, suppose

A = {multiples of 2 less than 14} = {2, 4, 6, 8, 10, 12}

B = {multiples of 3 less than 15} = {3, 6, 9, 12}

The intersection of A and B, written A ∩ B, is {6, 12}. On the **Venn diagram**, the shaded region represents A ∩ B.

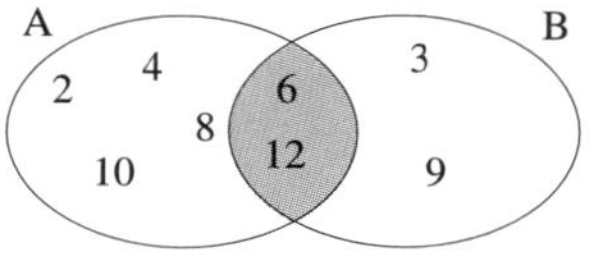

■ See **Union of sets**

Interval

The interval from 2 to 3 inclusive is the set of all **real numbers** between 2 and 3, including 2 and 3, and can be pictured on a **number line** as shown.

It consists of the real numbers x such that $2 \le x \le 3$.

More generally, the interval from a to b inclusive is the set of real numbers x such that $a \le x \le b$. When the end points are not included, the interval from a to b consists of the real numbers x such that $a < x < b$.

■ See **Class interval**.

Invariant

A property which stays the same in a **transformation** is called an invariant. For example, when an object is transformed by an **enlargement**, angles stay the same but lengths are altered. Thus in an enlargement angles are invariant but lengths are not invariant.

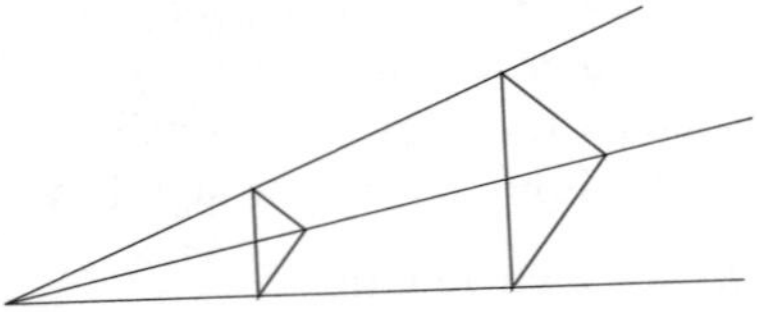

■ See **Isometry**, **Shear** and **Topology**.

Inverse element

The inverse of an **element** under a particular **operation** is the element which combines with it to give the **identity** for the operation. For example, the inverse of 4 under addition is −4 because $4 + (-4) = 0 = (-4) + 4$. The inverse of 4 under multiplication is $\frac{1}{4}$ because $4 \times \frac{1}{4} = 1 = \frac{1}{4} \times 4$. The inverse of $\begin{pmatrix} 2 & 3 \\ 3 & 5 \end{pmatrix}$ under **matrix multiplication** is $\begin{pmatrix} 5 & -3 \\ -3 & 2 \end{pmatrix}$

$$\text{because } \begin{pmatrix} 2 & 3 \\ 3 & 5 \end{pmatrix}\begin{pmatrix} 5 & -3 \\ -3 & 2 \end{pmatrix} = \begin{pmatrix} 1 & 0 \\ 0 & 1 \end{pmatrix} = \begin{pmatrix} 5 & -3 \\ -3 & 2 \end{pmatrix}\begin{pmatrix} 2 & 3 \\ 3 & 5 \end{pmatrix}$$

The inverse of the **function** $x \mapsto 3x$ is the function $x \mapsto \frac{1}{3}x$ because the combination of the two functions is the identity function $x \mapsto x$.

Inverse operation

An inverse **operation** has the opposite effect to the original one. For example, subtraction is the inverse operation to addition, and squaring is the inverse operation to square rooting.

Inverse proportion, inversely proportional to

When the average **speed** for a journey of 100 km is doubled, the time taken is halved. The time taken, t hours, is said to be inversely proportional to the speed u km per hour. As u increases, t decreases according to the algebraic **relationship**

$$t = \frac{100}{u}$$

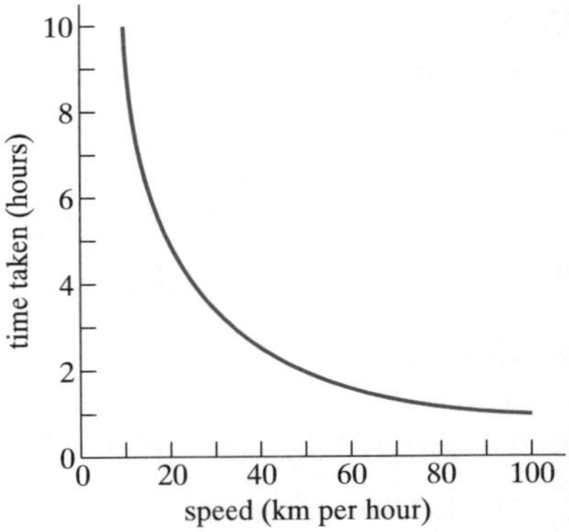

In general, when y is inversely proportional to x there is an algebraic relationship between x and y of the form

$$y = \frac{a}{x}$$

where a is a constant. y is inversely proportional to x is often written

$$y \propto \frac{1}{x}$$

See **Direct proportion** and **Varies inversely as**

Investigation

An investigation involves the explanation, analysis and generalisation of a mathematical problem. For example, a student investigated the problem

How many squares are there on a chessboard?

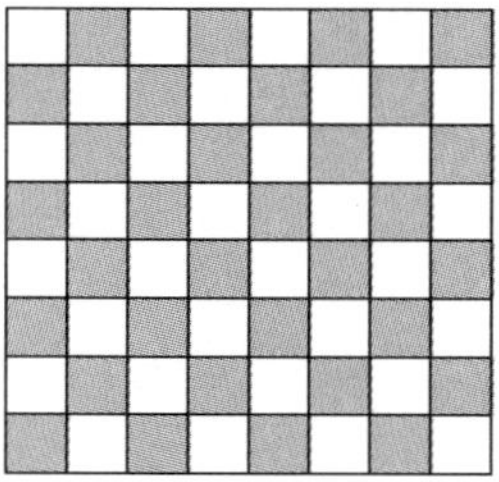

First the student realised that it could be interpreted to obtain an answer other than 64. She then simplified the problem by starting with small 'chessboards', (1 by 1, 2 by 2, etc.). From these special cases a pattern emerged and a **conjecture** was made. She then went on to **prove** the conjecture and was able to **generalise** it to obtain a **formula** for the number of squares on an n by n board. Other problems then suggested themselves, for example,

How many rectangles are there on a chessboard?

Can the problem be extended to three dimensions?

Irrational number

See **Rational number**.

Isometric paper

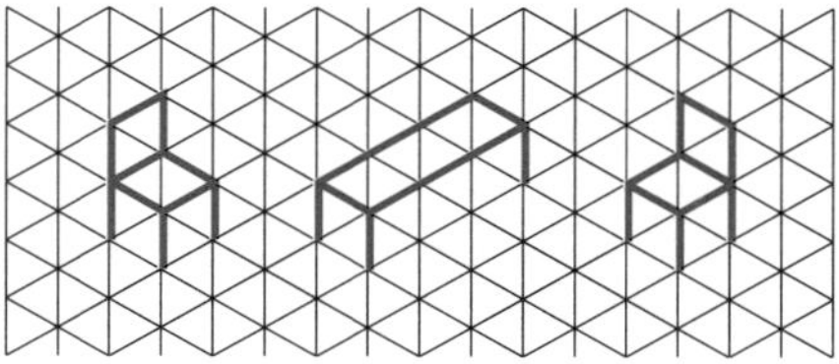

Isometric paper consists of a grid of **equilateral triangles**. It is useful for illustrating three-dimensional objects.

Isometry

The word *isometry* means 'equal measure'. An isometry is a **transformation** in which the distance between any two points is unchanged by the transformation. The effect is to map any shape onto an identical shape.

Rotations, **reflections** and **translations** are isometries, but **enlargements** are not because they alter lengths.

→

Isometries which do not alter **sense** are called *direct isometries*. Rotations and translations are direct isometries. Isometries which alter sense are called *opposite isometries*. Reflections and **glide reflections** are opposite isometries.

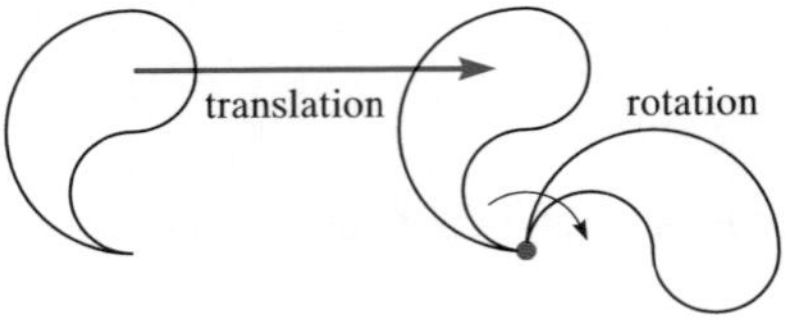

Isosceles triangle

An isosceles triangle is a **triangle** with two **sides** of equal length. It also has two equal **angles**, the angles opposite the equal sides. An isosceles triangle has one **line of symmetry**.

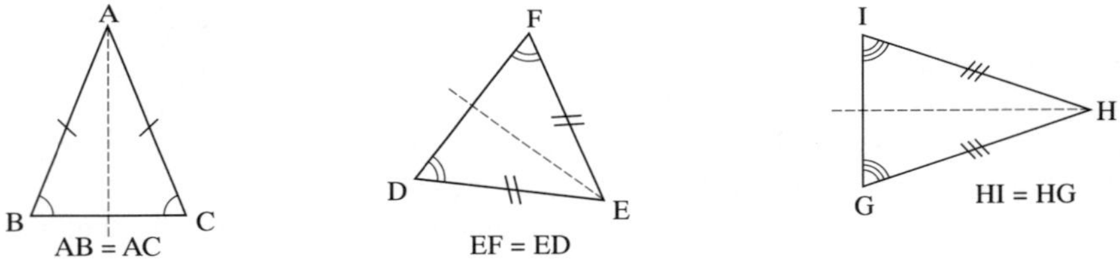

'Isosceles' comes from the Greek words *isos* and *celes*, meaning 'equal legs'.

Iterative procedure

In everyday language the word *reiterate* means to say again, to repeat. In mathematics an iterative procedure is a repetitive process. Here is an example.

A calculator can be used to find how a sum of money, £1000 say, grows when the **interest** rate is 7% per year by entering 1000 and then repeatedly multiplying by 1.07.

Sum invested	£1000
Amount at end of year 1	£1000 x 1.07 = £1070
Amount at end of year 2	£1070 x 1.07 = £1144.90
Amount at end of year 3	£1144.90 x 1.07 = £1225.043

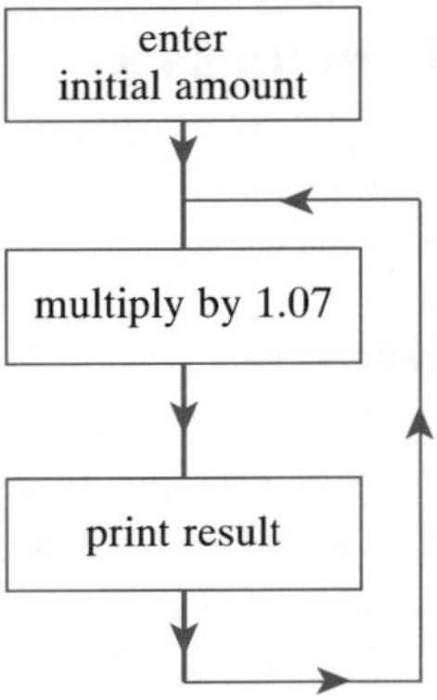

The amount £a_n at the end of year n and the amount £a_{n+1} at the end of year $n + 1$ are connected by the iterative relation

$$a_{n+1} = 1.07a_n$$

Kilogram

A kilogram is a unit of **mass** in the **metric system**.
It is equivalent to 1000 **grams**.
The prefix *kilo-* means 1000.
Kilogram is usually abbreviated to kg.

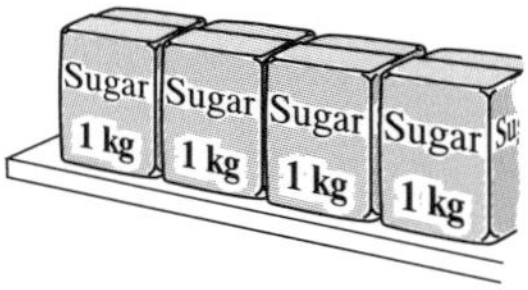

1000 kg = 1 **tonne**

Sugar is usually packed in 1 kilogram bags.

Kilometre

A kilometre is a unit of length in the **metric system**. 1 kilometre is 1000 **metres**.

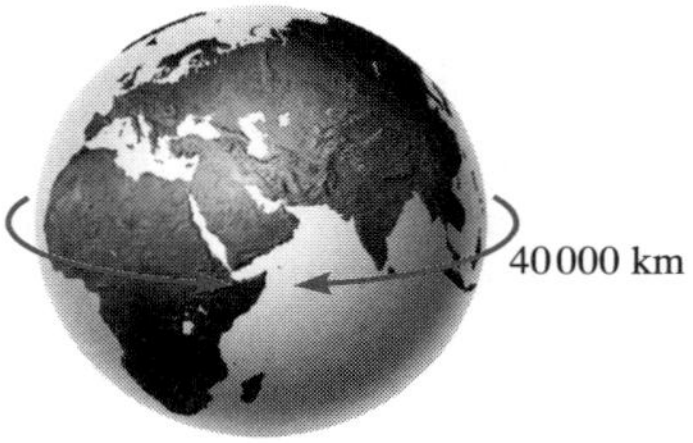

Kilometre is abbreviated to km.
8 km is approximately 5 **miles**.

The distance from London to Paris is about 340 km.

The distance round the Earth is about 40 000 km.

Kite

A kite is a convex **quadrilateral** with two pairs of equal **sides** and one line of **symmetry**.

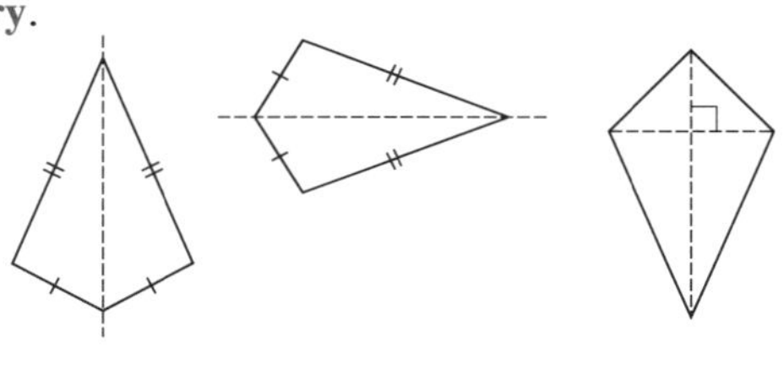

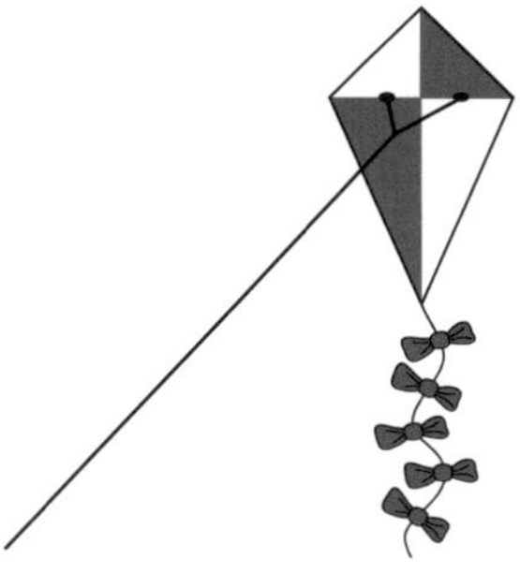

The **diagonals** of a kite are at **right angles**.

See **Arrowhead**.

Latitude

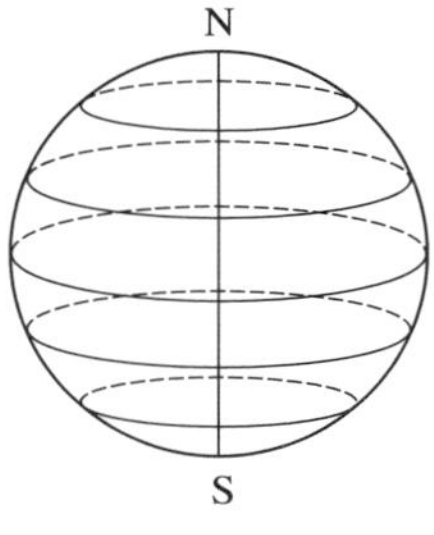

Circles on the Earth's surface with their centres on the line joining the north and south poles are called *circles of latitude*. All these circles are in planes **parallel** to the **plane** containing the equator. They are sometimes referred to as *parallels of latitude*.

To describe the parallel of latitude shown, take any point P on it, and let Q be a point on the equator below it. Then the circle of latitude is defined by the **angle** between OQ and OP.

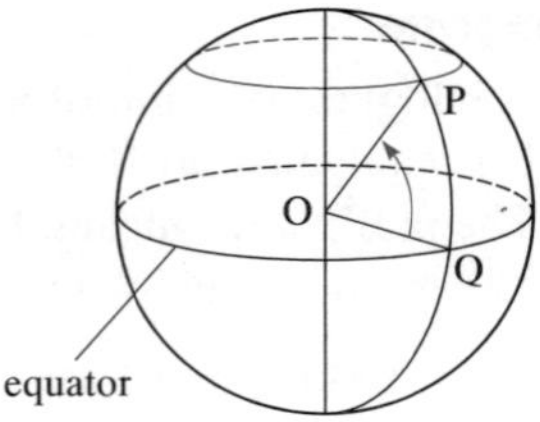

For the circle of latitude through London, the angle between OQ and OP is about 52°. London is said to be at latitude 52° north. Sydney, Australia, has a latitude of about 34° south.

■ See **Longitude**.

Leading diagonal

In a table or **matrix**, the line of elements from top left to bottom right is called the leading diagonal.

	a	*b*	*c*	*d*
a	*a*	*b*	*c*	*d*
b	*b*	*a*	*d*	*c*
c	*c*	*d*	*a*	*b*
d	*d*	*c*	*b*	*a*

$$\begin{pmatrix} 3 & 4 & 7 & 1 \\ 2 & 8 & 5 & 3 \\ 6 & 0 & 9 & 1 \\ 4 & 8 & 3 & 7 \end{pmatrix}$$

Less than

■ See **Inequality**.

Limit

A **sequence** of numbers has a limit L if the numbers get closer and closer to L as the sequence proceeds so that the difference between them and L approaches 0.

For example, the sequence 1.5, 1.25, 1.125, …, in which the nth term is $1 + \left(\frac{1}{2}\right)^n$, has a limit of 1. The terms of the sequence get closer and closer to 1 as n increases. The difference between the numbers and 1 is $\left(\frac{1}{2}\right)^n$, and this tends to 0 as n increases.

The sequence 2.9, 2.99, 2.999, …, in which the nth term is 2.99…9 with n nines, has a limit of 3.

A sequence of shapes can also have a limit. For example, the **polygons** in the diagram all have their vertices at a distance of 1 unit from the centre. As the number of sides increases the polygons get closer and closer to a **circle**.

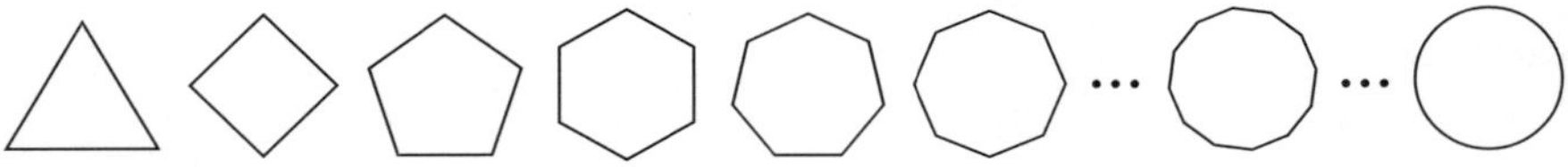

■ See **Converge**.

Linear equation

$$2x + 3y = 4 \qquad x + 2 = 0 \qquad 5x + 2y - 3z = 1$$

are examples of linear equations. In a linear equation the **degree** of the symbols such as x, y and z is 1. **Equations** containing terms involving degrees other than 1, for example x^2, y^3, $\frac{1}{x}$, are non-linear.

The **graph** of an equation such as $2x + 3y = 4$ is a straight line. For this reason it is said to be a linear equation.

See **Cubic function**, **Quadratic equation** and **Quadratic function**.

Linear relation

When the exchange rate is \$1.5 to the £, the number of dollars y you would get for £x can be found from

$$y = 1.5x$$

The **graph** of this **relationship** is a straight line. There is said to be a linear relation between the number of pounds and the number of dollars.

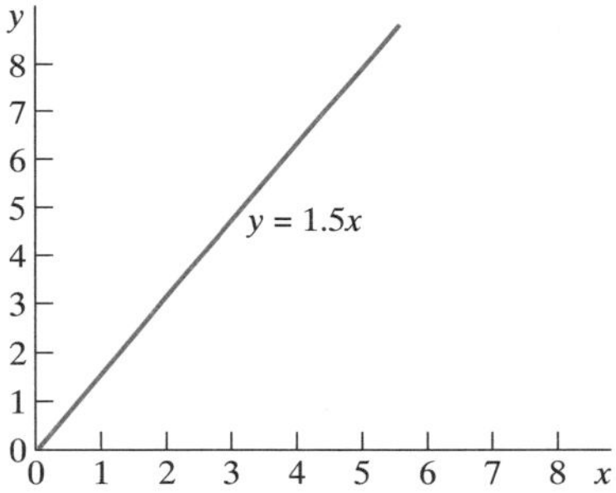

More generally, any relation of the form

$$y = ax + b$$

where a and b are constants, is a linear relation. The graph is a straight line. For example, a spring of unstretched length 6 cm is such that it stretches by 0.5 cm for every 100-gram load suspended on it. Its length y cm with a load of x hundreds of grams is given by $y = 0.5x + 6$. The graph of this relation is a straight line.

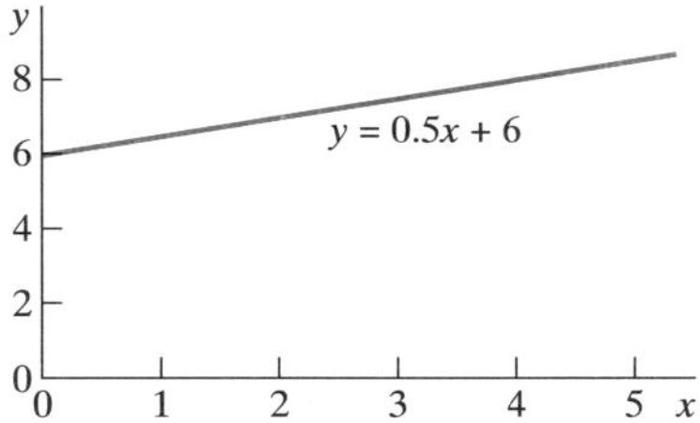

Linear scale factor

The diagram shows an **enlargement** in which the lengths of all lines have been multiplied by 2. The linear scale factor is 2.

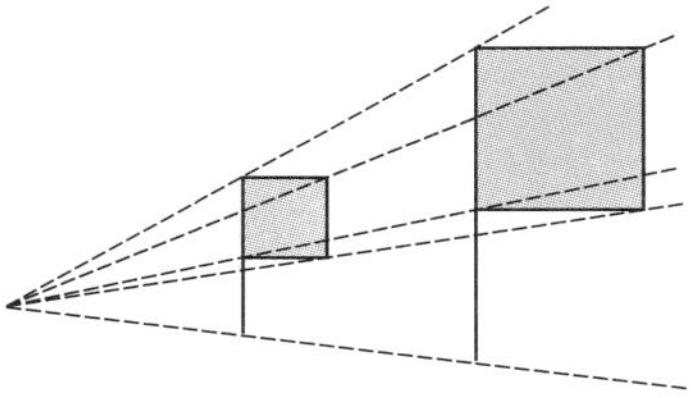

When an object is enlarged so that the lengths of all lines are multiplied by k, the linear scale factor is k.

See **Area scale factor**, **Scale factor** and **Volume scale factor**.

Line graph

The table shows the air temperature at hourly intervals during part of a day. These temperatures have been plotted on graph paper. The points have been joined by straight lines. The resulting graph is called a line graph.

Time (hours)	Temp. (°C)
2	15
3	17
4	14
5	16

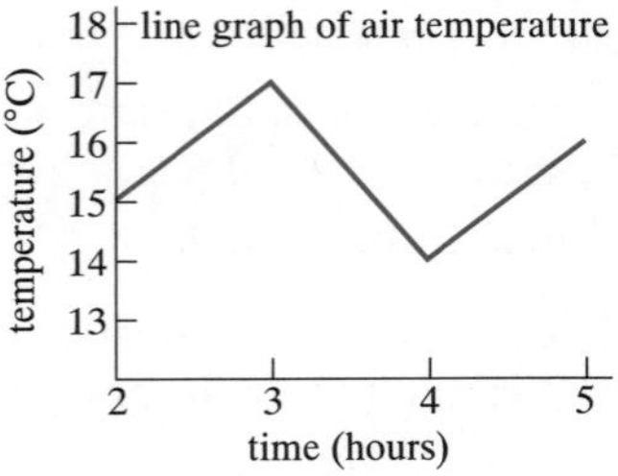

Line of best fit

The diagram shows the heights and weights of a group of 10 people. Although the points are not exactly on a straight line, the relation can be shown by drawing the best line possible through the points.

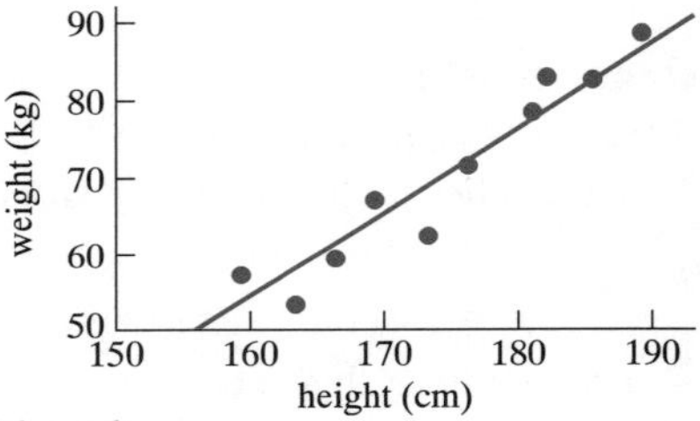

This line of best fit is often drawn by eye although there are ways to calculate it (according to various criteria).

■ See **Scatter diagram**.

Line of symmetry, line symmetry

A *line of symmetry* of a two-dimensional shape is a line such that when a mirror is placed on it one half of the shape reflects to the other half.

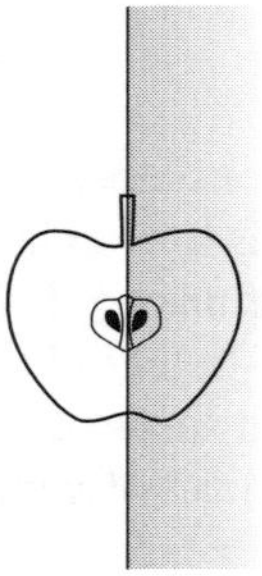

Shapes can have various numbers of lines of symmetry. If a shape has one or more lines of symmetry, it is said to have *line symmetry*. When a shape has only one line of symmetry, it is said to have *bilateral symmetry*.

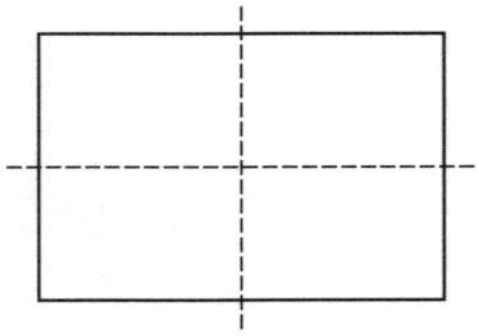

rectangle
2 lines of symmetry

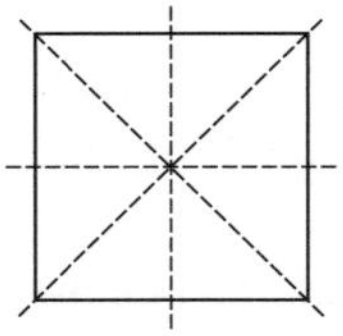

square
4 lines of symmetry

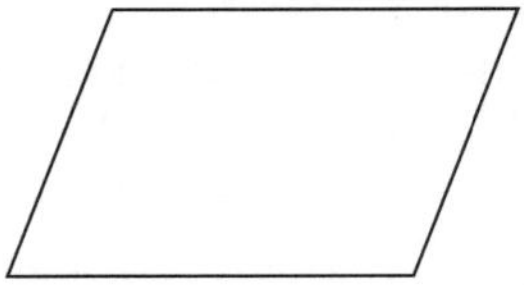

parallelogram
no lines of symmetry

■ See **Symmetry**.

Line segment

The part of a straight line between two given points is called a line segment.

the line segment AB

Litre

A litre is a measure of **capacity (volume)**.
1 litre is 1000 **cubic centimetres**, about $1\frac{3}{4}$ **pints.**
Litre is abbreviated to *l*.
1 gallon is about 4.55 litres.

The petrol tank of a typical small car holds about 40 litres. A bath uses about 90 litres; a shower is more economical, using only about 30 litres.

See **Centimetre** and **Gallon**.

Locus (*pl.* loci)

A locus is a set of points satisfying a condition.

For example, the locus of the points which are the same distance from two fixed points A and B is the red line in the diagram. It is the **perpendicular bisector** of AB.

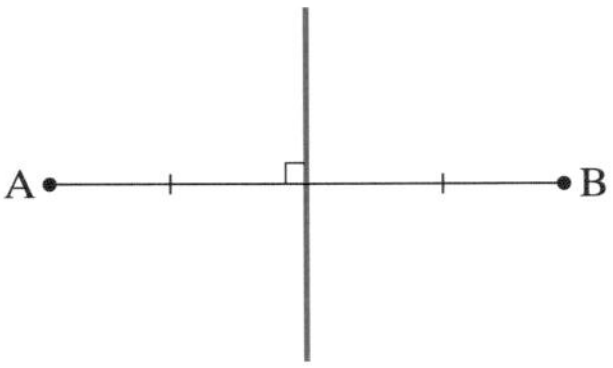

In two dimensions, the locus of a point which moves so that its distance from a fixed point O is 2 cm is a **circle** of **radius** 2 cm with its centre at O. In three dimensions, the locus is a **sphere** of radius 2 cm centred at O.

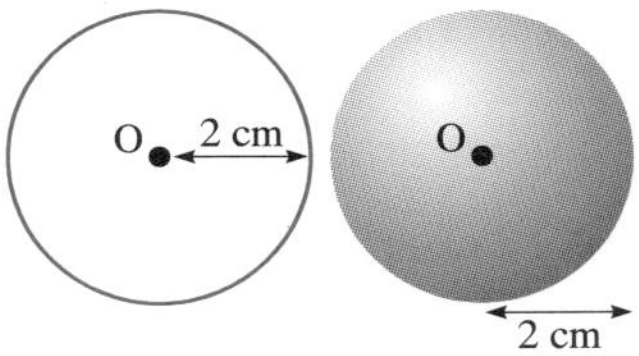

The diagram shows the locus of a **vertex** of a **square** as the square rotates along a straight line.

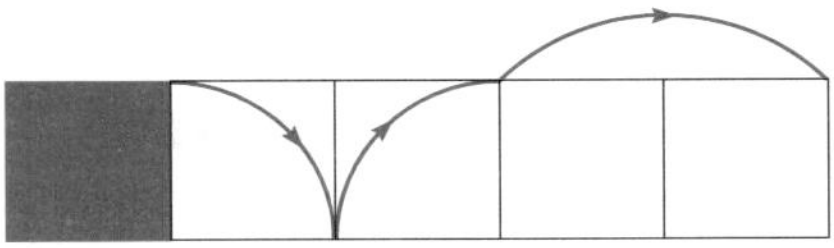

See **Curves of pursuit** and **Cycloid**.

Logo

Logo is a computer language. It is particularly useful in drawing shapes. For example, the command

```
repeat 6 [fd 50 lt 60]
```

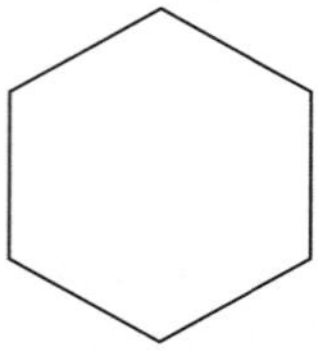

draws a regular hexagon.

`fd 50` means move forward 50 units.

`lt 60` means turn to the left through 60°.

These two instructions are repeated 6 times.

Longitude

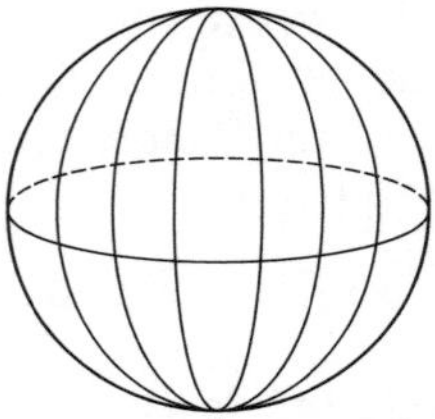

Lines of longitude are half-circles on the surface of the Earth passing through the north and south poles. They are used to fix the positions of places on the Earth.

The line of longitude passing through Greenwich in London is called the *Greenwich meridian*. The positions of other lines of longitude are given measured from the Greenwich meridian in the following way:

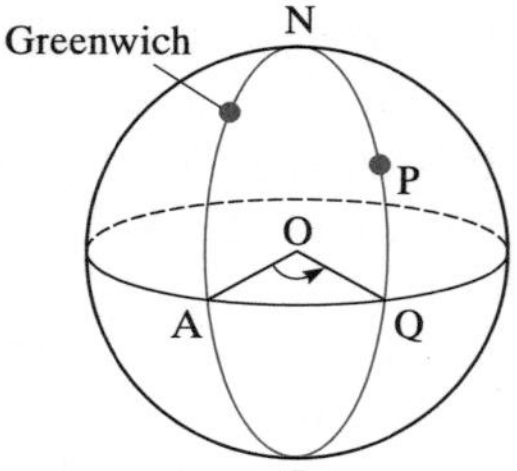

The diagram shows a line of longitude through a point P. This line **intersects** the equator at Q. In the diagram the Greenwich meridian intersects the equator at A, and O is the centre of the Earth. The line of longitude through P is determined by the **angle** between OA and OQ.

For example, if P represents Moscow, the angle between OA and OQ is about 38°. Moscow is said to have longitude 38°E. The longitude of New York is 74°W.

The position of any point on the Earth's surface is determined by its **latitude** and longitude.

Lowest common multiple (LCM)

See **Common multiple**.

Lowest terms

A **fraction** such as $\frac{10}{15}$ can be simplified as the numbers on the top and bottom have a **common factor** 5.

Dividing the top and bottom numbers by 5 gives

$$\frac{10}{15} \overset{\div 5}{=} \frac{2}{3} \quad (\div 5)$$

When no further cancelling of common factors is possible, as in this example, the fraction is said to be in its *lowest terms* or in its *simplest form.*

Algebraic fractions can similarly be reduced to simplest form. For example,

$\frac{5a^2b^3c}{20a^3bc}$ can be divided top and bottom by $5a^2bc$ to give $\frac{b^2}{4a}$.

See **Cancel** and **Equivalent fractions**.

Magic square

A magic square is an arrangement of numbers in a **square** so that each of the **rows and columns** and the two **diagonals** have the same total. Often the numbers from 1 to 9 or 1 to 16, etc. are used, but other sets of numbers can be used.

8	1	6
3	5	7
4	9	2

magic total 15

16	2	3	13
5	11	10	8
9	7	6	12
4	14	15	1

magic total 34

5	12	7
10	8	6
9	4	11

magic total 24

Magnitude

Magnitude means size. The magnitude of a number such as –2 is its size ignoring its sign, that is 2.

The magnitude of a displacement **vector** is its length.

The magnitude r of the vector $\binom{3}{4}$ can be found using **Pythagoras' theorem**:

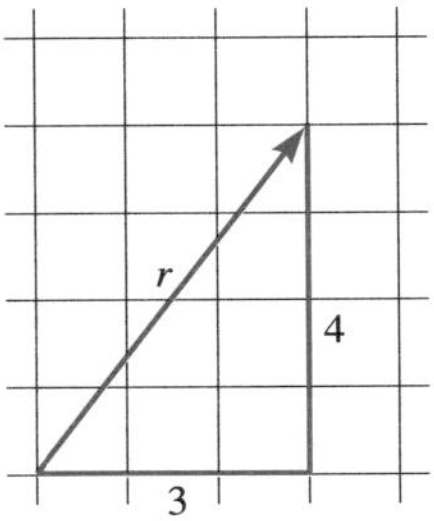

$$r^2 = 3^2 + 4^2 \quad \Rightarrow r^2 = 25 \quad \Rightarrow r = 5$$

→

The magnitude of a velocity vector gives the **speed.** For example, the **velocity** of a boat is given as $\begin{pmatrix} 5 \\ 12 \end{pmatrix}$, where the numbers refer to the boat's speed in km h^{-1} in the easterly and northerly directions. The magnitude of the vector is $\sqrt{5^2 + 12^2} = 13$ and so the boat's speed is 13 km h^{-1}.

Major arc

■ See **Minor arc**.

Major sector

■ See **Sector of a circle**.

Mapping

A mapping is another name for a **function**. It comes from the geographical idea of making a map in which for each point on the ground there is a unique point on the map.

This idea of transforming one set of points to another is used in mathematics, and **transformations** such as **reflections, rotations, translations, enlargements**, etc. are referred to as mappings.

Similarly, functions such as $x \mapsto x + 1$, where x is a **real number**, are sometimes called mappings. $x \mapsto x + 1$ '*maps*' the **number line** onto itself, each number having 1 added on. It can be illustrated using a *mapping diagram* as shown.

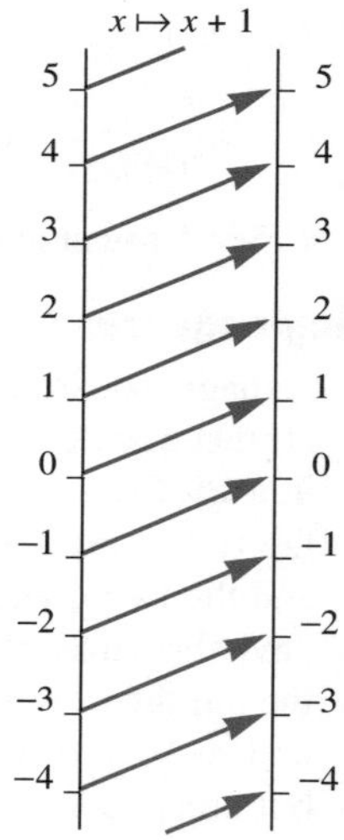

Mass

The mass of an object is the amount of matter in it. Mass is measured in **grams, kilograms** and **tonnes** in **metric units** and in **ounces**, **pounds**, stones, hundredweights and **tons** in **imperial units**.

■ See **Weight**.

Mathematical modelling

In order that a complex problem can be analysed mathematically some of its features are simplified or ignored initially. For example, in analysing the motion of a tennis ball a simple mathematical model could be made by treating the ball as a particle and ignoring air resistance and spin.

Matrix (*pl.* matrices)

A matrix is a set of numbers arranged in **rows and columns** in a rectangular or square array.

$$\begin{array}{c} \text{columns} \\ \downarrow\ \downarrow\ \downarrow \end{array}$$

$$\text{rows} \begin{array}{c} \rightarrow \\ \rightarrow \end{array} \begin{pmatrix} 2 & 3 & 4 \\ 6 & 1 & 8 \end{pmatrix} \qquad \begin{pmatrix} 3 & 4 \\ 7 & -5 \end{pmatrix} \qquad \begin{pmatrix} 6 & -2 & 1 \\ 8 & 3 & 4 \\ \frac{1}{2} & 0 & 5 \end{pmatrix} \qquad \begin{pmatrix} a & b \\ c & d \\ e & f \end{pmatrix}$$

The numbers and letters which make up the array are called its *elements* and can be referred to by giving their row and column. So, for example, the element in the second row and third column of the first matrix is 8.

See **Order of a matrix**.

Matrix addition

Matrices with the same number of rows and columns can be combined by adding corresponding elements. This process is called matrix addition. For example,

$$\begin{pmatrix} 2 & 3 & 4 \\ 6 & 1 & 8 \end{pmatrix} + \begin{pmatrix} 4 & 2 & 1 \\ 3 & 5 & 0 \end{pmatrix} = \begin{pmatrix} 2+4 & 3+2 & 4+1 \\ 6+3 & 1+5 & 8+0 \end{pmatrix}$$

$$= \begin{pmatrix} 6 & 5 & 5 \\ 9 & 6 & 8 \end{pmatrix}$$

Matrix multiplication

Two **matrices** A and B can be combined by matrix multiplication when the number of columns of A is the same as the number of rows of B. For example, the 2 by 3 matrix $A = \begin{pmatrix} 2 & 3 & 4 \\ 6 & 1 & 8 \end{pmatrix}$ can be combined with the 3 by 2 matrix

$$B = \begin{pmatrix} 5 & 6 \\ 4 & 0 \\ 1 & 2 \end{pmatrix}$$

Each row of A is combined with each column of B in the following way:

$$\underset{\text{2 by 3}}{\overset{\text{A}}{\begin{pmatrix} 2 & 3 & 4 \\ 6 & 1 & 8 \end{pmatrix}}} \underset{\text{3 by 2}}{\overset{\text{B}}{\begin{pmatrix} 5 & 6 \\ 4 & 0 \\ 1 & 2 \end{pmatrix}}} = \begin{pmatrix} 2 \times 5 + 3 \times 4 + 4 \times 1 & 2 \times 6 + 3 \times 0 + 4 \times 2 \\ 6 \times 5 + 1 \times 4 + 8 \times 1 & 6 \times 6 + 1 \times 0 + 8 \times 2 \end{pmatrix} = \underset{\text{2 by 2}}{\overset{\text{AB}}{\begin{pmatrix} 26 & 20 \\ 42 & 52 \end{pmatrix}}}$$

→

- The element in row 1 column 1 of AB has been obtained by 'running along' row 1 of matrix A, 'diving down' column 1 of matrix B, multiplying corresponding numbers and adding these products.
- For the element in row 1 column 2 of AB, run along row 1 of matrix A and dive down column 2 of matrix B.
- The other two elements are obtained by running along row 2 of A and diving down the columns of B.

In this case it is also possible to form BA:

$$\begin{pmatrix}5 & 6\\4 & 0\\1 & 2\end{pmatrix}\begin{pmatrix}2 & 3 & 4\\6 & 1 & 8\end{pmatrix} = \begin{pmatrix}46 & 21 & 68\\8 & 12 & 16\\14 & 5 & 20\end{pmatrix}$$

3 by 2   2 by 3   3 by 3

When A and B are both square matrices of the same **order** (shape), AB and BA will both be square matrices of the same order, but not necessarily equal. For example,

$$\overset{\text{A}}{\begin{pmatrix}2 & 3\\1 & 4\end{pmatrix}}\overset{\text{B}}{\begin{pmatrix}5 & 6\\0 & 2\end{pmatrix}} = \overset{\text{AB}}{\begin{pmatrix}10 & 18\\5 & 14\end{pmatrix}} \quad \text{and} \quad \overset{\text{B}}{\begin{pmatrix}5 & 6\\0 & 2\end{pmatrix}}\overset{\text{A}}{\begin{pmatrix}2 & 3\\1 & 4\end{pmatrix}} = \overset{\text{BA}}{\begin{pmatrix}16 & 39\\2 & 8\end{pmatrix}}$$

Matrix multiplication is not **commutative**.

Generalising, when A is a p by q matrix and B is a q by r matrix, the product AB is a p by r matrix:

A	B	=	AB
p by q	q by r		p by r

■ See **Identity element** and **Inverse element**.

Matrix transformations

Transformations of the plane which **map parallel** lines onto parallel lines can be described using 2 by 2 matrices. For example, the transformation which maps the grid of **squares** onto the grid of **parallelograms** as shown is described by

$$\begin{pmatrix}x\\y\end{pmatrix} \mapsto \begin{pmatrix}2 & 1\\1 & 3\end{pmatrix}\begin{pmatrix}x\\y\end{pmatrix}$$

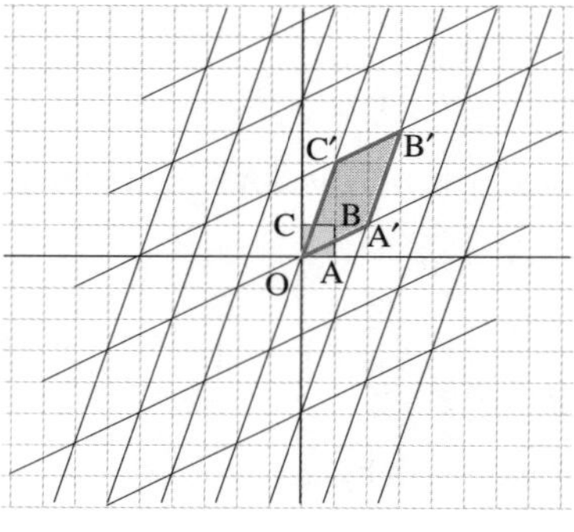

The vertices of the square OABC are then mapped as follows

$$\begin{pmatrix}0\\0\end{pmatrix} \mapsto \begin{pmatrix}2 & 1\\1 & 3\end{pmatrix}\begin{pmatrix}0\\0\end{pmatrix} = \begin{pmatrix}0\\0\end{pmatrix} \qquad \begin{pmatrix}1\\0\end{pmatrix} \mapsto \begin{pmatrix}2 & 1\\1 & 3\end{pmatrix}\begin{pmatrix}1\\0\end{pmatrix} = \begin{pmatrix}2\\1\end{pmatrix}$$

$$\begin{pmatrix}0\\1\end{pmatrix} \mapsto \begin{pmatrix}2 & 1\\1 & 3\end{pmatrix}\begin{pmatrix}0\\1\end{pmatrix} = \begin{pmatrix}1\\3\end{pmatrix} \qquad \begin{pmatrix}1\\1\end{pmatrix} \mapsto \begin{pmatrix}2 & 1\\1 & 3\end{pmatrix}\begin{pmatrix}1\\1\end{pmatrix} = \begin{pmatrix}3\\4\end{pmatrix}$$

to give the parallelogram OA′B′C′.

The matrix for an **enlargement**, centre (0, 0) with **scale factor** 2, is $\begin{pmatrix}2 & 0\\0 & 2\end{pmatrix}$

The matrix for **reflection** in the line $y = x$ is $\begin{pmatrix}0 & 1\\1 & 0\end{pmatrix}$

See **Rotation** and **Shear**.

Maximum

The maximum of a **function** is its greatest value.

Mean

See **Average**.

Median

See **Average**.

Median of a triangle

A median of a **triangle** is a line joining a **vertex** to the mid-point of the opposite side.

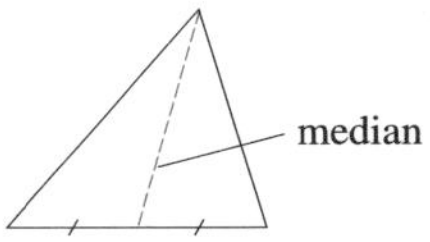

A triangle has three medians which always meet at a point. This point is one-third of the way up each median and is called the *centroid* of the triangle.

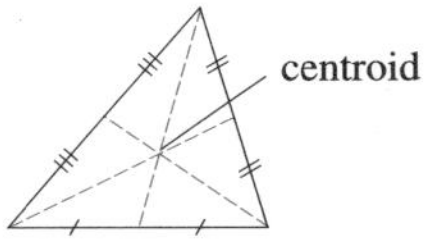

Mediator

A mediator is another name for a **perpendicular bisector**.

See **Bisector**.

Meridian

See **Longitude**.

Metre

A metre is a **metric unit** of length. A very long stride is about 1 metre.

Metre is abbreviated to m.

1 m = 100 cm   1000 m = 1 km

1 metre is about 39.4 **inches** (about 1.1 **yards**).

A metre was originally defined as one ten millionth of the distance from the equator to the north pole.

Metric units

Metric units are based on length in **metres**, and **mass** in **kilograms**.

The following prefixes are commonly used:

milli-	one thousandth
centi-	one hundredth
kilo-	one thousand

See **Centimetre**, **Gram**, **Litre**, **Millilitre** and **Millimetre**.

Mile

A mile is an **imperial unit** of distance. One mile is 1760 **yards** (5280 feet). A distance of 5 miles is about 8 **kilometres**.

Millilitre

A millilitre is one thousandth of a **litre**. It is abbreviated to ml.

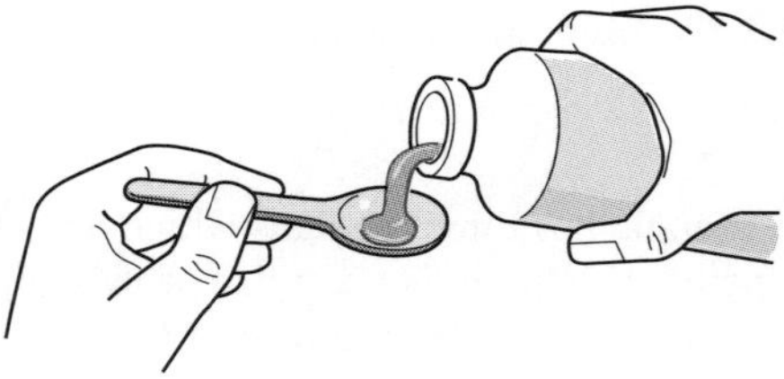

1 millilitre is the same as 1 **cubic centimetre** (cm^3).
A medicine spoon holds 5 ml.

Millimetre

A millimetre is one thousandth of a **metre**. It is abbreviated to mm.
There are 10 mm in 1 cm.
1 mm is the distance between each of the small marks on the ruler.

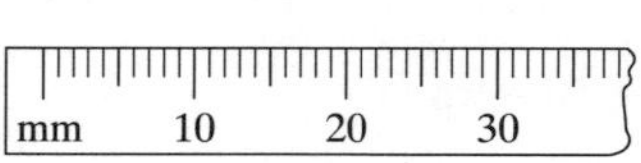

Million

A million is 1 000 000. In **index** notation, a million is written 10^6 (ten to the **power** of six).

The population of the United Kingdom in 1995 was about 60 million.

A million small cubes 1 cm by 1 cm by 1 cm would be needed to fill up a cube measuring 1 metre by 1 metre by 1 metre.

Minimum

The minimum value of a **function** is its smallest value.

Minor arc, major arc

When A and B are two points on a **circle** not at the ends of a **diameter**, the small part of the circumference from A to B is called the *minor arc* and the larger part of the circumference from A to B is called the *major arc*.

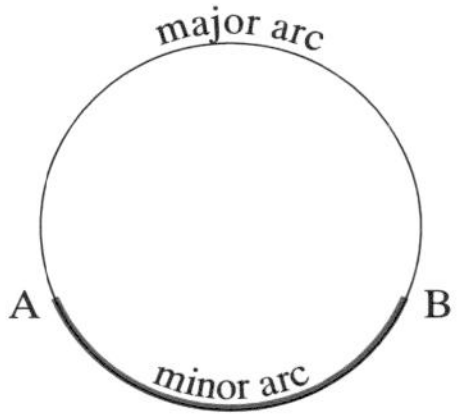

See **Arc of a circle**.

Minor sector

See **Sector of a circle**.

Minute (unit of angle)

A minute is a unit for measuring very small angles.
There are 60 minutes in 1 **degree**.

Minute (unit of time)

A minute is 60 **seconds**.
There are 60 minutes in an **hour**.

It takes about 5 minutes to soft-boil an egg.

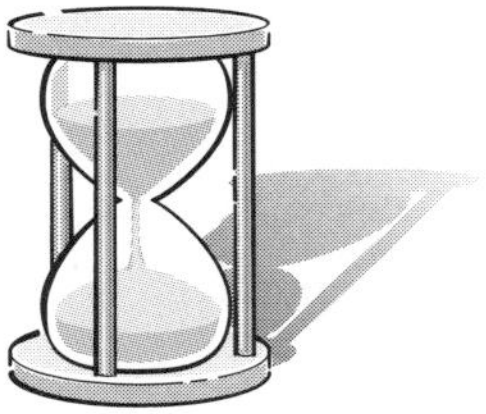

Mixed number

A mixed number consists of a **whole number** and a **fraction**.
For example, $2\frac{3}{4}$ is a mixed number.
It is $2 + \frac{3}{4}$ and could be written as $\frac{11}{4}$

Mode

See **Average**.

Modulo arithmetic

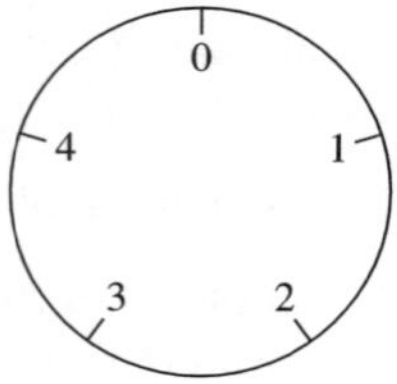

Arithmetic modulo 5 can be thought of as arithmetic on a 'clock' with the numbers 0, 1, 2, 3, 4. For example, to find 3 + 4, start at 3 and go round 4 spaces, arriving at 2. This can be written

$$3 + 4 = 2 \pmod 5$$

Similarly, 2 x 3 (2 lots of 3) can be interpreted as 3 + 3, which is 1 in clock arithmetic:

$$2 \times 3 = 1 \pmod 5$$

In this way, addition and multiplication tables can be drawn up:

+	0	1	2	3	4
0	0	1	2	3	4
1	1	2	3	4	0
2	2	3	4	0	1
3	3	4	0	1	2
4	4	0	1	2	3

x	0	1	2	3	4
0	0	0	0	0	0
1	0	1	2	3	4
2	0	2	4	1	3
3	0	3	1	4	2
4	0	4	3	2	1

When we make statements such as 'It's 9 o'clock now; the journey will take 5 hours; so I will arrive at 2 o'clock', we are in effect working in arithmetic mod 12.

In arithmetic mod n, the numbers 0, 1, 2, … , $n - 1$ are used.

Multiple

■ See **Common multiple**.

Multiplicative inverse

When working in the set of **rational numbers**, the multiplicative **inverse** of 3 is $\frac{1}{3}$ because $3 \times \frac{1}{3} = 1$ and 1 is the **identity element** for multiplication.

Also the multiplicative inverse of $\frac{1}{3}$ is 3 because $\frac{1}{3} \times 3 = 1$.

In **arithmetic modulo** 5 the multiplicative inverse of 3 is 2 because 3 x 2 = 1 and 1 is the identity element for multiplication mod 5.

The multiplicative inverse of the **matrix** $\begin{pmatrix} 3 & 1 \\ 5 & 2 \end{pmatrix}$ is $\begin{pmatrix} 2 & -1 \\ -5 & 3 \end{pmatrix}$ because

$$\begin{pmatrix} 3 & 1 \\ 5 & 2 \end{pmatrix}\begin{pmatrix} 2 & -1 \\ -5 & 3 \end{pmatrix} = \begin{pmatrix} 2 & -1 \\ -5 & 3 \end{pmatrix}\begin{pmatrix} 3 & 1 \\ 5 & 2 \end{pmatrix} = \begin{pmatrix} 1 & 0 \\ 0 & 1 \end{pmatrix}$$

and $\begin{pmatrix}1 & 0\\0 & 1\end{pmatrix}$ is the identity element for multiplication.

More generally, provided $ad - bc \neq 0$, the multiplicative inverse of

the matrix $\begin{pmatrix}a & b\\c & d\end{pmatrix}$ is $\begin{pmatrix}\frac{d}{ad-bc} & \frac{-b}{ad-bc}\\ \frac{-c}{ad-bc} & \frac{a}{ad-bc}\end{pmatrix}$

Natural numbers

The natural numbers (or **counting numbers**) are the numbers 1, 2, 3, 4, …. used for counting. 0 is sometimes included as a natural number.

See **Directed numbers**, **Integers**, **Positive number**, **Negative number**, **Rational numbers** and **Real numbers**.

Nautical mile

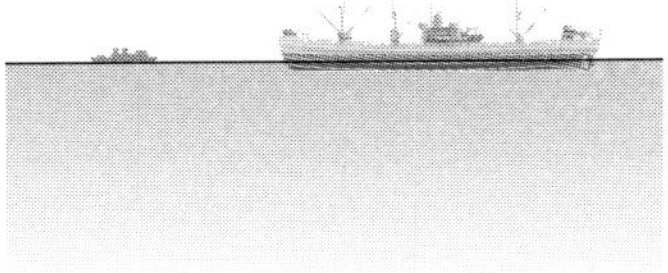

A nautical mile is a measurement of distance at sea. It is 6083 feet, which is about 1.15 'ordinary' miles. A nautical mile is one-sixtieth of the distance along the equator between two lines of **longitude** which differ by 1°.

A speed of 1 nautical mile per hour is known as a *knot*.

Negative number

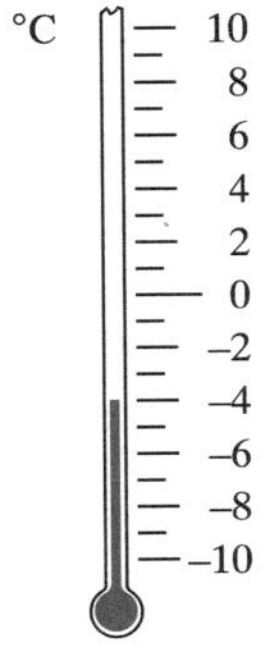

Negative numbers are **directed numbers** used to measure in the opposite sense to **positive numbers**. They are written with a minus sign. For example, -3, -1.5, $-\frac{7}{4}$.

Sometimes upper height minus signs are used to distinguish the sign from subtraction: $^{-}3$, $^{-}1.5$, $\frac{^{-}7}{4}$.

Temperatures below zero are described using negative numbers. For example, a temperature of 4 degrees below zero is called 'negative 4', or more usually 'minus 4', and is written -4.

See **Integers**.

Net

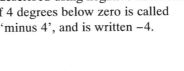

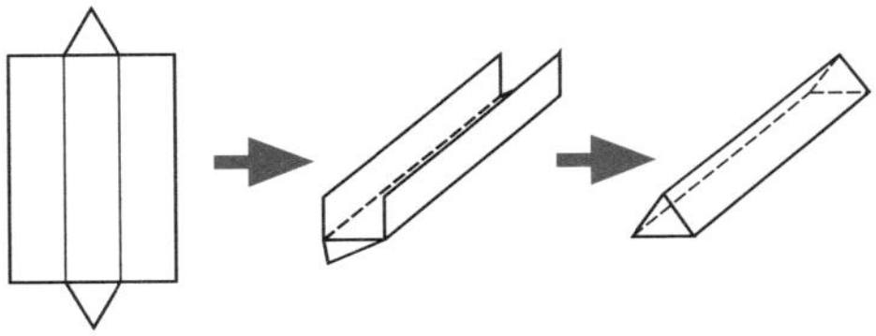

The net of a three-dimensional object is the shape which when folded can be made into the object. The diagram shows a possible net for a triangular **prism**.

Network

A network is a set of connected lines. The lines are called **arcs**. The points at which the lines meet are called *nodes* and the spaces formed are called **regions**.

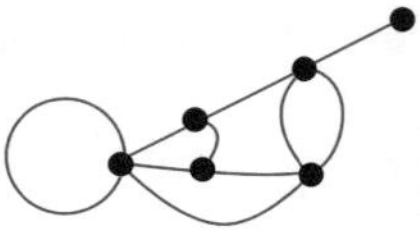

■ See **Order of a node**.

Node

■ See **Network**.

Nonagon

A nonagon is a 9-sided **polygon**. A regular nonagon has all its sides equal in length and all its **interior angles** equal (140°).

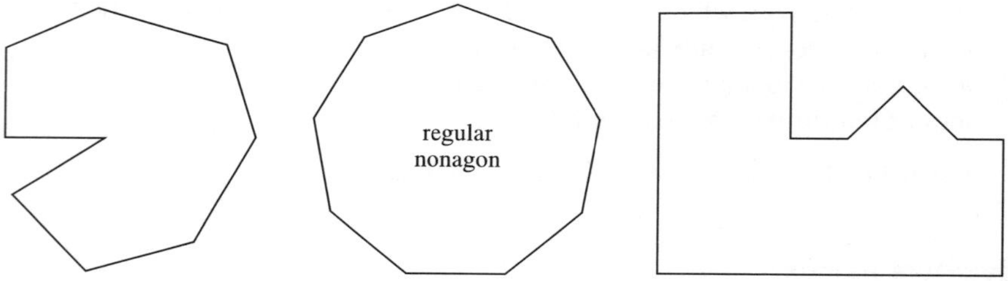

■ See **Polygon**.

Normal distribution

Normal distributions arise when measuring many naturally-occurring variables such as heights of people or lengths of leaves on a tree.

When the measurements are grouped in small **class intervals** the resulting **histogram** has a characteristic bell-shape. This is called a *normal distribution curve*.

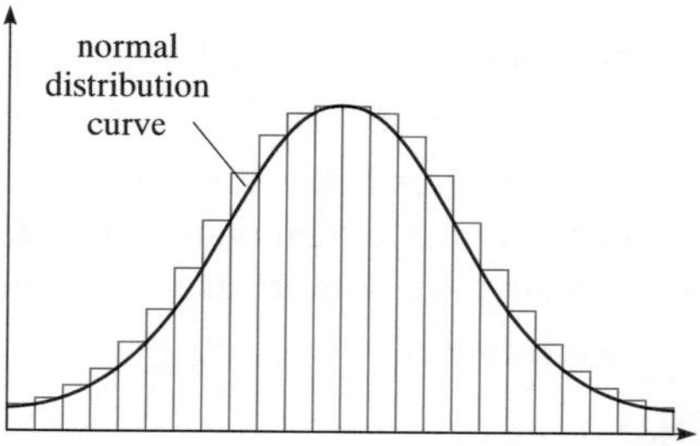

Null set

■ See **Empty set**.

Number line

Numbers can be represented on a number line like a ruler scale.

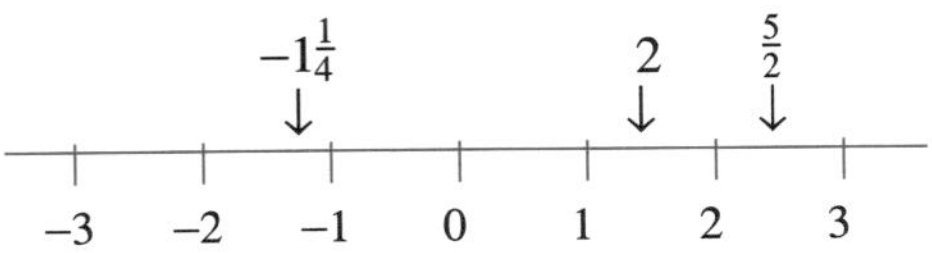

This picture can be helpful in adding and subtracting **directed numbers**.

See **Difference**.

Number patterns

A pattern can sometimes be seen in a **sequence** of numbers which leads to a rule for finding further numbers in the sequence.

For example, consider the sums of **odd numbers**:

$$1 = 1 = 1^2$$
$$1 + 3 = 4 = 2^2$$
$$1 + 3 + 5 = 9 = 3^2$$
$$1 + 3 + 5 + 7 = 16 = 4^2$$

A conjecture might be made:

the sum of the first n odd numbers is n^2.

The pattern can be illustrated with a 'dot' diagram. The diagram suggests that the pattern continues and can be used to lead to a general algebraic **proof**.

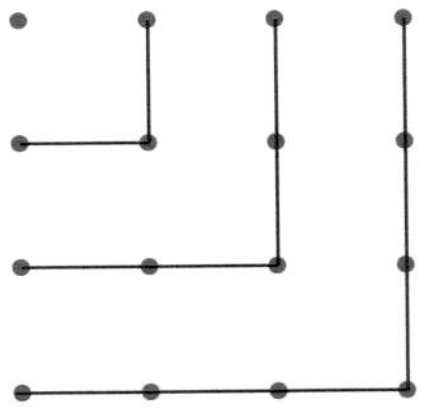

See **Fibonacci sequence** and **Triangle number**.

Numeral

The symbols used for showing the number of items in a set are called numerals.

You would write the number of stars on the right using the numeral 5. Two thousand years ago the Romans would have used the numeral V. Chinese people would use the numeral 五.

Numerator

The numerator of a **fraction** is the number on the top. For example, the numerators of

$$\frac{3}{4}, \quad \frac{11}{7}, \quad \frac{a}{b}, \quad \frac{x^2}{2y}$$

are 3, 11, a and x^2 respectively.

Object

The object of a **transformation** is the shape or set of points which is being transformed. The shape or set of points onto which it is transformed is called the **image**.

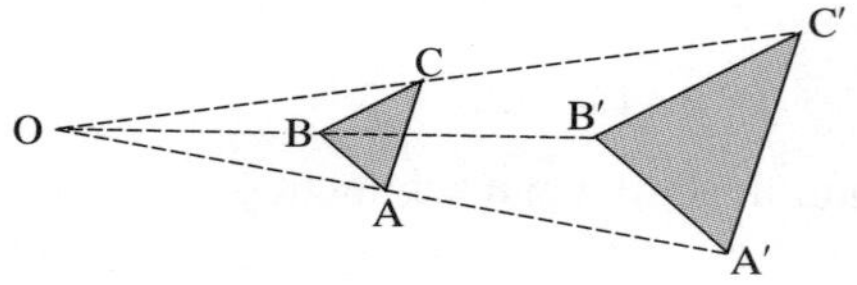

In the example shown, **triangle** ABC is the object which has been enlarged from O, with **linear scale factor** 2, and triangle A′B′C′ is its image.

Oblique cone or pyramid

■ See **Right cone** or **pyramid**.

Oblong

■ See **Rectangle**.

Obtuse angle

An obtuse angle is an **angle** whose size is between 90° and 180°.

Octagon

Octa means 'eight'. An octagon is an 8-sided **polygon**. A regular octagon has all its sides of equal length and all its **angles** equal to 135°, as shown.

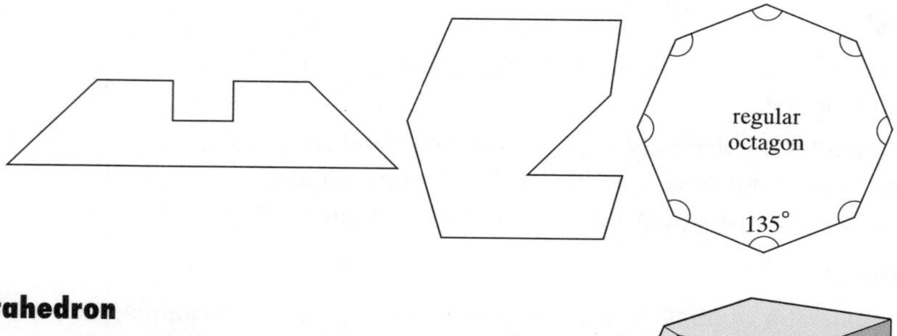

Octahedron

An octahedron is a **polyhedron** with eight **faces**. For example, a **cube** with two of its corners cut off is an octahedron.

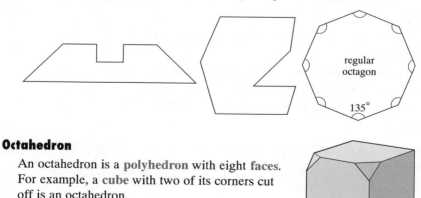

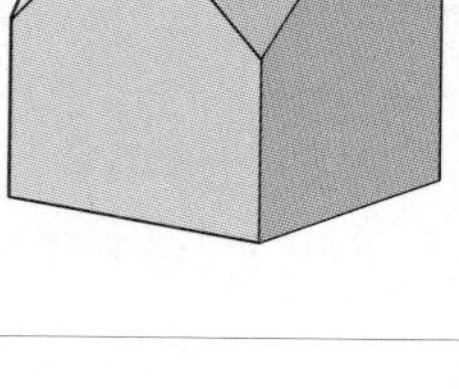

A regular octahedron has eight identical **equilateral triangle** faces, meeting four at each of its vertices. Picture it as two square-based **pyramids** with their bases stuck together. The crystals of some chemical compounds occur naturally as regular octahedra, for example, alum.

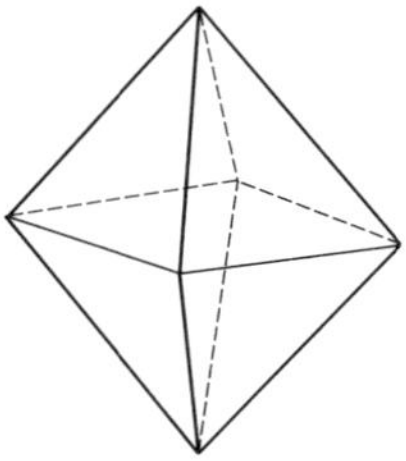

See **Polyhedron**.

Odd numbers

1, 3, 5, 7, 9, 11, 13, ... is the set of odd numbers. Any **whole number** which ends in 1, 3, 5, 7 or 9 is odd. All odd numbers leave a **remainder** of 1 when divided by 2. Examples of odd numbers are

89, 467, 4563, 36 821, 9 162 875

See **Even numbers**.

Odds

The odds of an **event** happening is a measure of the chance of that event happening expressed using a **ratio**.

For example, the odds of obtaining a three with one roll of a die is 1 to 5 (written 1 : 5), as only 1 face has a three, to 5 faces with other numbers. Compare this with the probability of the same event which is $\frac{1}{6}$.

The odds of drawing a jack, queen, king or ace from a standard pack of cards is 4 : 9.

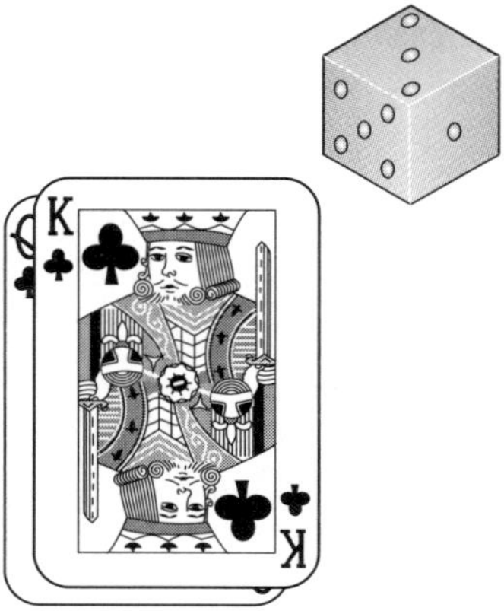

Ogive

An ogive is an alternative name for a **cumulative frequency** diagram.

Operation

+, −, x, ÷, √ are symbols which represent the arithmetic operations of adding, subtracting, multiplying, dividing, and finding the **square root**.
Intersection and **union** (∩ and ∪) are operations on **sets**.
In general, an operation is a rule for determining a new **element** from one or more elements.

Opposite angles

In the **quadrilateral** ABCD, the **angle** at A and the angle at C are said to be opposite angles, as are the angles at B and D. In all **parallelograms** both pairs of opposite angles are equal. In a **kite** the two opposite angles on either side of the **line of symmetry** are equal.

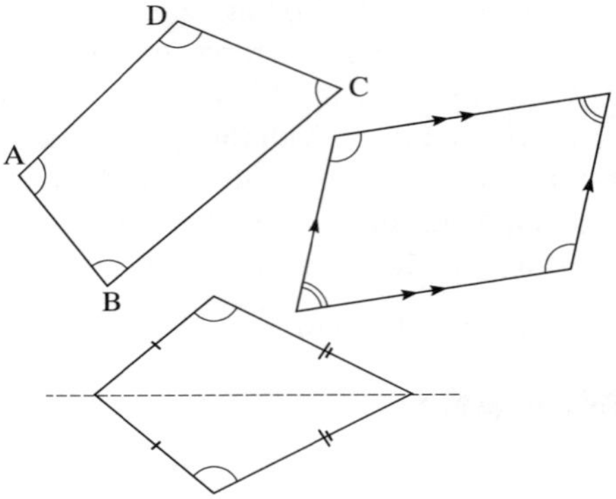

■ See **Vertically opposite angles**.

Opposite side(s)

In a **triangle** ABC, side BC is opposite to **angle** A. Its length is often given as a. Similarly b and c are used for the lengths of the sides opposite angles B and C. The longest side is opposite the largest angle, and the shortest side is opposite the smallest angle.

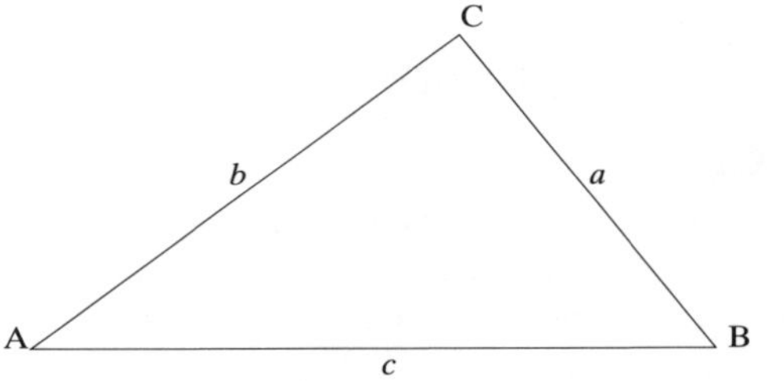

In a **quadrilateral** ABCD, there are two pairs of opposite sides: AB and DC, AD and BC. When both pairs of opposite sides are equal, the quadrilateral is a **parallelogram**.

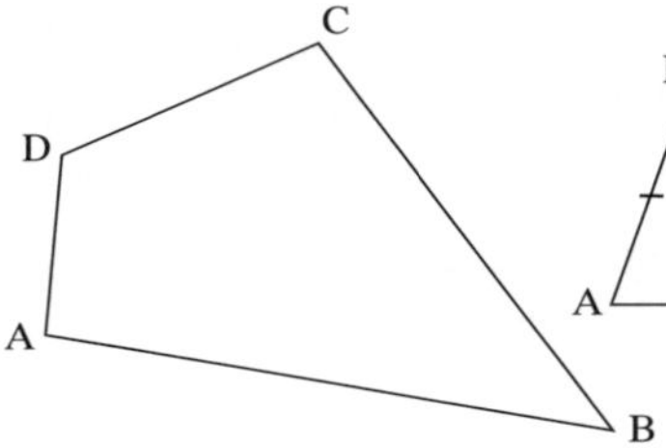

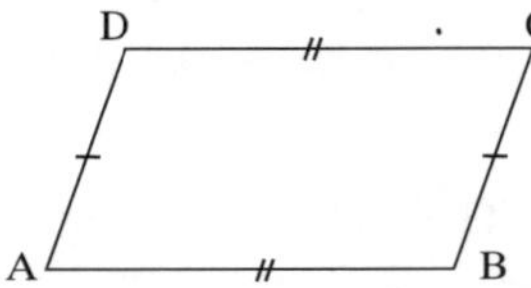

Opposite isometry

■ See **Isometry**.

Order of a matrix

A **matrix** is a rectangular array of numbers. The size and shape of the array is given by the number of **rows** and **columns** it contains, called its order. So a matrix with 3 rows and 2 columns is described as having order 3 by 2 (written 3 x 2). This is not the same as a matrix of order 2 by 3, which has 2 rows and 3 columns. For example,

$$\begin{pmatrix} 3 & 0 \\ 5 & 9 \\ 1 & 2 \end{pmatrix} \qquad \begin{pmatrix} 7 & -1 & 2 \\ 4 & 6 & 8 \end{pmatrix}$$

3 by 2 2 by 3

In general, a matrix of order *m* by *n* has *m* rows and *n* columns.

Order of a node

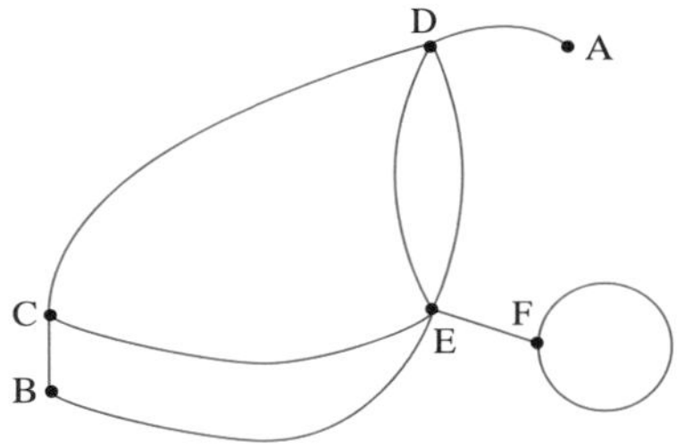

The number of **arc** ends which meet at a **node** of a **network** is called the order of the node. In the example given: A is of order 1, B is of order 2, C and F are of order 3, D is of order 4, and E is of order 5.

■ See **Euler's formula** and **Traversable**.

Order of rotational symmetry

■ See **Rotational symmetry** and **Symmetry**.

Ordered pair

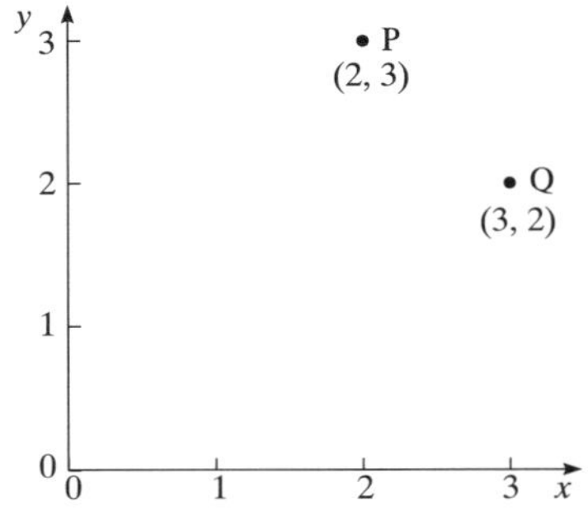

When a pair of numbers such as (2, 3) is represented as a point on graph paper, then the order of the numbers is important. In this case the first number, 2, is the x-coordinate and the second number, 3, is the y-coordinate. See point P. The pair (3, 2) is represented by point Q whose x-coordinate is 3 and y-coordinate 2.

When the order of two numbers is taken into account they form an ordered pair. In contrast, consider a game where someone wants to score a total of 5 from the roll of two dice. It makes no difference whether a 2 follows a 3, or a 3 follows a 2.

Ordinal numbers

Ordinal numbers describe order or position. For example:

'James lives in the fifth house from the corner.'

'Katy finished second in the cross-country race.'

■ See **Cardinal number**.

Origin

An origin is a starting point. It is the **zero** mark on a **number line**, or the point where coordinate axes cross. In two dimensions it is the point with **coordinates** (0, 0) and in three dimensions it is the point with coordinates (0, 0, 0).

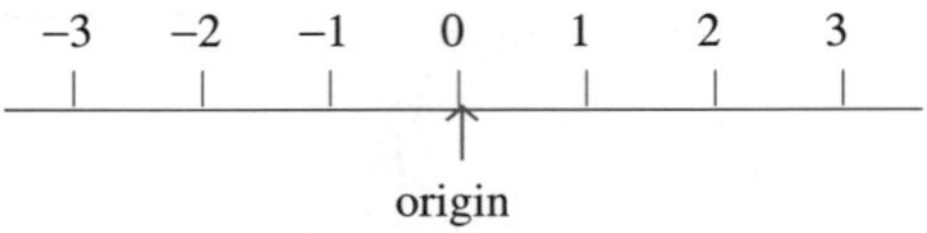

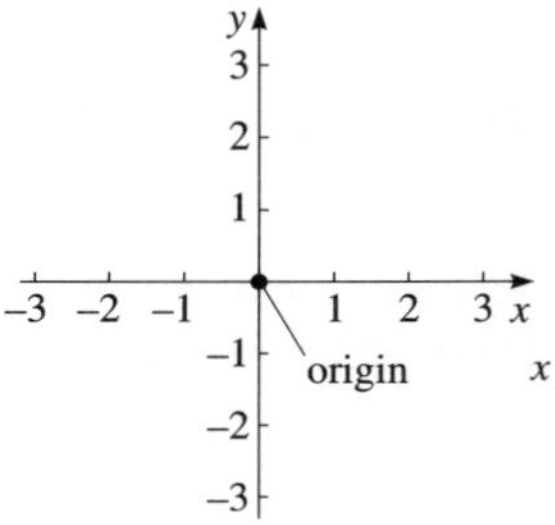

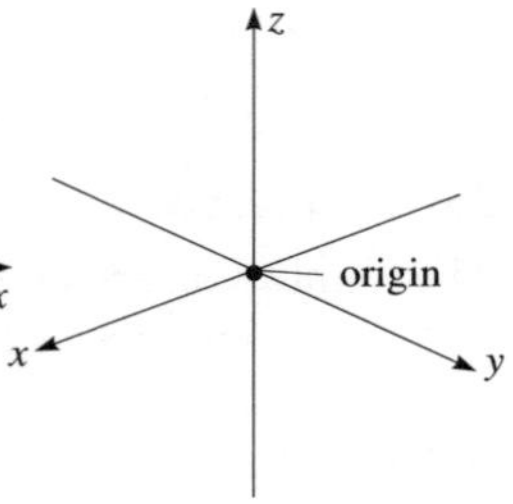

Orthocentre

See **Altitude of a triangle**.

Ounce (*abbreviation* oz)

An ounce is an **imperial unit** for measuring **mass**. 16 ounces equal 1 **pound**.

Outcome

An outcome is the word used in statistics for the result of an experiment. For example, if three coins are tossed there are 8 ways in which they might land with head (H) or tail (T) uppermost, namely:

HHH HHT HTH THH HTT THT HTT TTT

These are the possible outcomes of the experiment.

Palindromic number

171 23632 55 8998 7346437

are examples of palindromic numbers. Their **digits** read the same backwards as forwards.

Parabola

A parabola is the shape of the **graph** of $y = x^2$, and of any **quadratic** function. It is the approximate path followed by any projectile in flight such as a shell, a ball or a stone. It has the property that when used as a reflector it concentrates a parallel beam of light or radio waves to a single point, the **focus**. This fact is

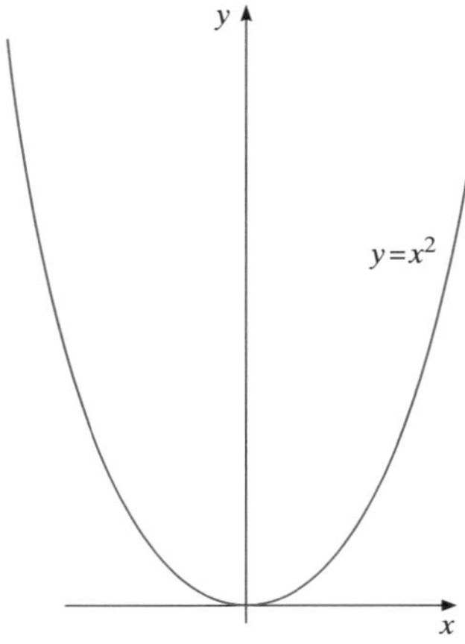

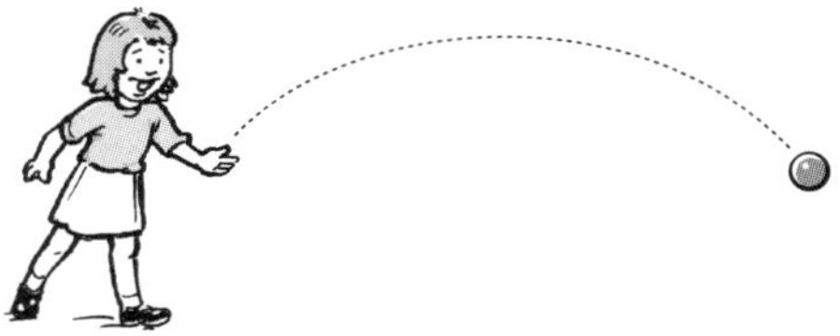

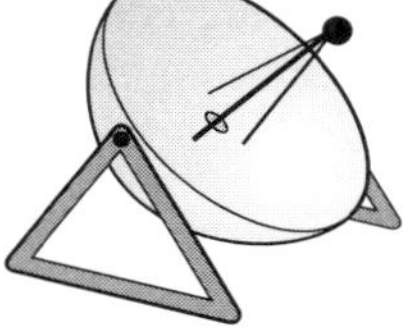

used in the design of telescopes and television aerials for sending and receiving messages from satellites. The shape taken up by the supporting cables of a suspension bridge is parabolic, and some modern motorway bridges have parabolic arches.

See **Conic section** and **Envelope**.

Parallel

When lines never meet, no matter how far they are extended, they are said to be parallel. To indicate when lines are parallel, small arrows are drawn on them.

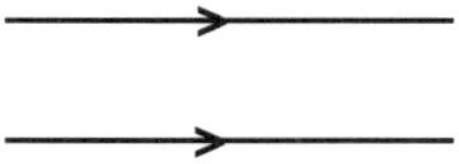

The lines in an exercise book are parallel. The horizontal lines of mortar between brickwork are also parallel, as are railway lines.

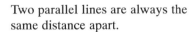

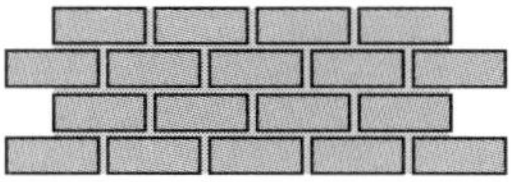

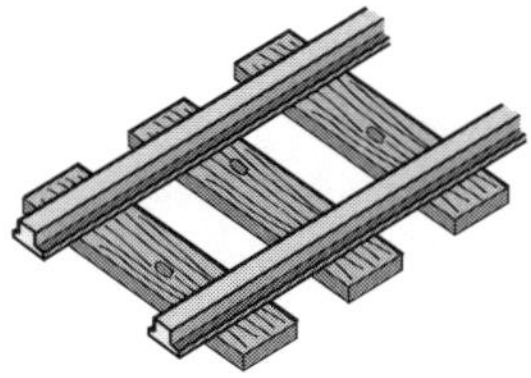

Two parallel lines are always the same distance apart.

In the same way, two **planes** (flat surfaces) are parallel when they are the same distance apart. For example, the ceiling and floor of a room are parallel (usually!).

See **Transversal**.

Parallelogram

A parallelogram is a **quadrilateral** with both pairs of opposite sides **parallel**. The opposite sides of a parallelogram are equal in length and the opposite **angles** are equal. The **diagonals** cut each other in half.

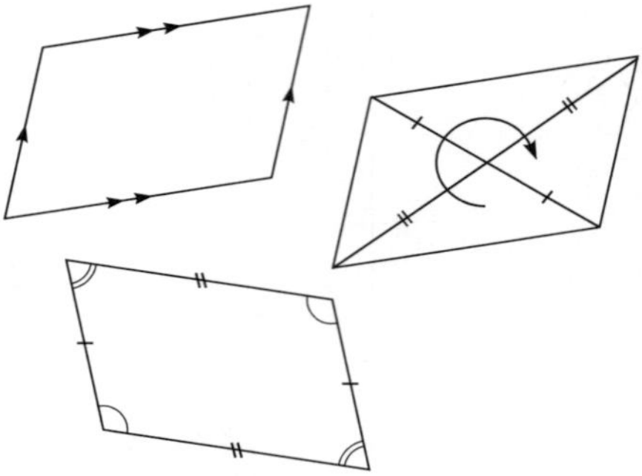

All parallelograms have **rotational symmetry** about the point of intersection of their diagonals.

Pascal's triangle

Pascal's triangle is a number pattern which starts with a 1 at the **vertex**, has a 1 at the end of each line, and each other number is found as the sum of the two numbers immediately above it. This triangular pattern is important in **algebra** and **probability**.

1
1 1
1 2 1
1 3 3 1
1 4 6 4 1
1 5 10 10 5 1

Path

A path is another name for a route around a **network** or in space. The diagram shows the path followed by a ball around a snooker table.

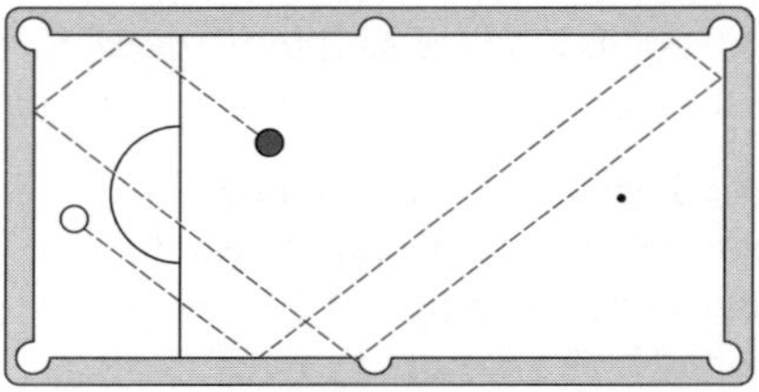

■ See **Locus**.

Pentagon

'Penta' means 'five'. A pentagon is a 5-sided **polygon**.

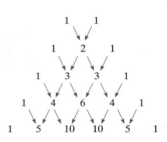

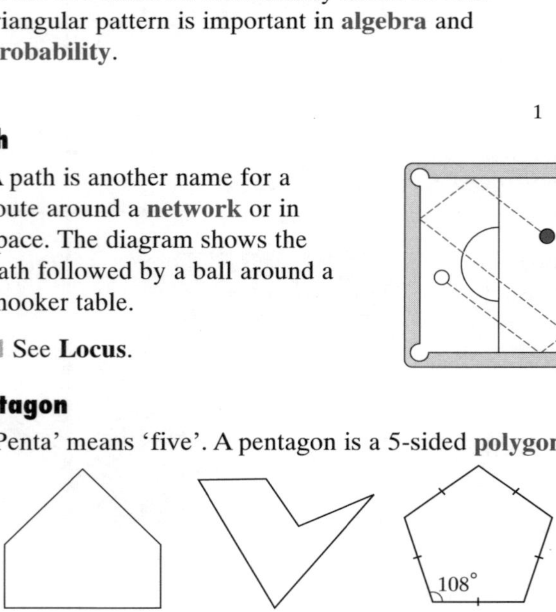

A regular pentagon has all its sides equal in length and all its **interior angles** equal to 108°. The Pentagon building in Washington DC is so named because of its shape.

Pentagram

A pentagram is a five-pointed star. It is the shape formed by the **diagonals** of a regular **pentagon**. It is also the approximate shape of a starfish.

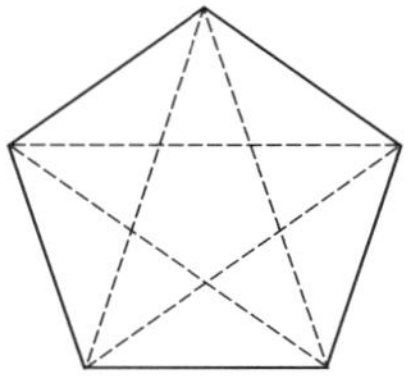

Percentage (%, per cent)

'Per cent' means 'per 100'. A percentage is a way of expressing a **fraction**, as so many parts in 100. For example, since $\frac{1}{4} = \frac{25}{100}$, it is equivalent to 25 parts in 100. This is written as 25%, pronounced 'twenty-five per cent'. The % symbol can be seen as 100 in disguise!

Any fraction can be turned into a percentage. To see how many parts out of 100 it is equivalent to, multiply the fraction by 100. For example,

$$\frac{4}{5} = \left(\frac{4}{5} \times 100\right)\% = 80\% \qquad \frac{3}{8} = \left(\frac{3}{8} \times 100\right)\% = 37.5\%$$

Similarly any percentage can be turned into a fraction by dividing by 100. For example,

$$29\% = 29 \div 100 = \frac{29}{100}$$

Note that 1% of £1 is 1 penny.

Percentage change

Suppose the value of a house has changed from £64 000 to £80 000, then it has increased in value by £16 000. So its **fractional change** is

$$\frac{16\,000}{64\,000} = \frac{1}{4}$$

and its percentage change is

$$\frac{1}{4} \times 100\% = 25\%$$

Charlbury
3 bedroom modern detached
house in quiet country village
2 WC, joined garage, large garden
£ 80 000
view by appointment

When a percentage change is given, for example, in a sale at a sports shop all the goods may be advertised as 15% off marked prices, then the reduction in price of a tennis racket marked as £80 can be found by finding 15% of £80 as follows:

$$\frac{15}{100} \times £80 = £12$$

SALE
BIG SAVINGS
15% off

Percentile

When a large quantity of **data** is arranged in order by size and then divided into 100 equal groups, with the first group containing the smallest, and so on, until the 100th group contains the largest, the sizes of the data at the boundaries of the groups are called the percentiles. Imagine, for example, that all of Tokyo's population were put in a line with the youngest first and the oldest last. If 15% of the population are 9 years of age or less, and the remaining 85% are older than 9 years, then 9 years would be the 15th percentile.

The 50th percentile divides the population in two so it is equivalent to the **median** (see **Average**), while the **quartiles** correspond to the 25th and 75th percentiles.

Perfect number

A **whole number** is a perfect number when it is equal to the sum of all its **factors** (not including itself). The two smallest perfect numbers are 6 and 28:

$$6 = 1 + 2 + 3 \quad \text{and} \quad 28 = 1 + 2 + 4 + 7 + 14$$

Very few perfect numbers are known. The next three are 496, 8128 and 33 550 336.

Perfect square

Any number such as $64 = 8^2$, which is equal to the square of a whole number, is called a perfect square. The first 8 square numbers are

$$1 = 1^2, \quad 4 = 2^2, \quad 9 = 3^2, \quad 16 = 4^2, \quad 25 = 5^2,$$
$$36 = 6^2, \quad 49 = 7^2, \quad 64 = 8^2$$

All such numbers can be represented by a **square** array of dots.

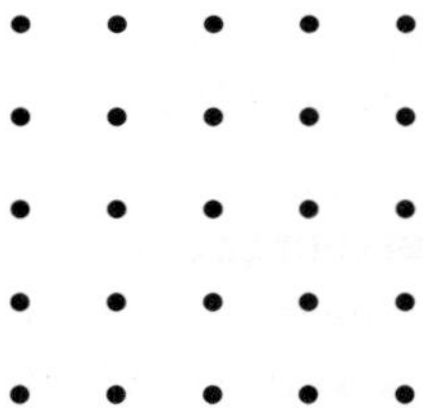

25 = 5 x 5

Perimeter

The perimeter of a shape is the name given to the boundary of the shape.

It is also sometimes used to mean the length of the boundary. The perimeter of the building plot shown can be interpreted as its five sides or the total distance you would walk to go all the way around it:

$$(25 + 25 + 35 + 40 + 30)\text{ m} = 155\text{ m}$$

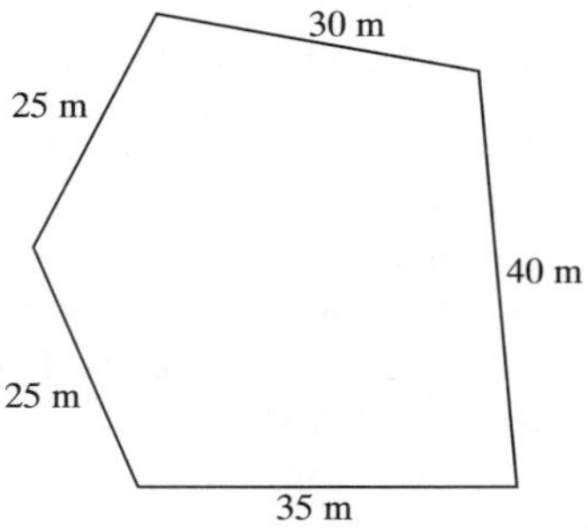

■ See **Circumference of a circle**.

Permutation

A rearrangement of a number of objects is called a permutation.

Suppose Ann, Bob and Carole are to sit on three chairs side by side. Then there are 6 different orders in which they could be placed on the chairs, each being a permutation of the 3 people.

ABC BCA CAB BAC CBA ACB

Perpendicular

Perpendicular means 'at **right angles**'. Two lines are perpendicular when they cut at 90°. A line can be perpendicular to a **plane**, for example, the edge of a room is perpendicular to the floor. Also two planes can be perpendicular to each other such as two faces of a shoe box with a common edge.

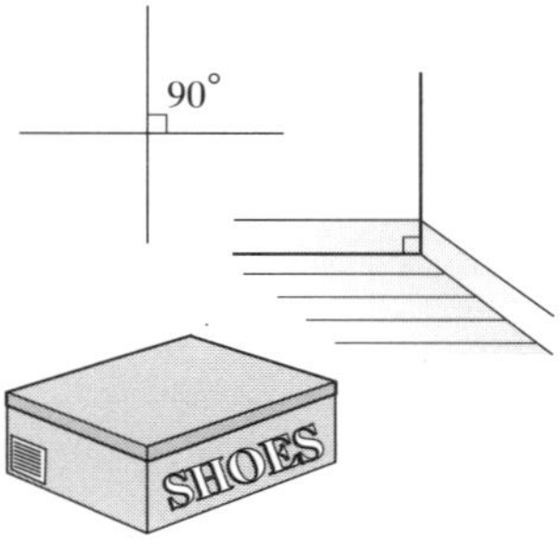

The symbol $\perp$ is used to show when two lines are perpendicular.

Perpendicular bisector

A line which is drawn at **right angles** to a **line segment** AB and divides it in half is called its *perpendicular bisector*. Any point P on this line is the same distance from A as it is from B.

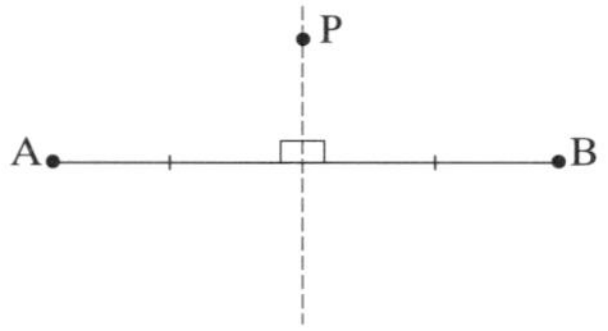

The perpendicular bisector can be constructed by using compasses to draw circular **arcs** of equal **radius** centred on A and B, and joining the two points where they intersect by a straight line.

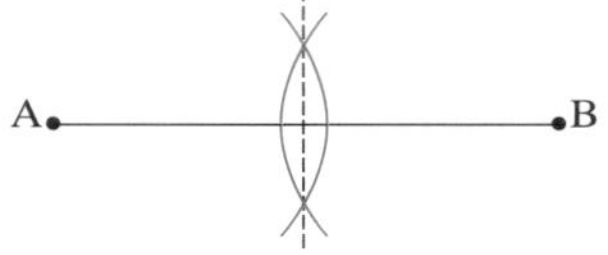

The three perpendicular bisectors of the sides of a **triangle** meet at the same point. This is the centre of the triangle's *circumcircle*, the circle through its vertices.

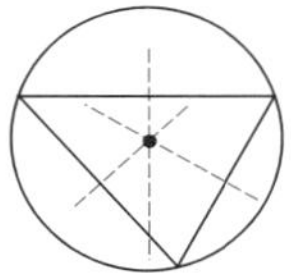

See **Bisect**.

Pi (π)

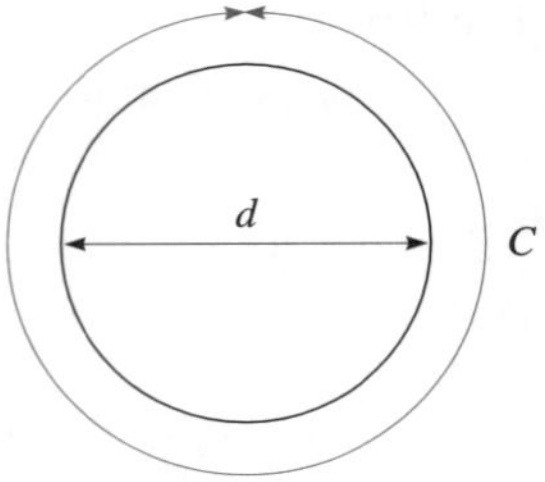

When the length of the **circumference of a circle** is divided by the length of its **diameter**, the result is always the same number. This number is slightly more than 3 and is symbolised by the Greek letter π, pronounced pi.

$$\frac{C}{d} = \pi \quad \text{or} \quad C = \pi d$$

An electronic calculator gives π as 3.1415927. This is not exact, but accurate enough for most practical purposes. π is an **irrational number** so it cannot be expressed exactly as a **fraction**. $\frac{22}{7}$ is often used as a good approximation to π, but $\frac{355}{113}$ proposed by the ancient Chinese astronomer Ch'ung-Chi is much better.

π occurs in all the formulae for measuring the **areas** and **volumes** of circular objects such as the **circle**, **sphere**, **cylinder** and **cone**.

Pictogram

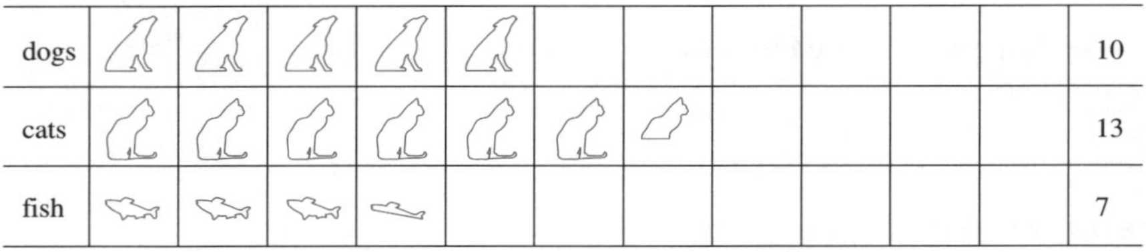

A pictogram is a way of representing statistical **data** making use of symbolic figures to correspond to the **frequencies** of the different kinds of data. For example, the pictogram here shows the result of a survey of the pets owned by the students in a class. In this case each symbolic pet represents 2 animals, and a half symbol represents 1 pet. It shows 10 dogs, 13 cats and 7 fish. Note that the different pet symbols must each be the same width.

Pie chart

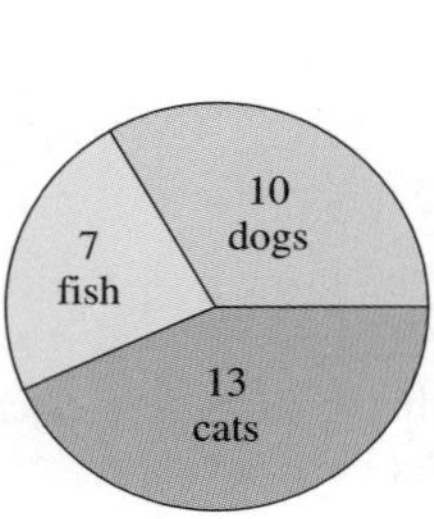

A pie chart, like a **pictogram**, is a way of presenting statistical **data** in a visual form which can be easily understood. A **circle** is divided up, like a pie, into **sectors** in proportion to the **frequencies** of the data. The pie chart shown represents the same information about pets as the pictogram above, namely 10 dogs, 13 cats and 7 fish. The **angle** for each type of pet is found by first dividing 360° by the total number of pets, 30 in this case, to give 12° for each pet. Then the angle required for 10 dogs is 10 x 12° = 120°, for 13 cats is 13 x 12°= 156°, and for 7 fish is 7 x 12° = 84°.

Pint

A pint is an **imperial unit** for measuring the volume of liquid and is familiar as the standard size of milk bottle and beer mug. 2 pints make 1 quart and 8 pints make 1 **gallon**. 1 **litre** is about 1.76 pints.

Place value

The **digit** 5 occurs in each of the numbers

563 258 1025 67.51

but it has a different value in each case because of its position. In 563 the 5 stands for 500. In 258 the 5 stands for 50. In 1025 the 5 stands for 5 units. In 67.51 the 5 stands for 5 tenths. In the **decimal** number system, the value of each position is multiplied by 10 as you move from right to left.

Th	H	T	U •	t	h	th
1000	100	10	1	$\frac{1}{10}$	$\frac{1}{100}$	$\frac{1}{1000}$

See **Base of a number**.

Plane

A plane is a flat surface, like a sheet of glass or a table top, or the surface of a lake when there is no wind to create ripples or waves. In mathematics a plane is imagined as stretching for ever in all directions with no edges to it.

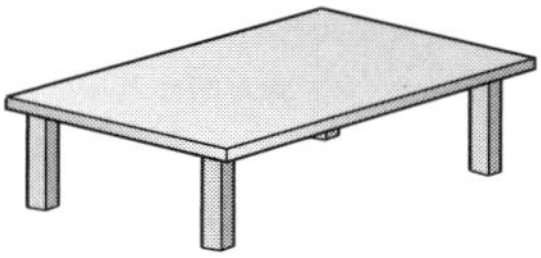

Plane of symmetry

See **Symmetry**.

Plan view

When an object is looked down on from above, as if hovering in a helicopter, or hot air balloon, what can be seen is called its plan view. The example shows the plan view of a detached house and garage.

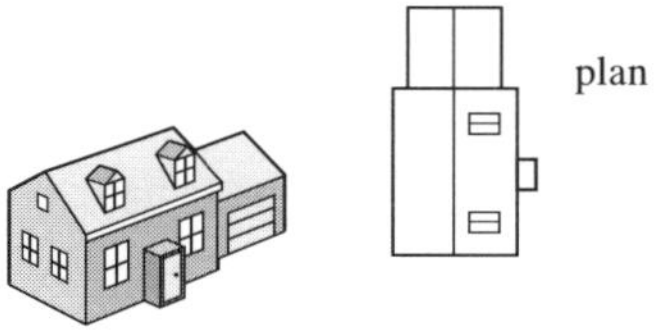

See **Elevation**.

Point

A point is a position in space which can be fixed by giving its **coordinates**. Although usually represented by a small dot it has no size.

Point symmetry

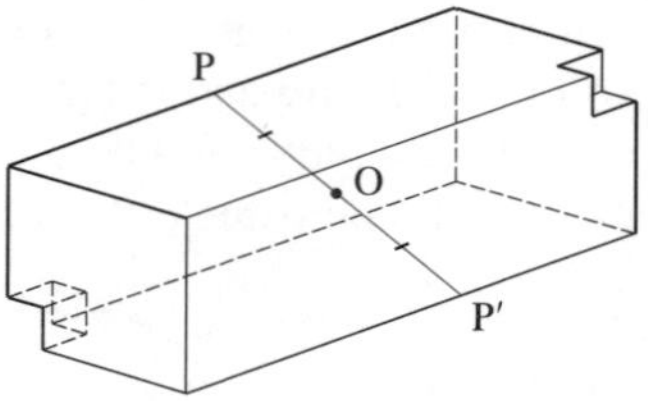

Consider a **cuboid** with a small **cube** cut out of a pair of opposite corners. This modified block has no axis of rotational symmetry or plane of symmetry, but it has **symmetry** about its centre O. For every point P on the block there is another point P′ such that O is the mid-point of PP′.
This kind of symmetry is called point symmetry. A two-dimensional object can only have point symmetry when it has **rotational symmetry** about its centre of even order.

■ See **Symmetry**.

Polar coordinates

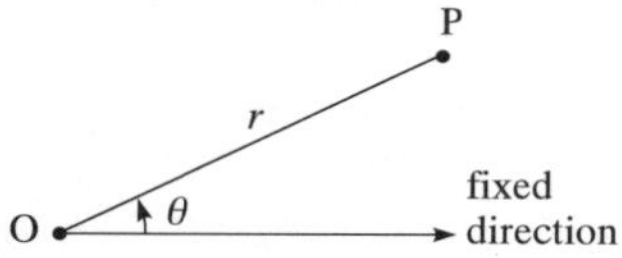

The position of a point P in a plane can be described by giving its distance *r* from a fixed point O, called the *pole*, and the **angle** θ of OP from a fixed direction. The coordinates of P are given as (r, θ) and known as polar coordinates.

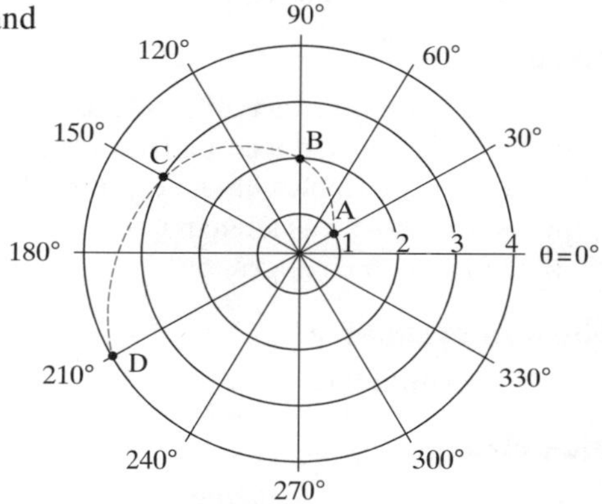

The diagram shows a polar graph with the points A (1, 30), B (2, 90), C (3, 150) and D (4, 210) plotted on a spiral curve.

When the position of a ship or an aircraft is given relative to its base by using its distance from base and its **bearing** from the base, then polar coordinates are being used.

Polygon

A polygon is a plane shape whose boundary is formed from 3 or more straight lines. Many of the polygons have special names which correspond to the number of lines forming their boundary.

No. of sides	Name	No. of sides	Name
3 sides	**triangle**	7 sides	**heptagon**
4 sides	**quadrilateral**	8 sides	**octagon**
5 sides	**pentagon**	9 sides	**nonagon**
6 sides	**hexagon**	10 sides	**decagon**

See **Regular polygon**.

Polyhedron (*pl.* polyhedra)

A polyhedron is a solid shape whose **faces** are all **polygons**. Polyhedra occur naturally as the shapes of crystals, for example, alum, copper sulphate and common salt.

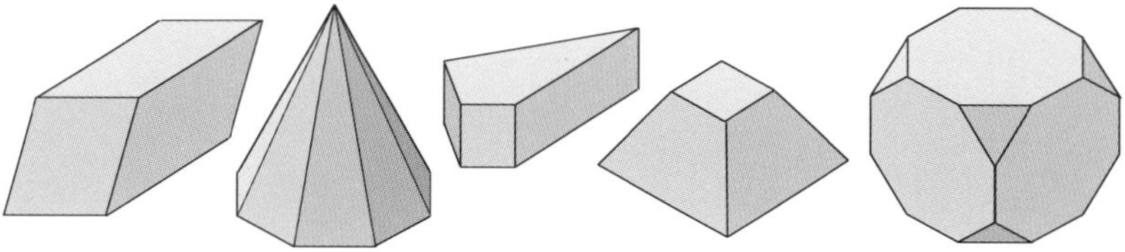

See **Cube**, **Cuboid**, **Dodecahedron**, **Icosahedron**, **Octahedron**, **Prism**, **Pyramid**, **Regular polyhedron** and **Tetrahedron**.

Polynomial

$$2x^3 + 5x^2 - 8x + 1 \qquad y^2 - 7y + 6 \qquad 4z + 3 = 0$$

are examples of polynomials. A polynomial function is a **function** whose terms each consist of a **constant** multiplied by a **power** of a **variable**, such as $2x^3$, $7y$ and $4z$.

See **Linear equation**, **Quadratic equation** and **Root of equation**.

Population

The word 'population' is used in statistics for the set of **data** being looked at. It may concern people, but could equally well be concerned with the size of pebbles on a beach.

See **Sample**.

Positive number

A positive number is any number greater than **zero**. On a **number line** positive numbers correspond to any number to the right of the zero mark. Positive numbers may be denoted by a plus sign to distinguish them from **negative**

numbers, but it is often left out. For example, +3, +2.4, +5892 are positive while –3, –2.4 and –5892 are negative.

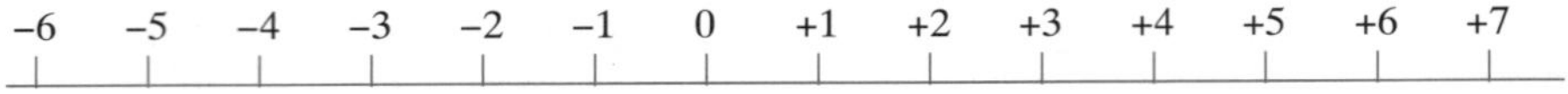

Sometimes an upper-height plus sign is used to distinguish between a number such as $^{+}3$, meaning 'positive 3', from the operation + 3, meaning 'add 3'.

■ See **Integers**.

Possibility space, probability space

The possibility space or probability space is the term for all the possible outcomes in an experiment used to determine probability. If the triangular and pentagonal shaped spinners are spun, then there are 15 possible ways in which they could come to rest. This possible set of outcomes is the possibility space:

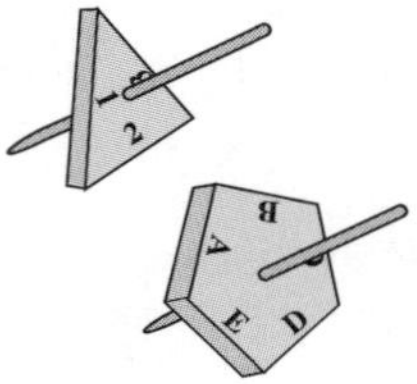

(1, A), (2, A), (3, A), (1, B), (2, B), …, (3,E).

■ See **Outcome**.

Pound (*abbreviation* lb)

A pound (lb) is an **imperial unit** for measuring **mass**. A bag of sugar has a mass of about 2.2 lb, while an average man has a mass of about 160 lb.

Power of a number

When a **product** is formed by multiplying a number by itself, such as

$$7 \times 7 = 7^2 \qquad 2 \times 2 \times 2 = 2^3 \qquad 5 \times 5 \times 5 \times 5 \times 5 \times 5 \times 5 \times 5 = 5^8$$

then the power of the number is the number of times it has been used in the product. So in the examples given:

7 is said to be raised to the power of 2;

2 is said to be raised to the power of 3;

5 is said to be raised to the power of 8.

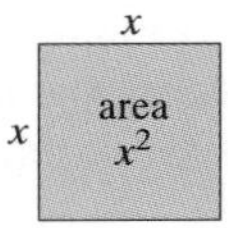

When a number x is raised to the power of 2 it is said to be squared, and when it is raised to the power of 3 it is said to be cubed. These names come from the **area** of a **square** of side x and the **volume** of a **cube** of edge x.

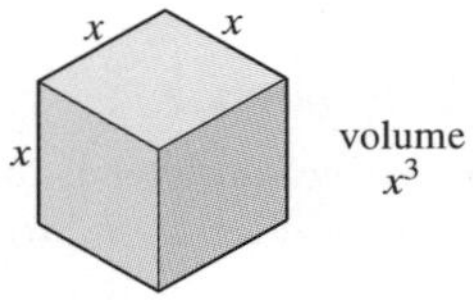

■ See **Index** and **Square number**.

Prime factors

The **factors** of 36 are 1, 2, 3, 4, 6, 9, 12, 18 and 36. Two of these numbers, namely 2 and 3, are prime numbers and are called the prime factors of 36.

Every number can be written as a product of its prime factors only. For example,

$$36 = 2 \times 18 = 2 \times 2 \times 9 = 2 \times 2 \times 3 \times 3$$

$$96 = 2 \times 48 = 2 \times 2 \times 24 = 2 \times 2 \times 2 \times 12 = 2 \times 2 \times 2 \times 2 \times 6 = 2 \times 2 \times 2 \times 2 \times 2 \times 3$$

■ See **Common factor** and **Common multiple**.

Prime number

A number is called prime when its only **factors** are 1 and itself. The first ten prime numbers are

2, 3, 5, 7, 11, 13, 17, 19, 23, 29

Note that:

- 1 is not considered a prime number;
- 2 is the only even prime number;
- there is an infinity of prime numbers.

All prime numbers other than 2 or 3 are of the form $6n + 1$ or $6n - 1$. This can be seen by writing the **natural numbers** in 6 columns as shown, where the prime numbers are shown in red.

1	**2**	**3**	4	**5**	6
7	8	9	10	**11**	12
13	14	15	16	**17**	18
19	20	21	22	**23**	24
25	26	27	28	**29**	30
31	32	33	34	35	36
37	38	39	40	**41**	42

■ See **Common factor**.

Prism

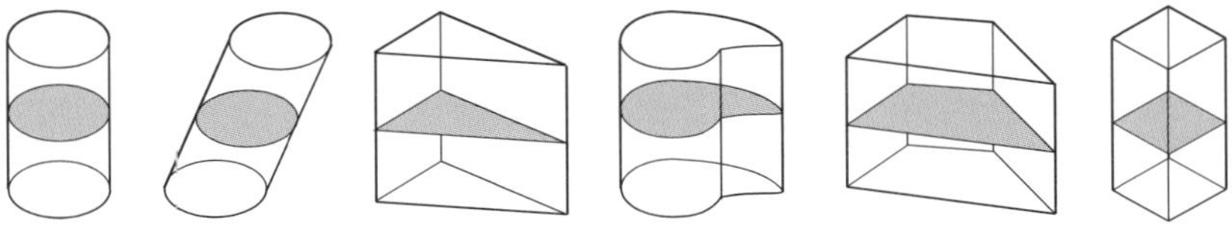

A prism is a solid shape whose **cross-sections** parallel to an end are all identical. The diagram shows a range of prisms, from a circular **cylinder** to a **cuboid**. In every case the **volume** V of the prism is equal to the **area** of its cross-section A multiplied by its height h:

$$V = Ah$$

■ See **Right prism**.

Probability

There are many situations where we have an intuitive idea of how likely they are to happen based on past experience. We may, for example, look at the sky and the barometer and decide that there is a good chance that it will rain. Mathematicians try to put a number to such an **event** to give a clearer idea of how likely it is to happen. When an event is a certainty, such as the chance that you will die one day, it is given the number 1. When the chance of an event happening is zero, such as you swimming the Atlantic Ocean, then it is given the number 0. Tossing a coin to see whether it comes up head or tail is used to start many games because the likelihood of either happening is the same, so it is given the number $\frac{1}{2}$. This numerical value of the likelihood of an event happening is called its probability, and it always takes a value between 0 and 1.

When a die is rolled there are six possible **outcomes** which are all **equally likely**, so as only one of these gives a 5 uppermost, the probability of scoring a 5 is said to be $\frac{1}{6}$. In a standard pack of 52 playing cards there are 4 kings, so the probability that if you take one card from the pack it will be a king is $\frac{4}{52} = \frac{1}{13}$. The probability of drawing a **prime number** from the pack would be $\frac{16}{52} = \frac{4}{13}$, as there are 16 prime numbers in the pack, namely the 2, 3, 5 and 7 of clubs, hearts, diamonds and spades.

Probability is also determined by keeping records of similar events over a long run. For example, a sheep farmer may know from her records that on average one-third of her ewes have twin lambs, so she would give the probability of having twins at each birth as $\frac{1}{3}$.

Generally, the probability of a particular outcome for equally likely events is given by

$$\frac{\text{number of ways of getting the required outcome}}{\text{number of possible outcomes}}$$

■ See **Odds**, **Possibility space** and **Relative frequency**.

Product

The result of multiplying two or more numbers or **matrices** together is called their product.

$$72 \times 369 = 26\ 568$$

$$5 \times 8 \times 2.43 = 97.2$$

$$\begin{pmatrix} 1 & 3 \\ 2 & -1 \end{pmatrix}\begin{pmatrix} 2 & 1 \\ 0 & 5 \end{pmatrix} = \begin{pmatrix} 2 & 16 \\ 4 & -3 \end{pmatrix}$$

Program

A program is a set of instructions given to a computer to get it to perform a particular task.

See **BASIC** and **Logo**.

Proof, prove

A *proof* is a reasoned argument to establish the truth of a mathematical result. For example, the **sequence**

$1^2 = 1$

$3^2 = 9 = 8 + 1$

$5^2 = 25 = 24 + 1$

$7^2 = 49 = 48 + 1$

$9^2 = 81 = 80 + 1$

suggests that the **square** of an **odd number** is always 1 more than a multiple of 8. But is it always true? A proof follows:

Any odd number can be expressed as $2n + 1$ where n is a **whole number**.

$$\begin{aligned}(2n + 1)^2 &= 4n^2 + 4n + 1\\ &= 4(n^2 + n) + 1\\ &= 4n(n + 1) + 1\end{aligned}$$

Now n and $n + 1$ are consecutive numbers so one of them is even and has a factor of 2. Hence $n(n + 1) = 2m$ for some whole number m, and it follows that $(2n + 1)^2 = 8m + 1$.

To *prove* a result is to construct a proof for the result.

Proper fraction

$\frac{1}{2}$, $\frac{3}{5}$, $\frac{7}{8}$ and $\frac{29}{101}$ are examples of proper **fractions**. To be a proper fraction the number on top must be smaller than the number on the bottom.

See **Improper fraction**.

Properties

Properties are facts which are always true about a set of numbers, or geometrical shapes, or transformations. For example:

2 is a **factor** of an **even number**;

the **diagonals** of a **rhombus** cross at **right angles**;

a **matrix transformation** maps lines onto lines.

Proportion

Two sets of numbers are proportional to one another when one set is a **constant** times the other. For example, {1, 2, 5, 7} and {3, 6, 15, 21} are in proportion, because the numbers in the second set are 3 times the numbers in the first.

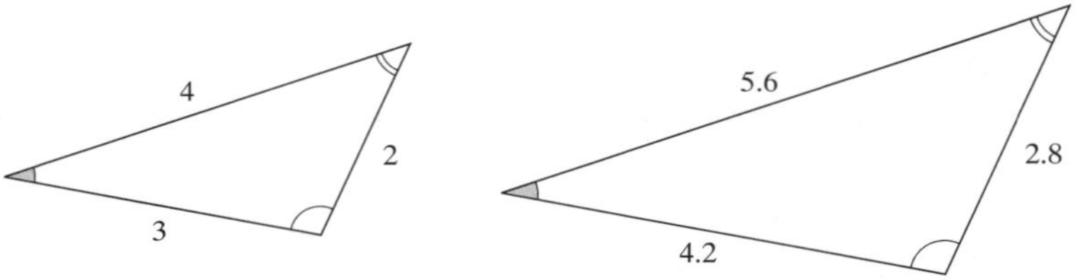

When two **triangles** are **similar**, the lengths of their sides are proportional. In the triangles shown the constant multiplying factor is 1.4.

$$\{3, 2, 4\} \times 1.4 = \{4.2, 2.8, 5.6\}$$

Scale models are made so that all the dimensions of the model are the same constant fraction of the real object, so the dimensions of the model are proportional to the dimensions of the real object.

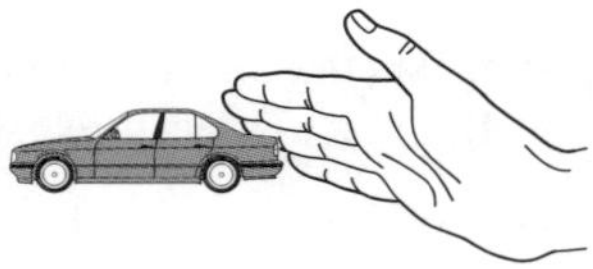

Pyramid

The name comes from the Egyptian square-based pyramids. But in general a pyramid is a **polyhedron** formed by joining the edges of a **polygon** to a point to form sloping triangular **faces**.

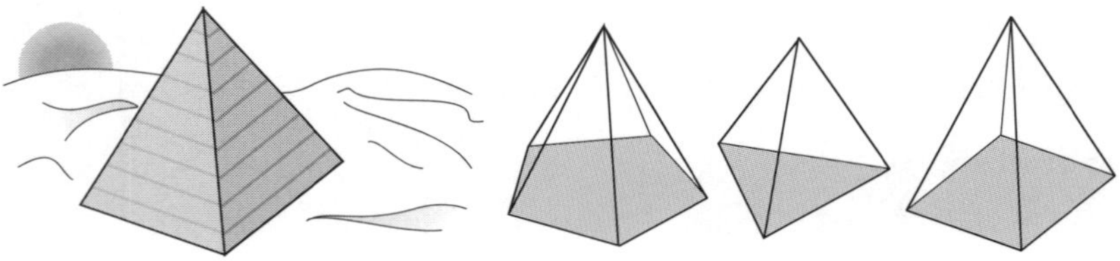

The **volume** of any pyramid is equal to $\frac{1}{3}Ah$, where A is the **area** of its **base** polygon and h is its height. The diagram shows three identical square-based pyramids fitting together to form a **cube** to illustrate this result.

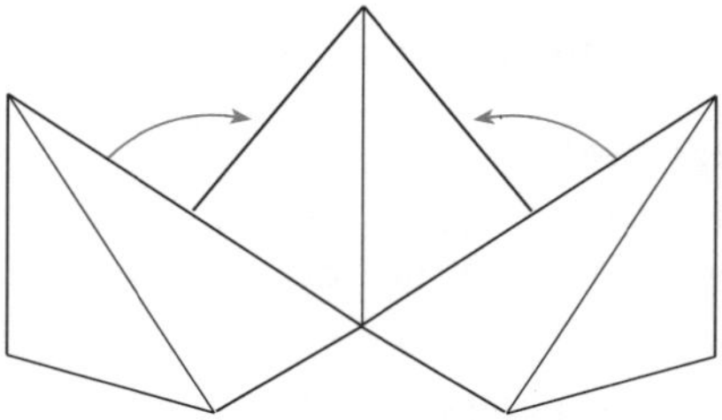

■ See **Right pyramid**.

Pythagoras' theorem

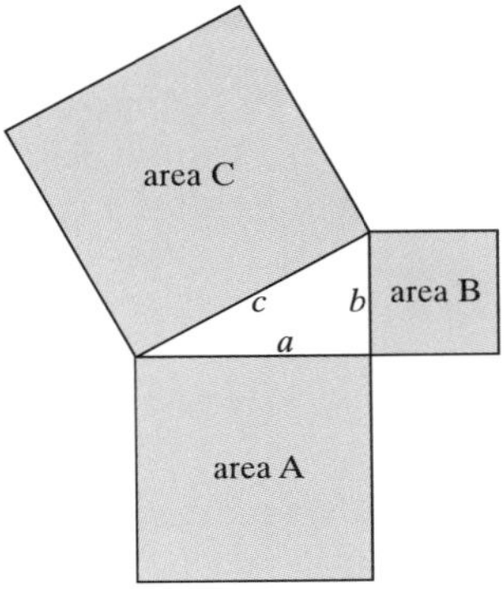

Pythagoras was a Greek mathematician who lived around 500BC and discovered a significant fact about **right-angled triangles** known as his **theorem**:

> The **area** of the **square** on the side opposite to the **right angle** is equal to the sum of the areas of the squares on the sides forming the right angle.
>
> area C = area A + area B

which is equivalent to

$$c^2 = a^2 + b^2$$

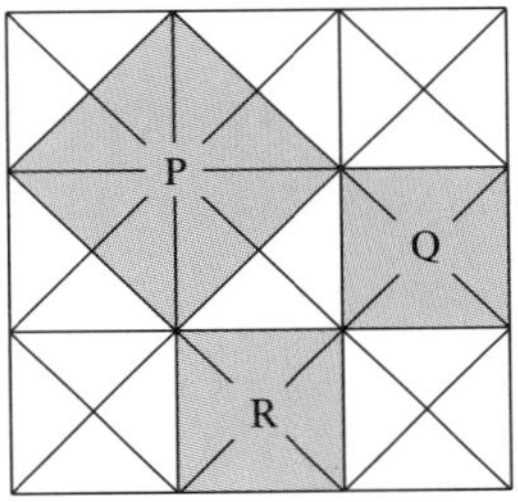

where a, b and c are the lengths of the sides of the triangle. For example, the tiling pattern of right-angled triangles has square R and square Q each made from 4 tiles while square P is made from 8 tiles.

It is also true that whenever the lengths a, b, c of the sides of a triangle satisfy the relation $c^2 = a^2 + b^2$ then the triangle is right-angled. This is the converse of Pythagoras' theorem. For example, when $a = 3$, $b = 4$ and $c = 5$ then

$$a^2 + b^2 = 3^2 + 4^2 = 25 = 5^2 = c^2$$

and the triangle is right-angled.

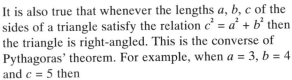

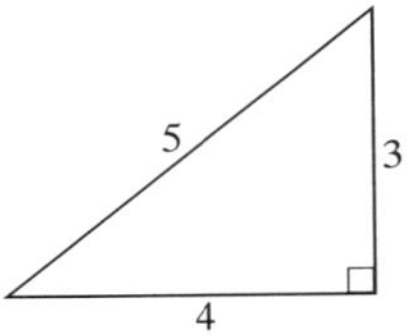

Pythagorean triples

Any three **whole numbers** a, b and c such as 3, 4 and 5 satisfying the relation $a^2 + b^2 = c^2$ of **Pythagoras' theorem** are called Pythagorean triples. There is an infinity of such triples. The best known are:

(3, 4, 5): $3^2 + 4^2 = 5^2$

(5, 12, 13): $5^2 + 12^2 = 13^2$

(8, 15, 17): $8^2 + 15^2 = 17^2$

(7, 24, 25): $7^2 + 24^2 = 25^2$

They can easily be found using the formulae

$$a = m^2 - n^2 \qquad b = 2mn \qquad c = m^2 + n^2$$

where m and n are whole numbers. For example, when $m = 3$ and $n = 2$,

$$a = 3^2 - 2^2 = 5 \qquad b = 2 \times 3 \times 2 = 12 \qquad c = 3^2 + 2^2 = 13$$

Quadrant

A **circle** can be cut into four equal **sectors** by two **diameters** at **right angles**. Each of these quarters of the circle is called a quadrant.

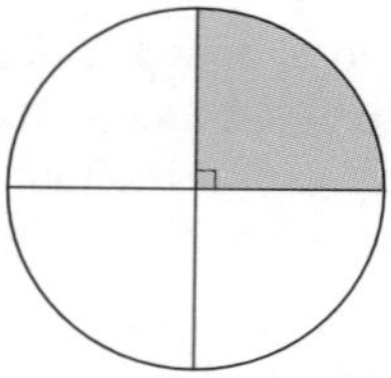

Each of the four **regions** into which the x-**axis** and the y-**axis** divide the plane is also called a quadrant. They are numbered as shown.

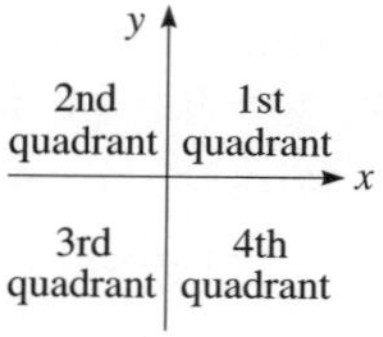

Quadratic equation

$$4x^2 = 9 \qquad (x - 3)(x + 4) = 0 \qquad 2x^2 - 5x + 2 = 0$$

are examples of quadratic **equations**, for they can all be written in the form

$$ax^2 + bx + c = 0$$

where $a \neq 0$. They each have two **solutions**, which can be found in a variety of ways.

The first example is easily solved by first dividing by 4 to get

$$x^2 = \frac{9}{4}$$

from which

$$x = \frac{3}{2} \quad \text{or} \quad x = -\frac{3}{2}$$

In the second example, as the **product** of the two **factors** $(x - 3)$ and $(x + 4)$ is zero, then either $x - 3 = 0$ or $x + 4 = 0$, from which $x = 3$ or $x = -4$.

In the third example, $2x^2 - 5x + 2 = 0$ can be **factorised** to give $(2x - 1)(x - 2) = 0$

from which $2x - 1 = 0$ or $x - 2 = 0$ giving $x = \frac{1}{2}$ or 2.

But factors are not always easy to spot so a quadratic equation can be solved by the method known as *completing the square*, illustrated here by solving

$$x^2 + 8x + 5 = 0$$

In this method the first two terms of $x^2 + 8x$ are replaced by $(x + 4)^2 - 16$. The 4 is half of 8, the **coefficient** of x in the equation, and the 16 comes from the 4^2

needed to cancel out the unwanted 4^2 produced from $(x + 4)^2$. This enables the equation to be written as

$$(x + 4)^2 - 16 + 5 = 0 \Rightarrow (x + 4)^2 = 11$$

from which

$$x + 4 = +\sqrt{11} \quad \text{or} \quad x + 4 = -\sqrt{11}$$

so $\quad x = -4 + \sqrt{11} \quad$ or $\quad x = -4 - \sqrt{11}$

In general, the solutions to $ax^2 + bx + c = 0$ are given by the **formula**

$$x = \frac{-b \pm \sqrt{b^2 - 4ac}}{2a}$$

Using the third example given, $a = 2$, $b = -5$ and $c = 2$, gives

$$x = \frac{5 \pm \sqrt{25 - (4 \times 2 \times 2)}}{4} = \frac{5 \pm 3}{4} = 2 \text{ or } \frac{1}{2}$$

Quadratic function

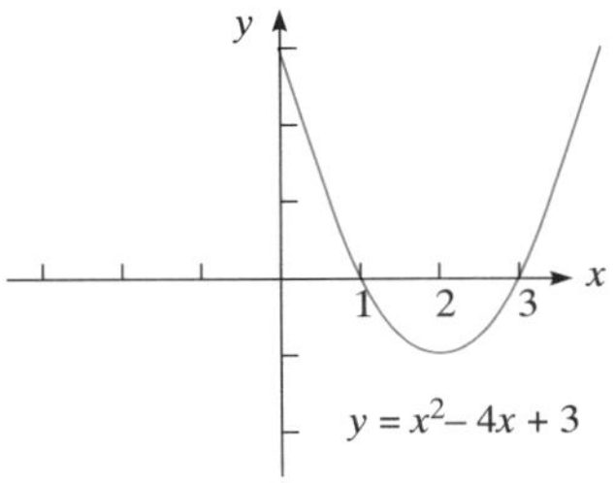

A quadratic function is a **polynomial function** in which the highest power of the variable is 2. For example, $x \mapsto x^2 - 4x + 3$ and $t \mapsto 6t^2 + 3t - 1$ are quadratic functions. The most general form of a quadratic function is $x \mapsto ax^2 + bx + c$, where a, b and c are constants.

The graph of the quadratic function $x \mapsto x^2 - 4x + 3$ is shown here. The graph is a **parabola**.

Quadrilateral

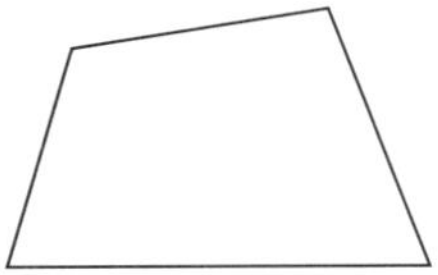

The prefix ‘quad’ always means ‘four’. A quadrilateral is a **polygon** with four sides. There are many kinds of quadrilateral with special features which have their own names.

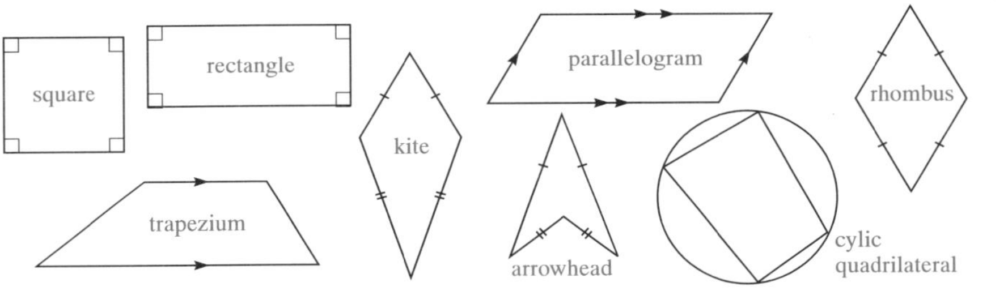

Quartile

Imagine a class of 23 children standing in line in order of their height with the shortest to the left and the tallest to the right. Then the height of the 6th child, the child a quarter of the way along, is called the *lower quartile*. Similarly, the height of the 18th child, three-quarters of the way along, is called the *upper quartile*.

In general, if there are N numbers, then the lower quartile is the value of the $\frac{1}{4}(N + 1)$th number and the upper quartile is the value of the $\frac{3}{4}(N + 1)$th number. For large populations these can be taken as the values of the $\frac{1}{4}N$th and $\frac{3}{4}N$th numbers.

The values of the quartiles can be found from a **cumulative frequency** diagram of the data. The example shows the cumulative frequency diagram of the weights of the 200 children on entry to a large secondary school. The lower quartile approximates to the weight of the 50th child in order, and the upper quartile approximates to the weight of the 150th child.

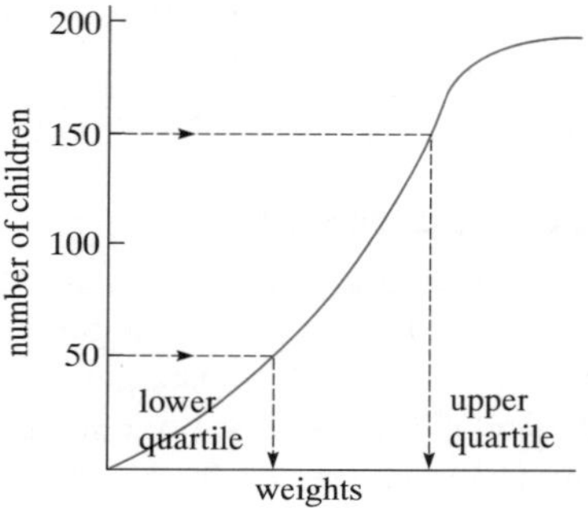

■ See **Interquartile range**, **Median** (under **Average**) and **Percentile**.

Quotient

A quotient is often taken to mean the result of dividing one number by another. Strictly speaking it is the **whole-number** part of the result. For example, using a calculator, $589 \div 17$ gives

34.647059

so the quotient is 34.

Radian measure

A radian is a unit of measure for **angles**. The angle formed at the centre of a **circle** of **radius** r by an **arc** of length s is defined as $\frac{s}{r}$ radians. It follows that 1 radian is formed by an arc of length r of a circle with radius r, and that a complete revolution is equal to

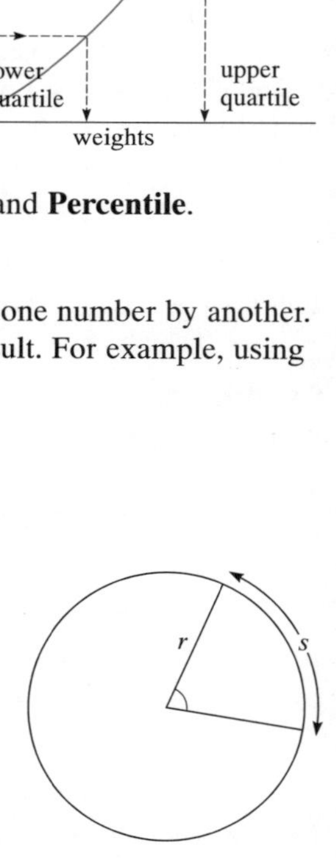

$$\frac{2\pi r}{r} = 2\pi \text{ radians } (\approx 6.3 \text{ radians})$$

$$2\pi \text{ radians} = 360° \quad \text{and} \quad 1 \text{ radian} \approx 57.3°$$

Most calculators are programmed so that either radians (rad) or **degrees** can be selected

Radius (pl. radii)

A radius of a **circle** is any straight line drawn from the centre of the circle to a point on its circumference. The phrase 'the radius of a circle' is often taken to mean the length of the radius of the circle. So, for example, if asked to find the radius of a bicycle wheel it is the length of its radius which is required.

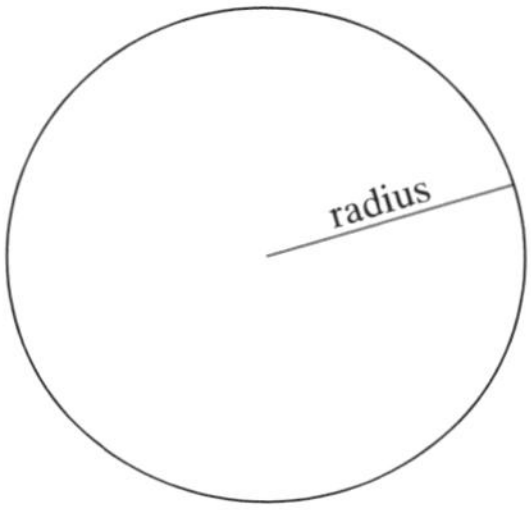

Random

When numbers or objects are chosen at random they are chosen freely without any rule or any obvious bias. For example:

- in the National Lottery the numbers which come up in a given week depend on the chance drop of the numbered balls;
- when the names of people are written on a piece of paper and put into a hat, and drawn one at a time, the draw is random.

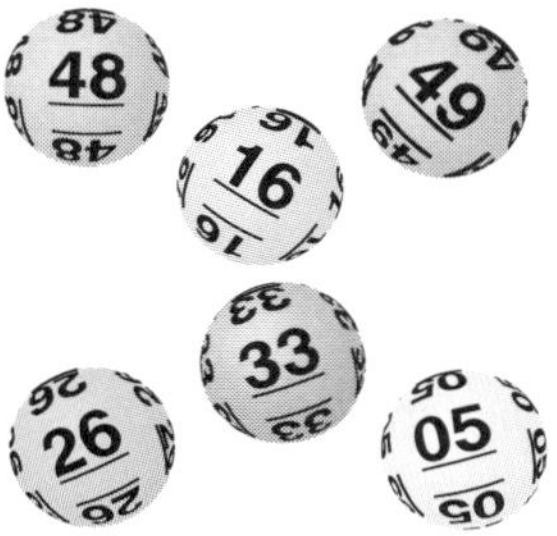

Range (of a function)

The set of numbers onto which a **function** maps the **domain** is called the range. For example, the function $x \mapsto 3x - 5$ maps $\{2, 3, 4, 5\}$, its domain, onto the set $\{1, 4, 7, 10\}$, its range, also called its **image** set.

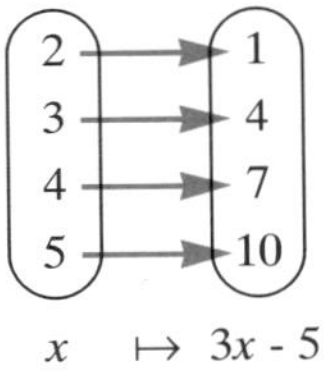

Range (of statistical data)

One of the measures of the **spread** of a set of statistical **data** is the difference in value between the highest and lowest values. For example, the times of the runners for a half marathon race are recorded. The fastest time was 72 minutes and the slowest time was 179 minutes. The range is $179 - 72 = 107$ minutes.

See **Interquartile range**.

Range of values

The set of values to be used for the **independent variable** when plotting a **graph** is called the range of values. For example, the graph $y = (x - 2)(x - 5)$ has been drawn using the range of values $0 \leq x \leq 7$.

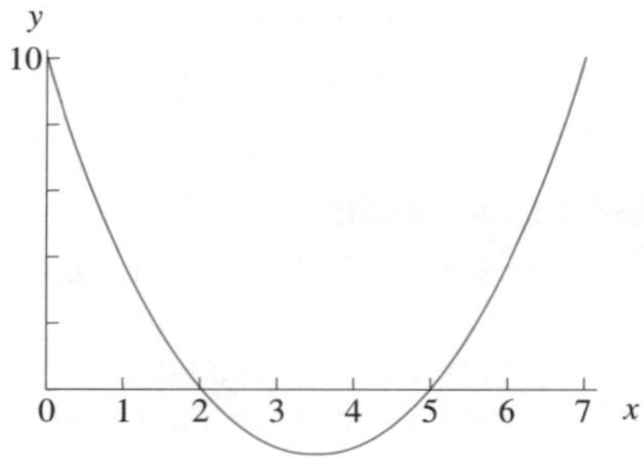

Rate of change

The rate at which an object changes its distance with time is its **speed**. So, for example, a train which covers 9 miles in 6 minutes is travelling at an average speed of 90 mph. On a straight line **graph** showing how far a train has travelled with time, the **gradient** of the graph gives the rate of change and hence the speed. The steeper the slope, the faster the train is travelling.

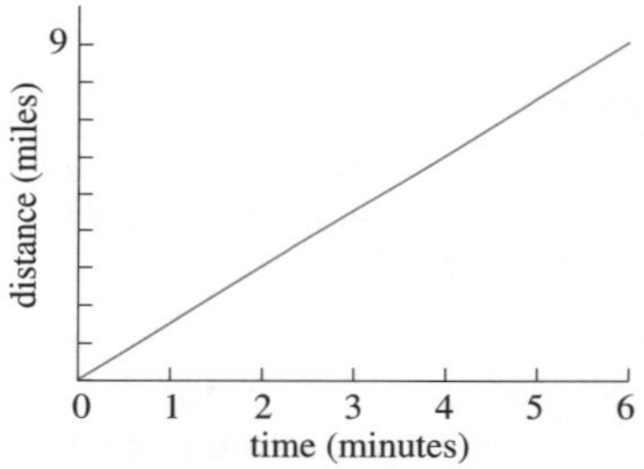

A record is kept of a baby's weight at weekly intervals from birth and the rate at which the baby's weight is changing is noted on a graph to see if it is progressing satisfactorily. Again the steepness of the graph's slope, measured by the slope of the **tangent** at a point, shows how fast the baby is growing.

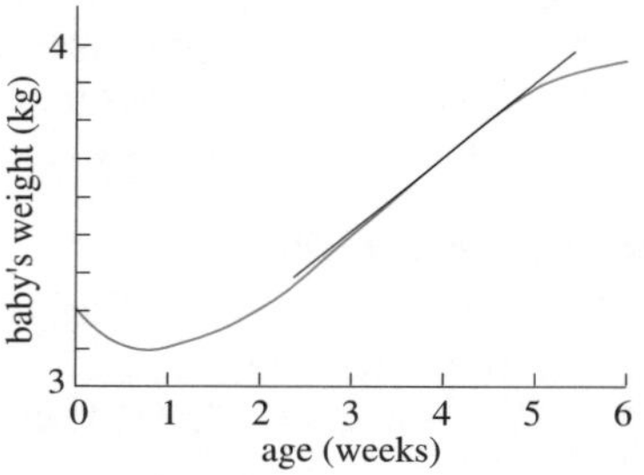

When money is invested in a bank or building society or National Savings, the money grows at a speed determined by the rate of **interest**

Ratio

Two quantities can be compared in a variety of ways. For example, if two brothers David and John weigh 50 kg and 75 kg respectively, then John could be described as 25 kg heavier than David, or $1\frac{1}{2}$ times as heavy as his brother.

Alternatively, their weights could be given as being in the ratio of 50 : 75, which **simplifies** on division by 25 to the ratio 2 : 3.

If a class of students has 12 boys and 16 girls then the ratio of boys to girls is 12 : 16, which simplifies to 3 : 4 on division by 4.

In general the value of a ratio is unchanged when the numbers forming it are both multiplied (or divided) by a **constant**. So, for example,

$$24 : 40 = 12 : 20 = 6 : 10 = 3 : 5 = 9 : 15 = 45 : 75$$

Rational number

Any number which can be expressed in the form $\frac{p}{q}$ where p and q are **positive** or **negative whole numbers** is called rational.
For example,

$$\frac{2}{3} \quad \frac{3}{5} \quad \frac{-5}{7} \quad \frac{49}{-56}$$

are rational numbers.

The **natural numbers** and **integers** are subsets of the rational numbers, which is easily seen by putting $q = 1$.

Any terminating or recurring **decimal** can be written as a rational number.
For example,

$$37.2567 = \frac{372\,567}{10\,000} \quad \text{and} \quad 0.1313131313\ldots = \frac{13}{99}$$

But numbers like $\sqrt{2}$, $\sqrt{3}$ and π cannot be expressed as rational numbers and are called **irrational**.

Real number

Any number which corresponds to a length on a **number line** is a real number, such as 3, 8.4, –9.2, 0, 26.98732, $\sqrt{2}$ or π. Real numbers can be written using **decimal** notation, whether the decimal terminates, is recurring, or goes on for ever without the pattern of digits repeating, such as

3.745 29.1313131313... 812.01001000100001...

Reciprocal

The reciprocal of a number x is the number obtained by dividing 1 by x. Thus a number multiplied by its reciprocal is 1. The reciprocal of a **fraction** $\frac{a}{b}$ is $\frac{b}{a}$ since $\frac{a}{b} \times \frac{b}{a}$ is 1. For example:

$\frac{1}{4}$ is the reciprocal of 4;

$\frac{3}{2}$ is the reciprocal of $\frac{2}{3}$;

5 is the reciprocal of 0.2.

Reciprocal function

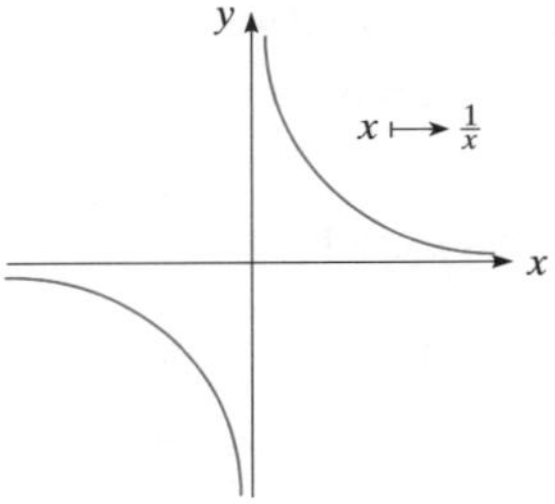

The **function** $x \mapsto \frac{1}{x}$ is called the reciprocal function, for it maps every number x (except 0) onto its reciprocal. Its **graph** is a **hyperbola**.

Rectangle

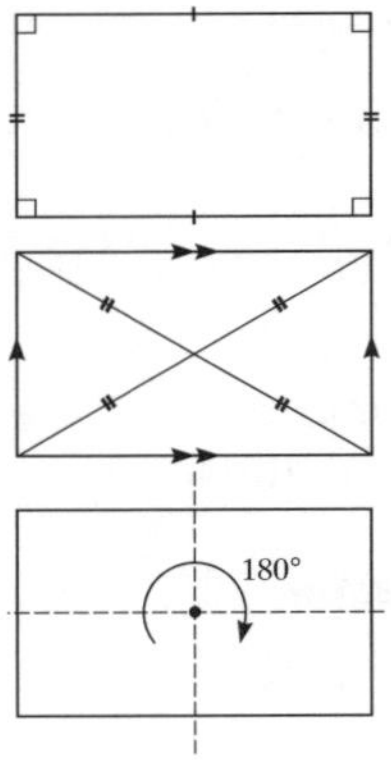

A rectangle is a **quadrilateral** all of whose **angles** are **right angles**, like a page of this book or the shape of most windows and doors.

In a rectangle: opposite sides are **parallel** and equal in length; **diagonals** are equal in length and cut each other in half. Except when it is a square it has two **lines of symmetry** and **rotational symmetry** of order two.

An *oblong* is a rectangle which is not a square.

Rectangle number

When a number of counters can be displayed in a rectangular pattern with more than one row or column, then the number concerned is called a rectangle number. It has at least two factors other than 1. Such numbers are also called **composite**. They are never **prime**, but may be **square**.

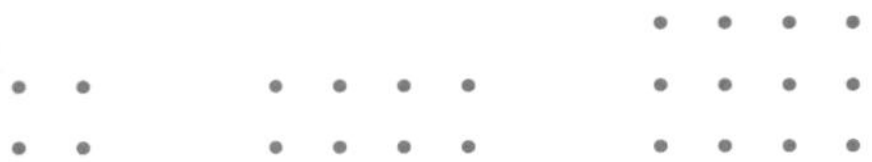

4 = 2 x 2   10 = 5 x 2   12 = 4 x 3

Rectangular prism

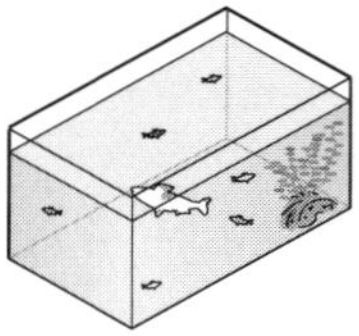

This is a **prism** whose **cross-section** is a **rectangle**, so it is equivalent to a **cuboid**.

Recurring decimal

A **decimal** where the pattern of digits after the decimal point keeps repeating itself is said to be recurring. It may be a single digit repeating as in 0.3333333333333… or a repeating sequence as with 0.238238238238238…., where the 238 is repeated endlessly. To indicate such a repetition a dot is placed over the first and last digit of the recurring sequence, so the above two numbers are written as $0.\dot{3}$ and $0.\dot{2}3\dot{8}$.

All recurring decimals can be turned into **fractions** by putting 9s under the recurring digits and treating the result as a fraction, so

$$0.\dot{3} = \frac{3}{9} = \frac{1}{3} \qquad 0.\dot{2}3\dot{8} = \frac{238}{999}$$

Most divisions if continued far enough turn out to give recurring decimals. For example,

$$3 \div 7 = 0.428571428571.... = 0.\dot{4}2857\dot{1}$$

and $6 \div 13 = 0.461538461538.... = 0.\dot{4}6153\dot{8}$

Reduce to simplest form

This phrase is used to indicate that **fractions** should have any **common factors** in their top and bottom numbers **cancelled** out. For example, $\frac{24}{36}$ can be divided top and bottom by 12 to give $\frac{2}{3}$.

■ See **Equivalent fractions**, **Lowest terms** and **Simplify**.

Re-entrant polygon

■ See **Concave polygon**.

Reflection

A reflection is a **transformation** which has the same effect as a mirror. Every point P in front of a mirror (line or plane) maps to an **image** point P′ on the other side of the mirror so that P′ and P are the same distance from the mirror, and PP′ is at **right angles** to it. The effect on any object is to produce an image of the same shape and size but in the opposite **sense**.

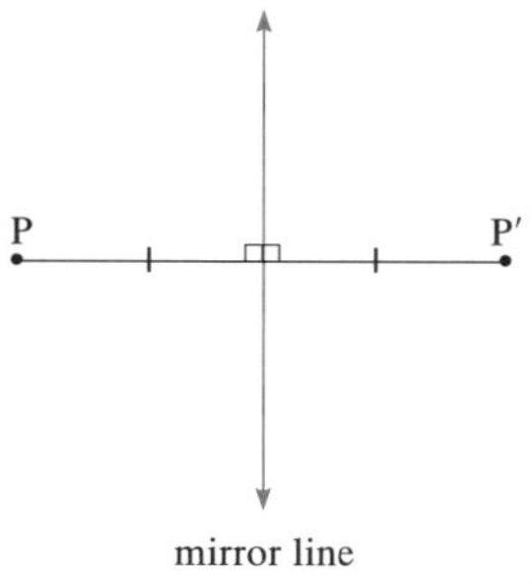

→

The **matrix** for reflection in a line through the **origin** at an **angle** α to the x-axis is

$$\begin{pmatrix} \cos 2\alpha & \sin 2\alpha \\ \sin 2\alpha & -\cos 2\alpha \end{pmatrix}$$

■ See **Isometry**.

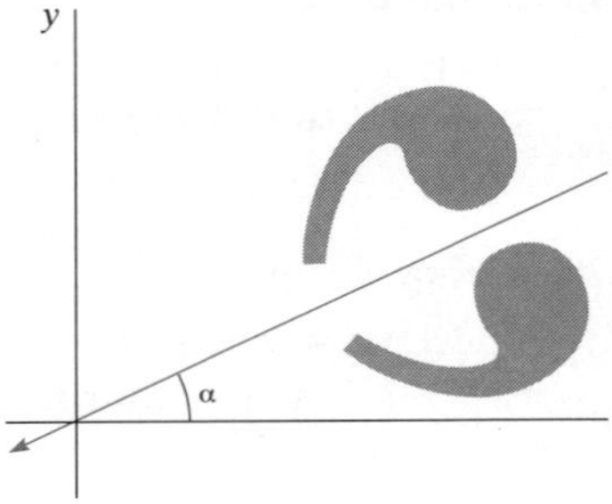

Reflex angle

An **angle** between 180° and 360° is a reflex angle.

Region

A **circle** drawn on a page divides it into two regions, that part of the surface inside the circle and that part outside.

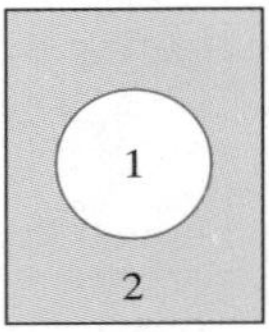

When a **network** is drawn on a piece of paper it will divide it into a number of regions each bounded by **arcs**. In the example there are 6 regions, 5 inside the network (like fields), and one region outside.

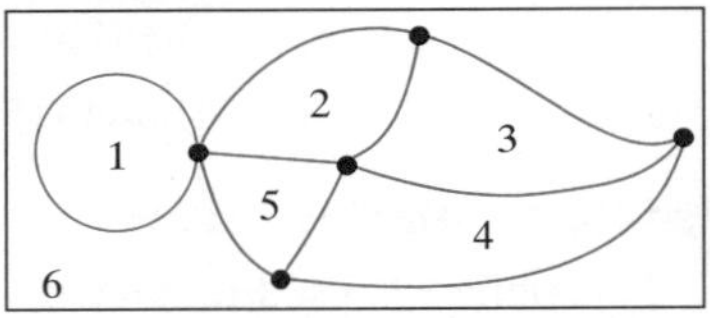

When a **graph** is drawn for an **equation** such as $x + y = 6$, the line representing it divides the **plane** into two regions which correspond to the **inequalities** $x + y > 6$ and $x + y < 6$ as shown.

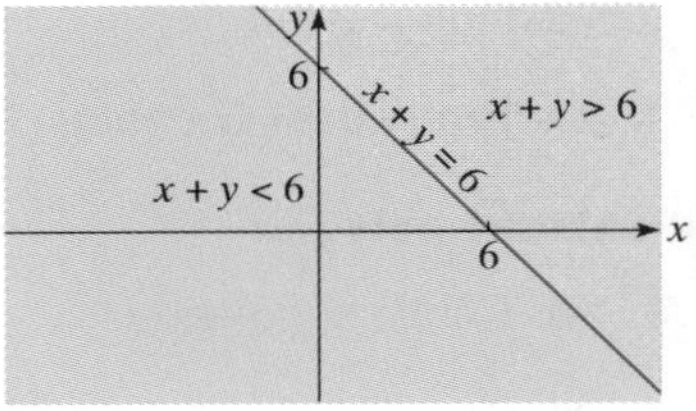

Equations such as $y = x^2$ divide the plane in a similar way but this time the boundary line is a **parabola**.

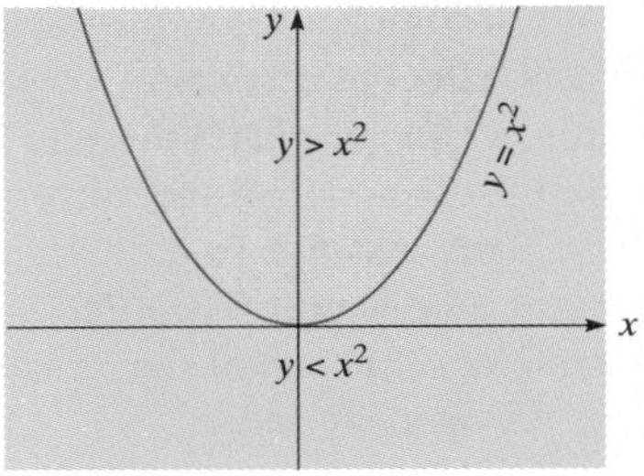

Regular polygon

A regular polygon is a **polygon** which has all its sides of equal length and all its **angles** equal. The simplest examples are an **equilateral triangle** and a **square**. A regular polygon with n sides can be easily drawn by starting with a **circle** and then drawing in radii at angles of $360° \div n$ to each other. The vertices of the polygon are at the ends of the radii. The drawings show a regular **pentagon** and regular **hexagon** produced in this way.

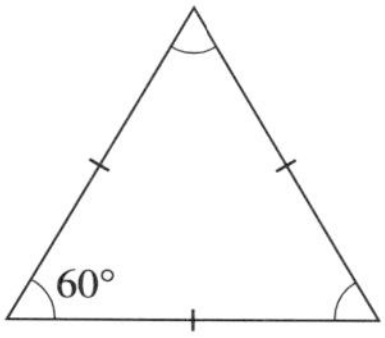

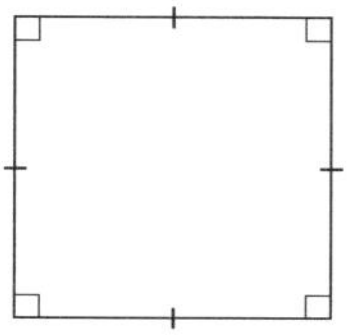

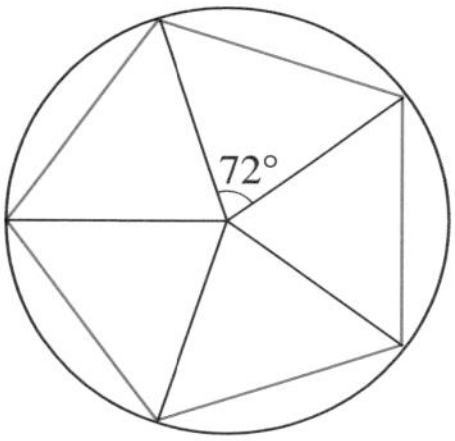

$$\frac{360°}{5} = 72°$$

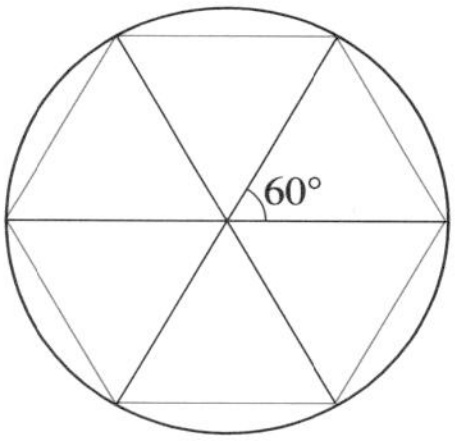

$$\frac{360°}{6} = 60°$$

Regular polyhedron

A regular **polyhedron** is a three-dimensional shape whose faces are all identical **regular polygons**, and whose corners are all the same as each other. There are only five. They are the **tetrahedron**, the **cube**, the **octahedron**, the **dodecahedron** and the **icosahedron**. The ending ‘hedron’ corresponds to **faces** and the prefix to the number of faces. ‘Tetra’ means ‘four’, ‘dodeca’ means ‘twelve’, and ‘icosa’ means ‘twenty’.

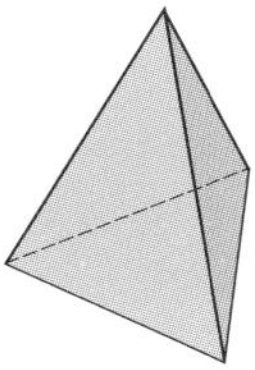

tetrahedron

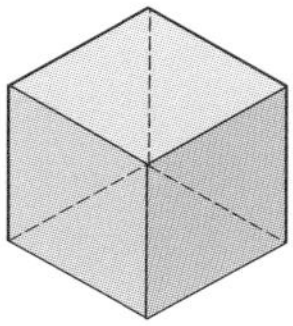

cube

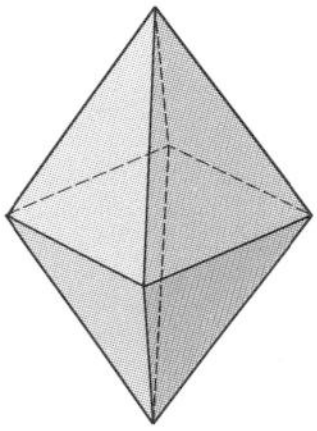

octahedron

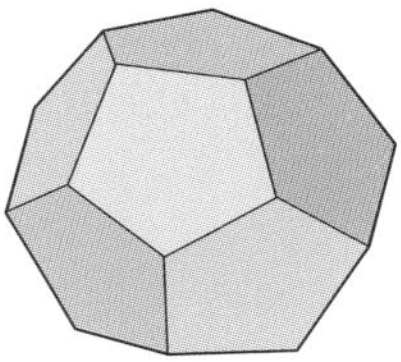

dodecahedron

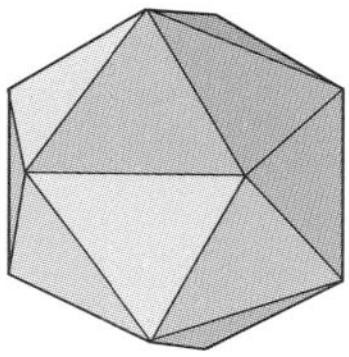

icosahedron

Relation(ship)

In general use a relation is someone in the same family, and the relationship is the connection between two members of a family such as aunt or cousin. In mathematics the words are used in a similar way to mean the connection between two sets of mathematical objects such as numbers or points.

For example, the following **sequences** of numbers are related by the equation $y = x^2$:

x	1	2	3	4	5	6	7
y	1	4	9	16	25	36	49

In the diagram, the shaded shape is related to the unshaded shape by a 90° **rotation** about the origin.

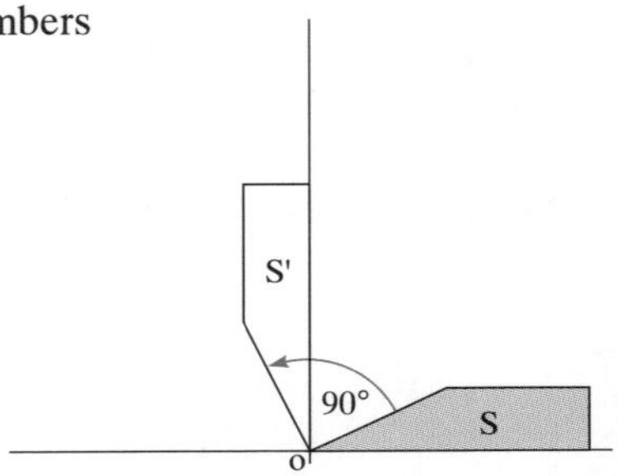

See **Function**.

Relative frequency

In an experiment two dice are rolled 600 times and their scores added together each time. A record is kept of the number of times the total is 2, 3, 4, …. , 12. The number of times a given total occurs divided by 600 is its relative **frequency**. So, if a total of 7 came up 104 times then its relative frequency would be $\frac{104}{600}$.

In general, the relative frequency of an event happening is the number of times the event happens divided by the number of trials made. It is the fraction of the occurrences.

Remainder

When one number is divided by another the result might be a **whole number** or, as is more likely, there will be something left over. What remains is called the remainder. For example, 1357 ÷ 23 = 59 exactly, but 1364 ÷ 23 = 59 with a remainder of 7. Using a calculator, 1364 ÷ 23 gives 59.304 348 from which the 59 is clear but not the remainder. This can be found in one of two ways:

- Multiply 23 by 59 and take the result from 1364, so 1364 – (23 x 59) = 7
- Take 59 from 59.304 348 to leave just the **decimal** part, 0.304 348, then multiply this number by 23. This gave 7.000 000 1 on one calculator. The 0.000 000 1 must be ignored as a **rounding error**, giving 7 as the remainder.

See **Quotient**.

Resultant vector

When two or more **vectors** are added, the single vector which results is called the resultant vector. The diagram shows the addition of **a**, **b** and **c**. The resultant vector is

$$\overrightarrow{OC} = \mathbf{a} + \mathbf{b} + \mathbf{c}$$

The vectors could, for example, represent **velocities**, **displacements**, **accelerations** or forces.

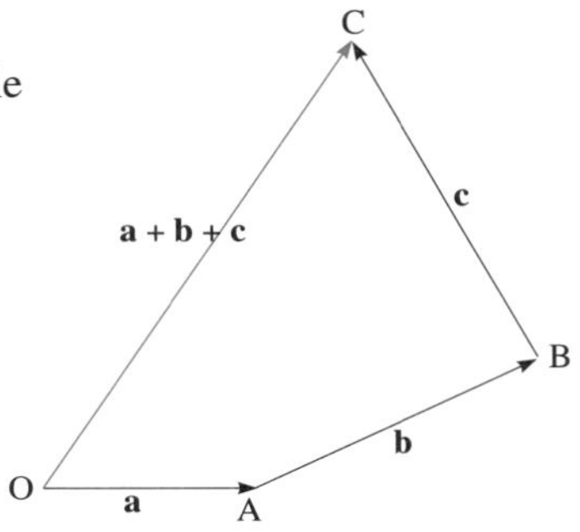

Rhombus

A rhombus is a **quadrilateral** which has its four sides equal in length. It is often described as a diamond because of the way it looks when standing on its end.

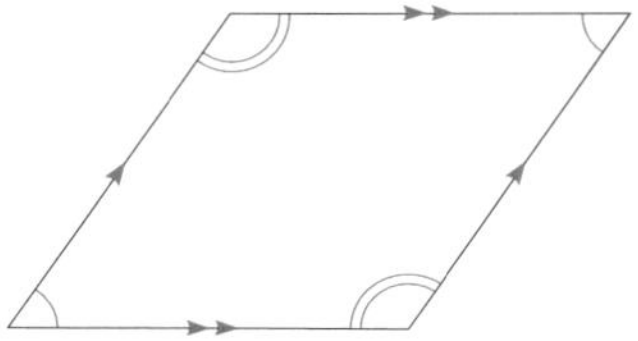

In a **rhombus**:

- opposite sides are **parallel** and opposite angles are equal;
- the **diagonals bisect** each other and are at **right angles** to one another;
- the diagonals bisect the **interior angles** and are **lines of symmetry**;
- there is **rotational symmetry** of order 2 about its centre.

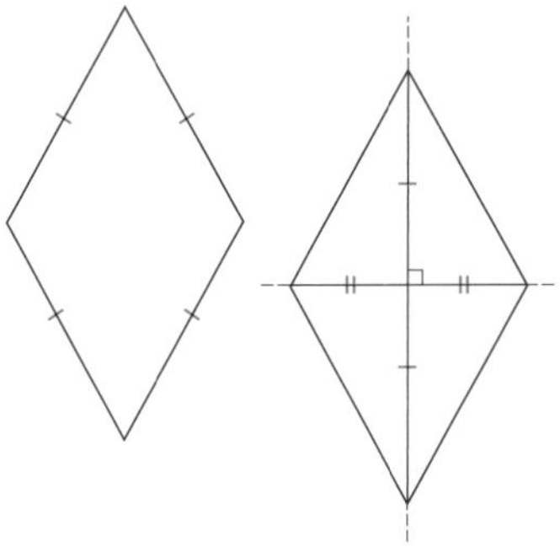

A **square** is a special case of a rhombus.

See **Parallelogram**.

Right angle

A right angle is the name given to a quarter of a turn and is equal to 90°. It is the angle between the **vertical** and **horizontal**, the angle between north and west, the angle at the corners of the pages of this book.

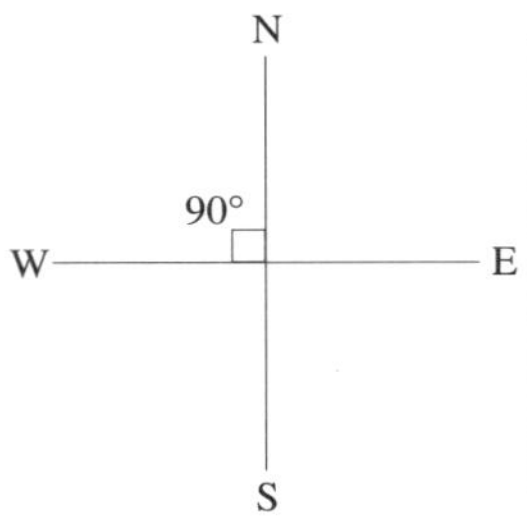

Many instruments have been designed to draw a right angle, such as a set square and T-square, because of its importance in construction and building.

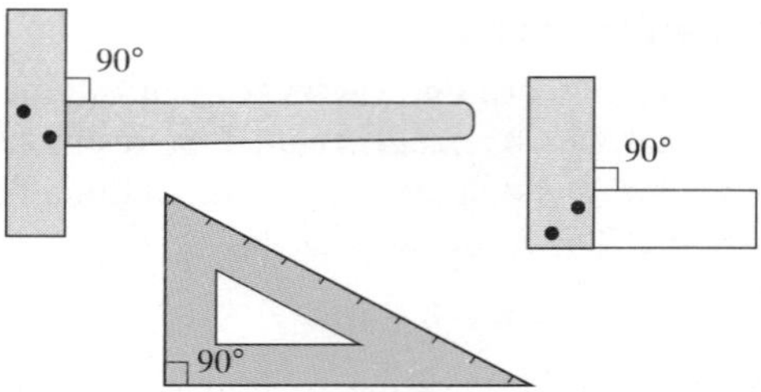

In mathematical drawings, a right angle is indicated by a small 'box'.

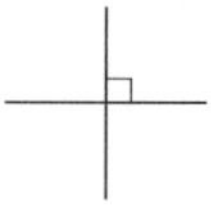

Right-angled triangle

This is a **triangle** in which one angle is a right angle. The side opposite to the right angle is called the **hypotenuse**.

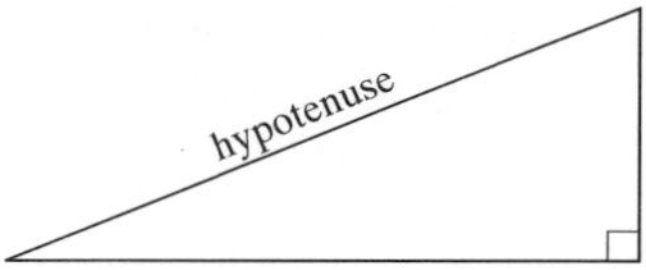

■ See **Pythagoras' theorem**.

Right cone or pyramid

A right **cone** or **pyramid** is one where the **vertex** V is right above the centre of its **base**. When this is not the case it is called *oblique*.

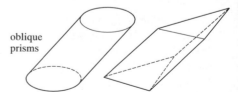

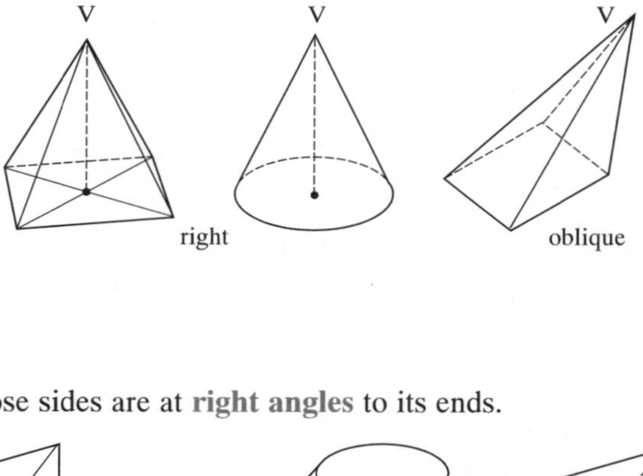

Right prism

A right prism is a **prism** whose sides are at **right angles** to its ends.

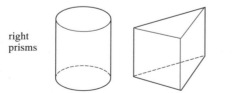

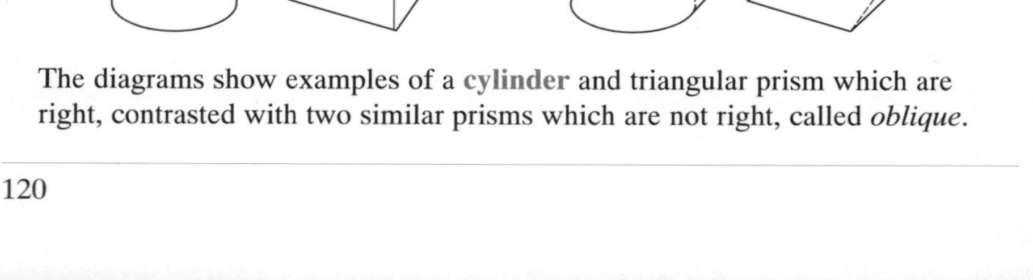

The diagrams show examples of a **cylinder** and triangular prism which are right, contrasted with two similar prisms which are not right, called *oblique*.

Roman numerals

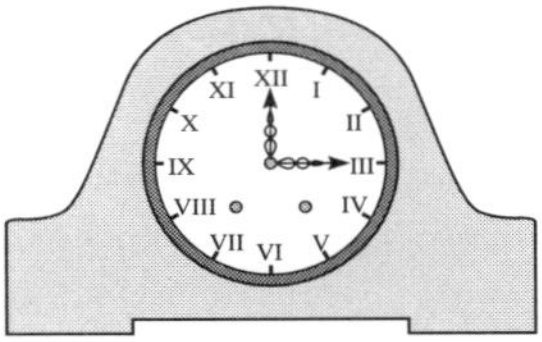

These are the symbols used by the ancient Romans to represent numbers, and can be seen, for example, on old clock faces. Often they can be seen on old buildings to indicate when they were built, or on old tombstones giving a person's date of birth.

The basic symbols and the numbers they represent are

I = 1 V = 5 X = 10 L = 50 C = 100 D = 500 M = 1000

Other numbers are obtained by placing these symbols beside each other, and the order in which they are placed indicates whether they are to be added or subtracted, as can be seen on a clock face. For example,

IV = 5 – 1 = 4 whereas VI = 5 + 1 = 6

IX = 10 – 1 = 9 while XV = 10 + 5 = 15

MCXXVII = 1000 + 100 + 10 + 10 + 5 + 1 + 1 = 1127

The Romans did not use a **place value** system.

Root of equation

The root of an **equation** is any number which satisfies the equation. It is a **solution** of the equation. For example, $x = 2$ is a root of $3x - 1 = 5$, as $3 \times 2 - 1 = 5$, and of $x^2 - 3x + 2 = 0$, as $2^2 - 3 \times 2 + 2 = 0$. But $x = 1$ is also a root of the second equation as $1^2 - 3 \times 1 + 2 = 0$.

Rotation

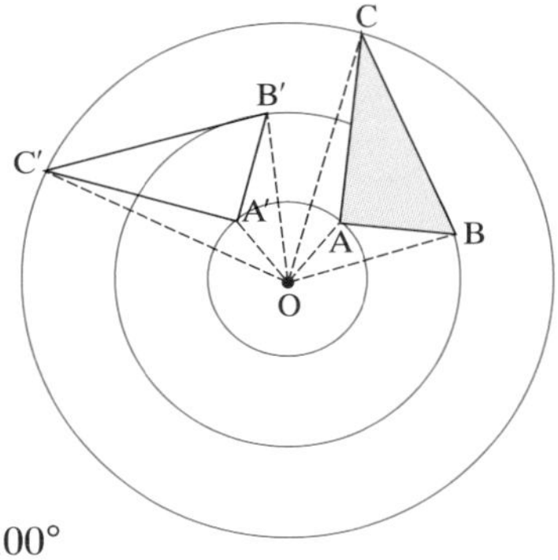

A rotation is a **transformation** which moves points so that they stay the same distance from a fixed point, the *centre of rotation*. The points are all turned through the same angle about the centre and appear to move along arcs of **concentric circles**.

In the diagram, the **triangle** ABC has been rotated about O through 100° to triangle A′B′C′.

angle AOA′ = angle BOB′ = angle COC′ = 100°

and every part of the triangle will have been turned through 100°.

A rotation is defined when its centre, the angle of rotation, and the direction of the turn are given. An **anti-clockwise** turn is said to be positive and a **clockwise** turn is negative.

See **Isometry**.

Rotation matrix

The **matrix** $\begin{pmatrix} \cos\theta & -\sin\theta \\ \sin\theta & \cos\theta \end{pmatrix}$ defines a **rotation** about the **origin** through an **angle** θ in an **anti-clockwise** direction. Special cases are

$$\begin{pmatrix} 0 & -1 \\ 1 & 0 \end{pmatrix}, \begin{pmatrix} -1 & 0 \\ 0 & -1 \end{pmatrix}, \begin{pmatrix} 0 & 1 \\ -1 & 0 \end{pmatrix},$$

which represent anti-clockwise rotations of 90°, 180° and 270° respectively.

Rotational symmetry

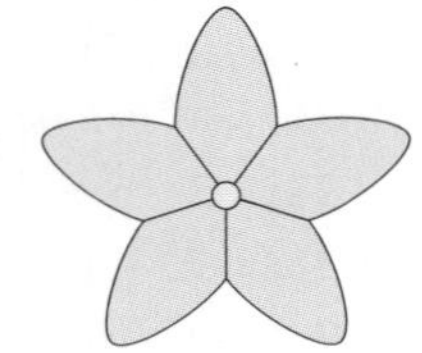

When a shape can be mapped onto itself by a **rotation** of less than 360° it is said to have rotational symmetry. The flower with 5 petals, for example, can be rotated about its centre to map onto itself through an **angle** of $\frac{1}{5}$th of a turn and any multiple of this angle, so it is said to have *rotational symmetry of order 5*. The box of chocolate mints, shaped like a hexagonal **prism**, can be rotated about its main axis through an angle of $\frac{1}{6}$th of a turn and any multiple of this angle, so it has rotational symmetry of order 6 about this axis.

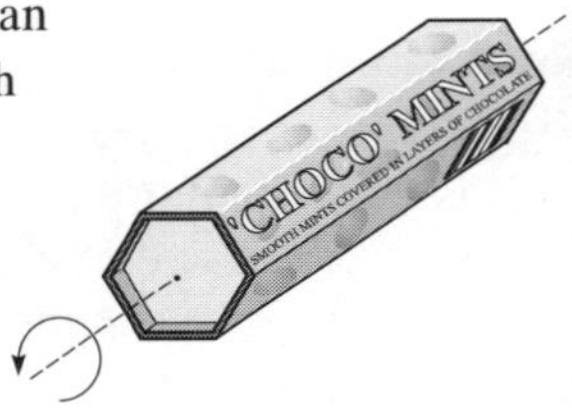

■ See **Symmetry**.

Rounding

A calculator often gives the result of a calculation to many more **digits** than is required. Approximating to the answer by giving it to a smaller number of **significant figures** or **decimal places** is known as 'rounding off'. The last digit to be ignored is the clue to how to round off the last digit kept. If it is 5 or more, the last digit kept is increased by 1; if less than 5, it is unchanged. The rounded number must be as near to the original as possible.

For example, 362.84518 becomes:

362.8 when rounded to 1 decimal place;

363 when rounded to the nearest whole number;

362.85 when rounded to 5 significant figures;

360 when rounded to 2 significant figures.

■ See **Approximation**.

Rounding error

When a number such as 362.84518 is rounded to 362.8, the rounding error is 362.84518 – 362.8 which is 0.04518.

The rounding error is

original number – rounded number.

Route matrix

A route matrix is a **matrix** used to give the number of direct routes between each pair of **nodes** in a **network**.

$$\begin{array}{cc} & \text{to} \\ & \begin{array}{cccc} \text{A} & \text{B} & \text{C} & \text{D} \end{array} \\ \text{from} \begin{array}{c} \text{A} \\ \text{B} \\ \text{C} \\ \text{D} \end{array} & \begin{pmatrix} 0 & 1 & 1 & 2 \\ 1 & 0 & 1 & 0 \\ 0 & 2 & 0 & 1 \\ 2 & 0 & 1 & 1 \end{pmatrix} \end{array}$$

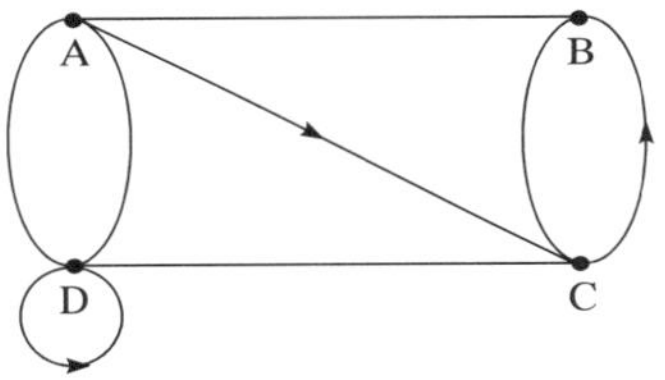

In the example shown, the arrows on some **arcs** of the network indicate one-way routes. So, for example, there is a route from A to C but not from C to A. The loop from D to itself gives an **anti-clockwise** route. If there had been no arrow then the loop could also have been traversed **clockwise**, giving 2 direct routes from D to itself. Matrices of this kind enable details of a network to be stored as numbers in a computer and manipulated as required.

Rows and columns

In a table or **matrix**, or array of numbers, a line of numbers across the page is called a *row*, in contrast to a line up and down the page called a *column*. In the matrix shown, (3 1 2 4), (1 2 0 1) and (5 6 7 2) are its rows. Its columns are

$$\begin{pmatrix} 3 & 1 & 2 & 4 \\ 1 & 2 & 0 & 1 \\ 5 & 6 & 7 & 2 \end{pmatrix}$$

$$\begin{pmatrix} 3 \\ 1 \\ 5 \end{pmatrix}, \begin{pmatrix} 1 \\ 2 \\ 6 \end{pmatrix}, \begin{pmatrix} 2 \\ 0 \\ 7 \end{pmatrix} \text{ and } \begin{pmatrix} 4 \\ 1 \\ 2 \end{pmatrix}.$$

Sample

When a survey is being carried out, for example, to see who might win an election, a selected **subset** of people are questioned about their voting intentions, and conclusions are then made about the whole population. The subset of people questioned is a statistical *sample*. The process of taking samples in this way is called *sampling*.

Inspectors in a factory will carefully examine a sample of the goods being produced to decide whether its quality comes up to scratch. In general, a sample is a selection from the **population** being studied.

Sample space

See **Possibility space**.

Scalar quantity

This is a quantity which has size but no direction, in contrast to a **vector** which has both size and direction. **Speed** is a scalar but **velocity** is a vector. Both the temperature and pressure of the air are scalar quantities.

Scale factor

Maps and models are made to a fixed **ratio** of what they represent, known as the scale factor. Maps used for walking, for example, are made to a scale of 1 : 25 000, which is more easily interpreted as 4 **centimetres** to 1 **kilometre**, or about $2\frac{1}{2}$ **inches** to 1 **mile**. Doll's house furniture is frequently made to a scale of 1 : 12 which is equivalent to 1 inch to 1 foot.

When making a scale drawing it is necessary to decide on the scale factor to be used and indicate it clearly. For example, in making a plan of a kitchen, a scale of 2 cm to represent 1 m might be appropriate.

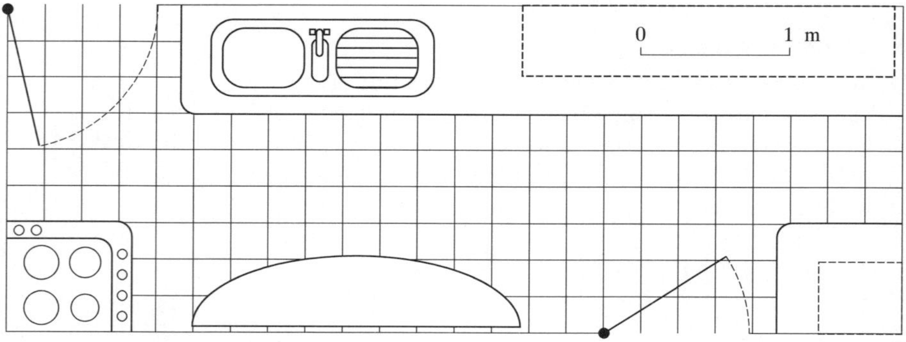

See **Area scale factor**, **Enlargement**, **Linear scale factor**, **Stretch** and **Volume scale factor**.

Scalene triangle

A **triangle** whose sides are all of different lengths is called scalene. Its **angles** are all different sizes.

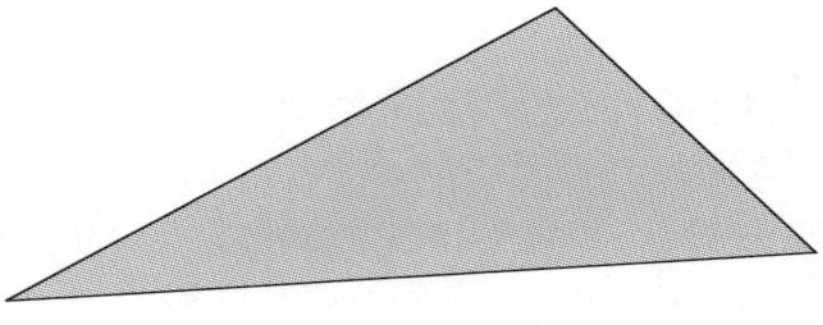

Scatter diagram

A scatter diagram is a diagram used in statistics to compare two quantities, often to show the **correlation** between them. For example, a group of people each have their height and shoe size recorded as a point on a graph. Because these measurements have a high correlation the points are all close to a line.

See **Line of best fit**.

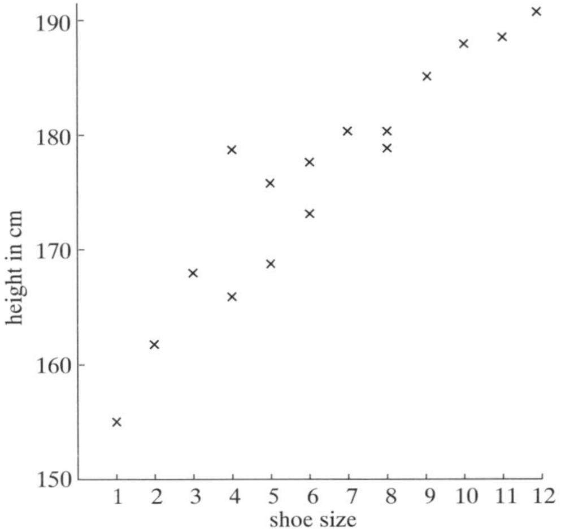

Second (unit of angle)

A second is a unit for measuring very small **angles**. 1 **degree** is divided into 60 minutes, and 1 minute of angle is divided into 60 seconds, so 3600 seconds make 1 degree.

Second (unit of time)

This is the smallest unit of time in everyday use. 60 seconds make up 1 **minute** and 60 minutes make up 1 **hour**. So there are 3600 seconds in 1 hour. 1 second is the time it takes a world-class sprinter to run 10 metres. It is also approximately equal to the time of 1 heart beat! Light travels at a speed of 186 000 miles in 1 second.

Sector of a circle

The region of a **circle** formed by two **radii** and part of the circle's **circumference** is called a sector of the circle. The smaller region formed is called the *minor sector*, the larger region formed is called the *major sector*.

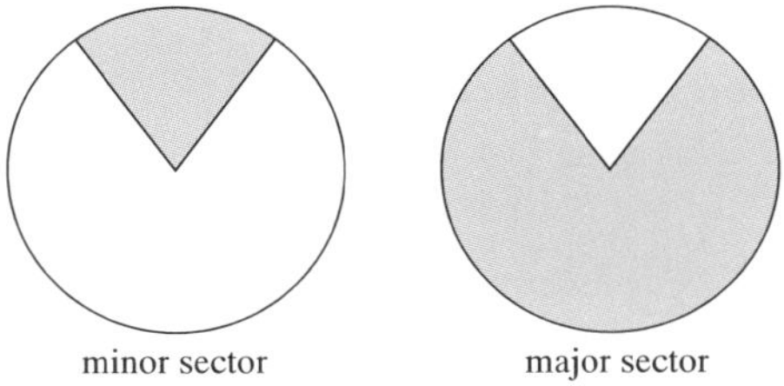

Some boxes of cheeses, sections of a flan, and the markings for a discus thrower are examples of sectors.

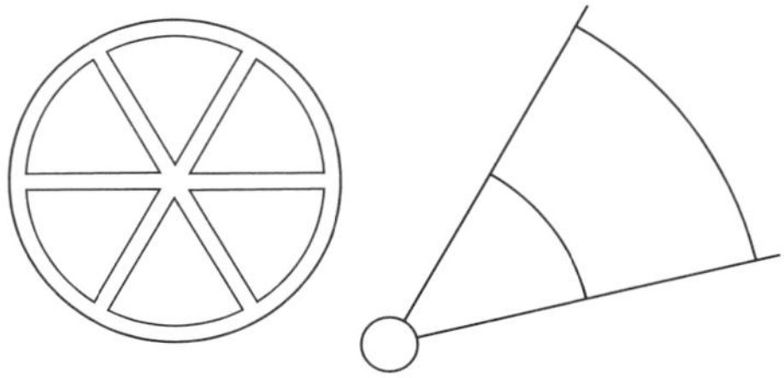

Segment of a circle

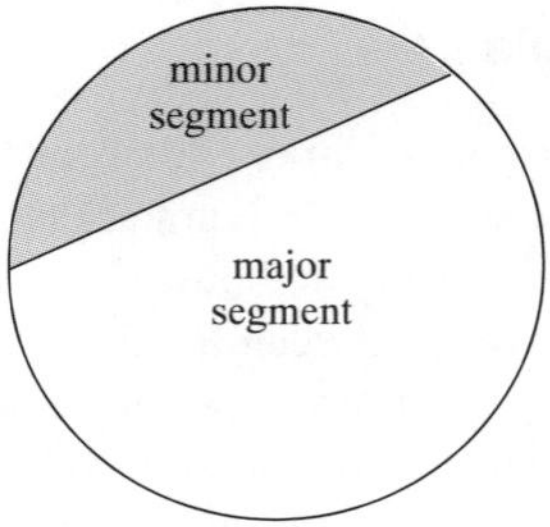

When a straight line is drawn joining two points on the **circumference** of a **circle** it divides it into two parts, the *minor segment* and the *major segment*.

Self-inverse

When an element combines with itself to produce the **identity element** it is said to be self-inverse. For example

$$-1 \times -1 = 1 \qquad \begin{pmatrix} 0 & 2 \\ \frac{1}{2} & 0 \end{pmatrix}\begin{pmatrix} 0 & 2 \\ \frac{1}{2} & 0 \end{pmatrix} = \begin{pmatrix} 1 & 0 \\ 0 & 1 \end{pmatrix}$$

A **reflection** when repeated gives the identity **transformation**, and the **function** $x \mapsto 1 - x$ when combined with itself gives the identity function, so these are also said to be self-inverse.

■ See **Inverse**.

Semi-circle

Semi means 'half'. A semi-circle is half of a **circle** formed by cutting along a **diameter**. Some protractors are semi-circles. The goal-scoring areas in hockey and netball are semi-circles.

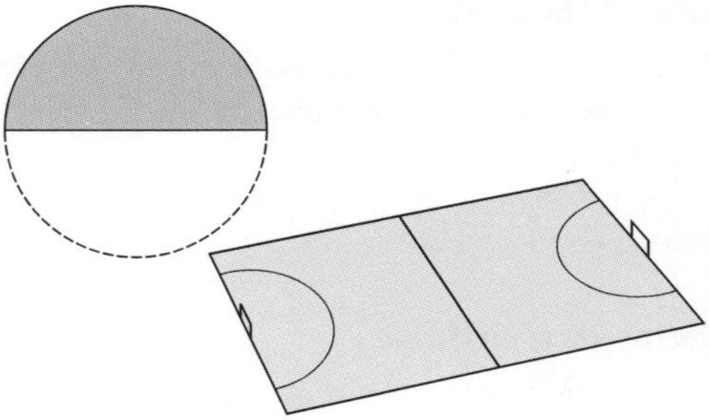

Semi-interquartile range

This is half of the distance from the lower **quartile** to the upper quartile.

■ See **Interquartile range**.

Sense

When a shape is traced out in a **clockwise** direction, its image after a **reflection** is traced out in an **anti-clockwise** direction. In every other way the **object** and its **image** are the same. What has changed is its *sense*.

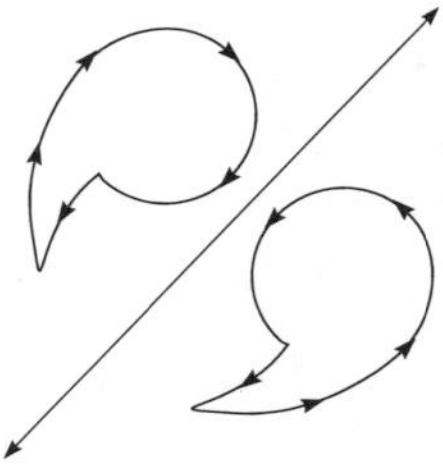

In the same way, a right glove or shoe is in the opposite sense to its partner, the left glove or shoe. It is this property of a reflection which distinguishes it from all the other common **transformations** such as **translations**, **rotations** and **enlargements**

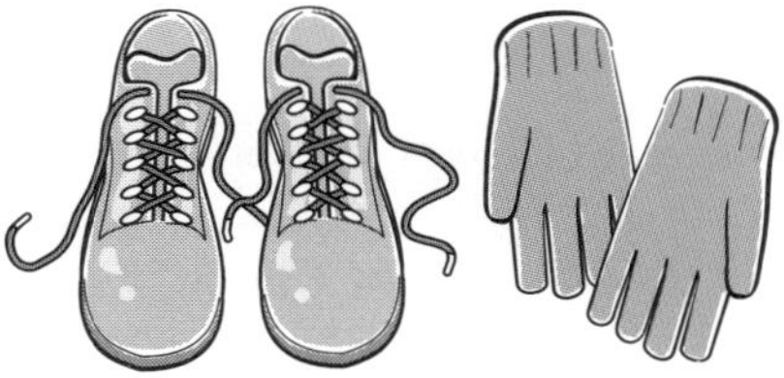

Whenever the **determinant** of a **matrix** is negative, the transformation it produces will change the sense of any shape on which it operates.

Sequence

A sequence is a set of numbers in a specified order. It is normally defined by some rule so that a **formula** can be given for a typical member of the sequence. For example,

$$5,\quad 8,\quad 11,\quad 14,\quad 17,\quad \ldots,\quad 3n+2,\quad \ldots,$$

$$6,\quad 9,\quad 14,\quad 21,\quad 30,\quad \ldots,\quad n^2+5,\quad \ldots$$

where n is a **natural number**.

▪ See **Fibonacci sequence**.

Series

A series is the sum of the numbers in a **sequence**. For example, the series

$$1 + 3 + 5 + 7 + 9 + 11 + 13 + 15 + 17 + 19$$

is formed from the first ten **odd numbers**, and its sum is 100. Similarly the series

$$1 + 2 + 4 + 8 + 16 + 32$$

is formed from the first six terms of the **powers** of 2, and its sum is 63.

Set

A set is a collection of objects, called the members or **elements** of the set. To show that the objects belong to a set they are put between curly brackets { }. For example, the set of **prime numbers** less than 12 is given as {2, 3, 5, 7, 11}, while the set of months whose names begin with J is given as {January, June, July}. Sets are often labelled with a single letter, for example,

F = {multiples of 5}

→

The symbol $\in$ is used to show that an object is a member of a set, and $\notin$ to show that it is not. So, for example, $20 \in F$ but $21 \notin F$.

When the elements of a set A are all members of a set B then A is called a *subset* of B, written $A \subset B$. For example, if A = {a, e, i, o, u} and B = {the letters of the alphabet}, then $A \subset B$.

It is important to note that the order in which the elements of a set are written is not important as it is just a collection of objects, so $\{2, x, \Delta\} = \{x, 2, \Delta\} = \{\Delta, x, 2\}$ etc.

See **Empty set**, **Intersection of sets** and **Union of sets**.

Shear

A shear is a **transformation** in which all the points move **parallel** to a fixed line or **plane**, in such a way that the distance a point moves is **proportional** to its distance from that line or plane. For example, if a pack of cards or pile of books on a table is pushed so that the **cross-section** of the pile changes from a **rectangle** to a **parallelogram**, then the pile will have undergone a shear. With a shear the **area** of a shape stays the same.

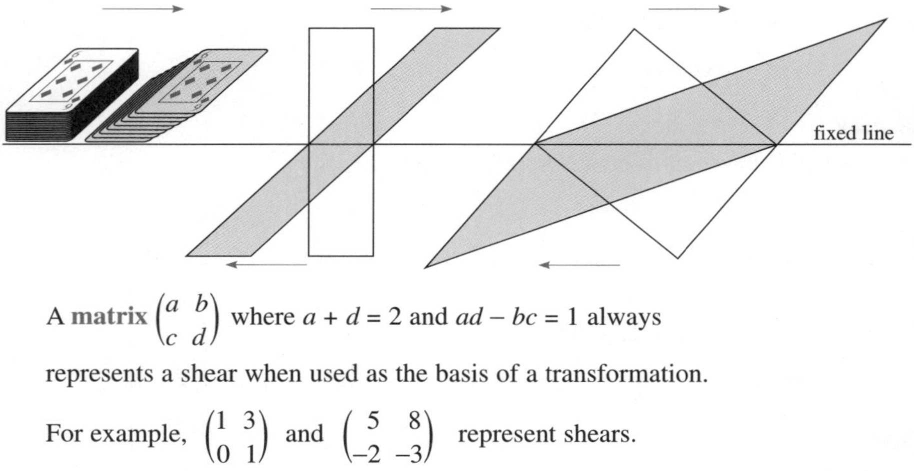

A **matrix** $\begin{pmatrix} a & b \\ c & d \end{pmatrix}$ where $a + d = 2$ and $ad - bc = 1$ always

represents a shear when used as the basis of a transformation.

For example, $\begin{pmatrix} 1 & 3 \\ 0 & 1 \end{pmatrix}$ and $\begin{pmatrix} 5 & 8 \\ -2 & -3 \end{pmatrix}$ represent shears.

Significant figures (s.f. or sig. fig.)

The most significant figure in a number is the first non-zero **digit** starting from the left. In the number 238.95, for example, although the left-hand digit is only 2 it represents 200, while the largest digit 9 only represents 9 tenths. The next most significant digit is the 3 for it represents 30, while the least significant digit is the 5 as it only represents 5 hundredths.

Numerical calculations are often rounded off to a specified number of significant figures, shortened to sig. fig. or s.f. The examples below show the result of various calculations, and the effect of rounding them to the number of significant figures stated:

9.434 285	to 4 s.f.	is 9.434
546.3287	to 3 s.f.	is 546
0.490 12	to 3 s.f.	is 0.490
0.002 054	to 2 s.f.	is 0.0021.

See **Rounding** and **Decimal places**.

Similar

Two objects are similar when they have the same shape but different size.

Paper is produced in different sizes, A1, A2, A3, A4 and A5, each one being half the size of the one before it, but all the same shape. When a photograph is enlarged to different sizes, all the objects in the photos change size but not shape, so they are similar. Different commodities such as soap powders and breakfast cereals are often sold in cartons of the same shape but different sizes.

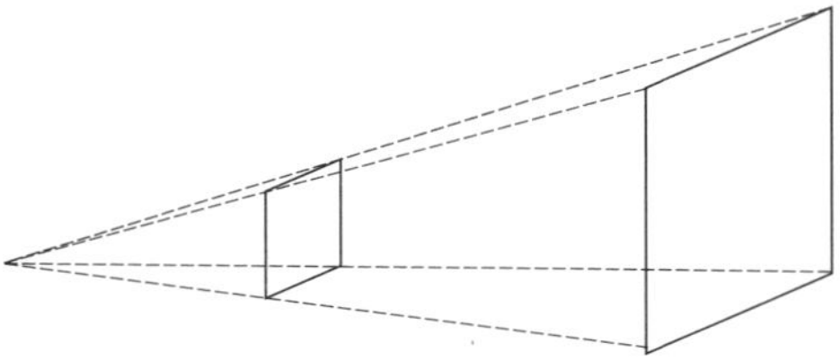

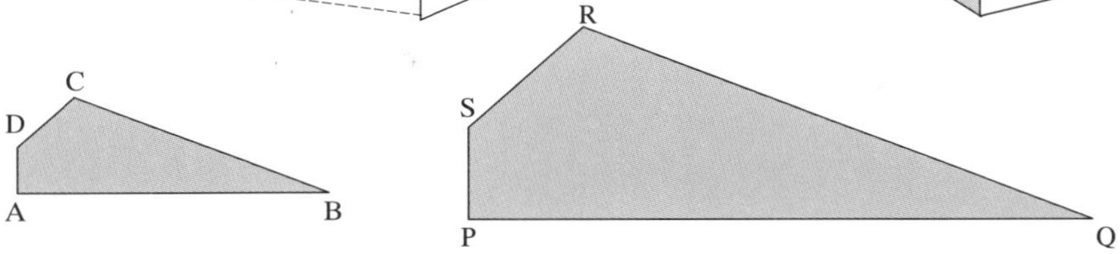

Two shapes such as the quadrilaterals ABCD and PQRS are similar when the angles which correspond to one another are equal:

$$\angle A = \angle P, \quad \angle B = \angle Q, \quad \angle C = \angle R, \quad \angle D = \angle S$$

and the **ratios** of the lengths of the corresponding sides are also equal. In the example shown,

$$PQ : AB = QR : BC = RS : CD = SP : DA = 2 : 1$$

where the **linear scale factor** is 2.

When two shapes are similar, the ratio of their **areas** is equal to the square of the ratio of their corresponding lengths. So the area of PQRS is $2^2 = 4$ times the area of ABCD.

The **enlargement transformation** maps any shape onto a similar shape.

■ See **Area scale factor** and **Volume scale factor**.

Simple closed curve

Imagine a loop of string on the table and consider the shapes it can take up without the string crossing over itself. All these shapes are simple closed curves. They divide the surface into two **regions**, inside and outside, like a **circle** to which they are all topologically equivalent.

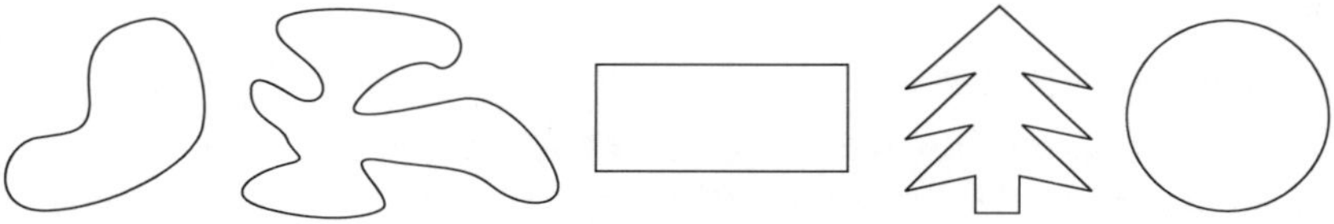

Simple interest

When a person is paid **interest** at regular intervals on a sum of money invested, without the interest being added to the sum invested, the investment is called *simple interest*. This contrasts with **compound interest** where the interest is added to the sum invested.

For example, when £240 is invested at 5% a year, then the person investing the money will be paid interest of 5% of £240, equal to £12, each year for which the money is invested.

In general the simple interest paid on a sum of money £P, invested at an annual interest rate of R% for T years, is given by the **formula**

$$\pounds\left(\frac{P \times R \times T}{100}\right)$$

Simplify

The word *simplify* means 'make simpler'. This may apply to working out a numerical problem or grouping together 'like' terms in an algebraic **expression** in the most concise way. For example,

$$3p^3q \times 2pqr = 6p^4q^2r$$

$$2(x + 3y) + 3(4x - y) = 2x + 6y + 12x - 3y$$

$$= 14x + 3y$$

■ See **Reduce to simplest form**.

Simultaneous equations

The word *simultaneous* means at the same time. When a problem involves two **variables** and they are related by two **equations**, then the equations have to be solved together, simultaneously.

For example, suppose you need to find the values of x and y so that

$$2x + y = 7 \quad \text{and} \quad x - y = 8$$

Adding the two equations together gives $3x = 15$, from which $x = 5$. Substituting $x = 5$ in the first equation gives $y = -3$. So the **solution** satisfying both equations is $(x, y) = (5, -3)$. This solution corresponds to the **coordinates** of the point of intersection of the two lines representing the equations.

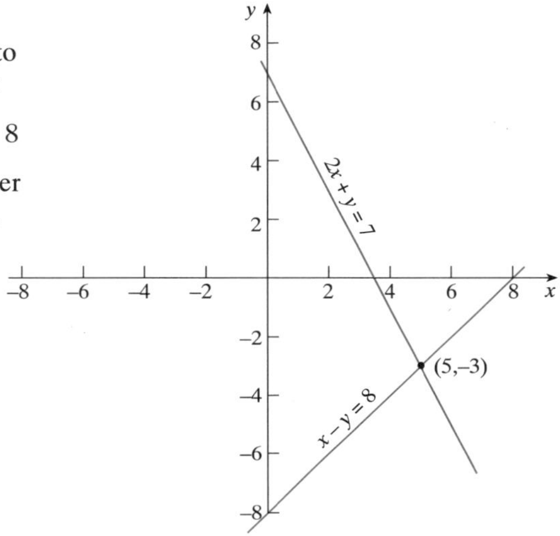

Sine of an acute angle

The sine of an **angle** θ ($\sin\theta$ as it is usually written) can be defined using a **right-angled triangle**, in which θ is one of the angles as shown, by

$$\sin\theta = \frac{BC}{AC} = \frac{\text{length of side opposite to } \theta}{\text{length of hypotenuse}}$$

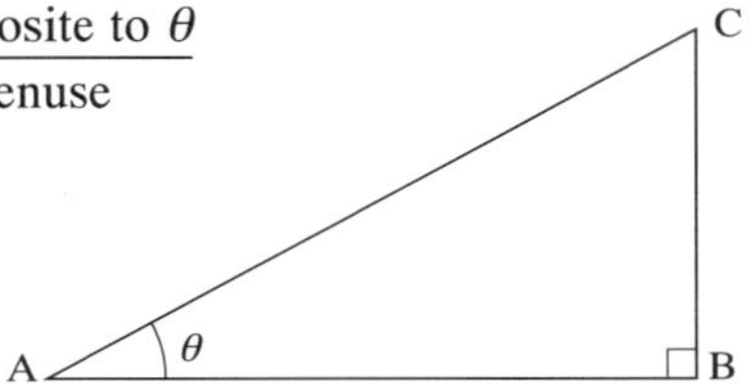

When AC = 1, then BC = $\sin\theta$,

so by **enlargement**, if A′C′ = r,

then B′C′ = $r\sin\theta$.

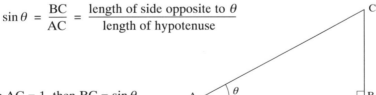

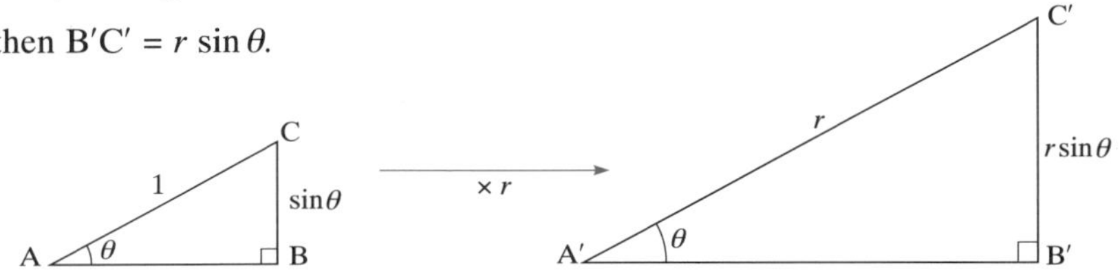

For example, if a ladder of length 5 metres leans against a wall at an angle of 65° to the horizontal, the height h metres at which it touches the wall is given by

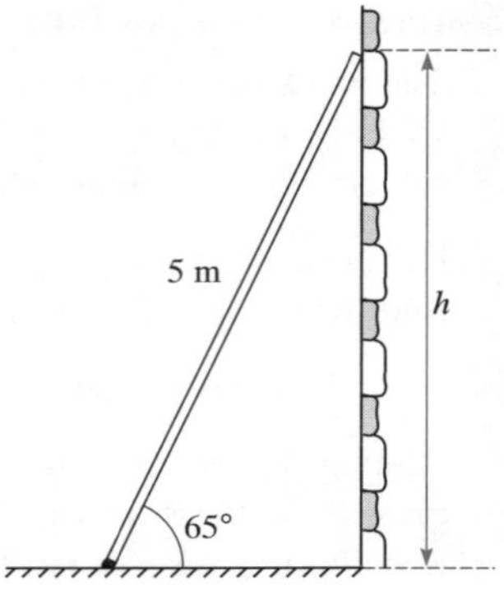

$$\frac{h}{5} = \sin 65°$$

so $h = 5 \sin 65° = 5 \times 0.906\,307\,8$
$= 4.531\,538\,9$
(to calculator accuracy)

The height is therefore 4.53 m to 2 **decimal places**.

Note: to use a scientific calculator to find sin 65°, enter 65 then press the sin key.

Sine of any angle

Consider a pointer OP of unit length rotating about the **origin**. When it has turned through an **angle** θ from the x-axis, as shown, the sine of θ is defined as the y-coordinate of the end of the pointer. This is consistent with the definition above for angles up to 90° and extends it for angles of any size.

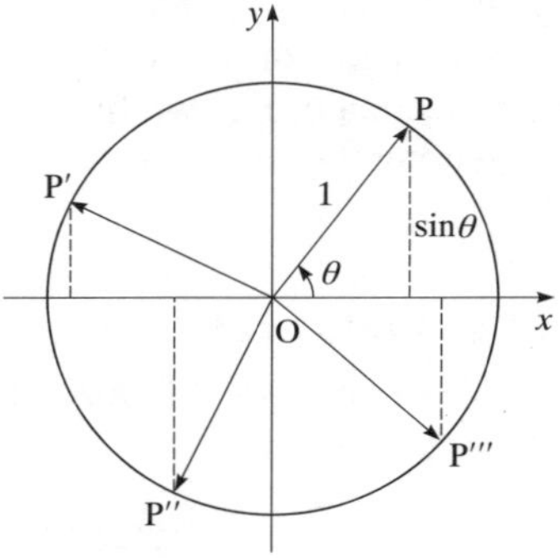

When P is at P′, $\sin\theta$ is positive, but when P is at P″ and at P‴, then $\sin\theta$ is negative.

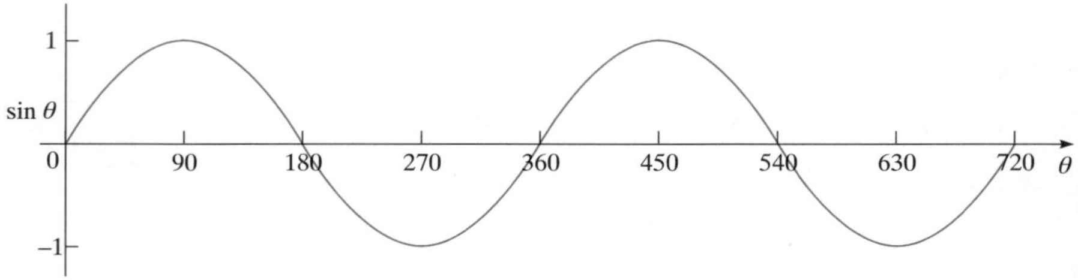

The graph of $\sin\theta$ plotted against θ gives the curve called the *sine wave* because of its wave-like shape.

See **Cosine** and **Tangent**.

Sine rule

In any **triangle**

$$\frac{a}{\sin A} = \frac{b}{\sin B} = \frac{c}{\sin C}$$

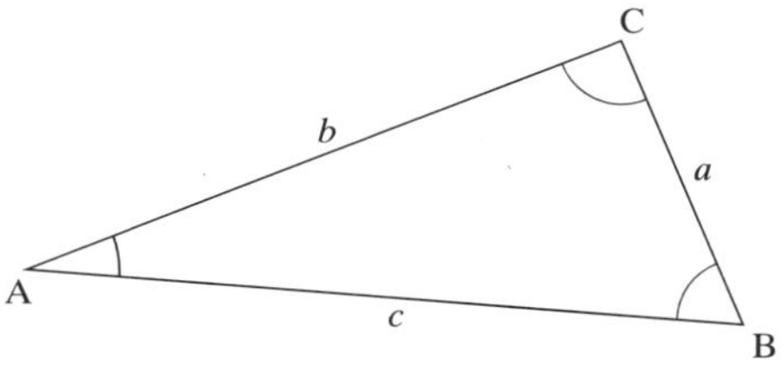

Singular matrix

A singular matrix is a **matrix** whose **determinant** is **zero**. It has no **inverse**.

For example, $\begin{pmatrix} 4 & 2 \\ 10 & 5 \end{pmatrix}$ is singular as its determinant is $4 \times 5 - 10 \times 2 = 0$.

A matrix whose determinant is not zero is called *non-singular*.

Skew distribution

This is the name given to a collection of statistical **data** which is clustered towards one end, rather than being evenly spread or symmetric about the middle as in a **normal distribution**. For example, the individual scores made by the members of a cricket club in a season may be skewed towards the lower scores in the range.

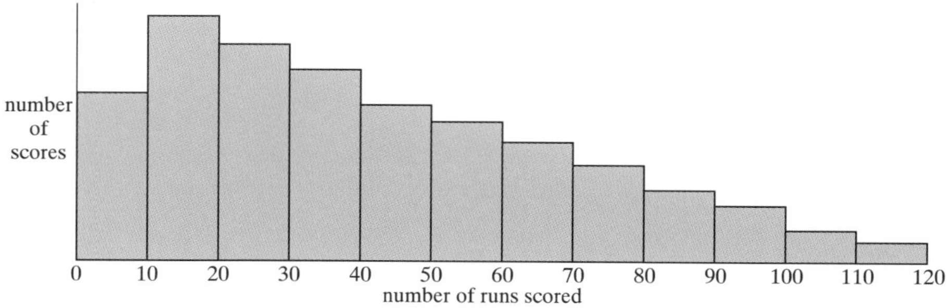

Skew lines

Two lines in space which are at an **angle** to each other and do not **intersect** are called skew. The two edges of the box drawn in red are skew to each other and to the red **diagonal**.

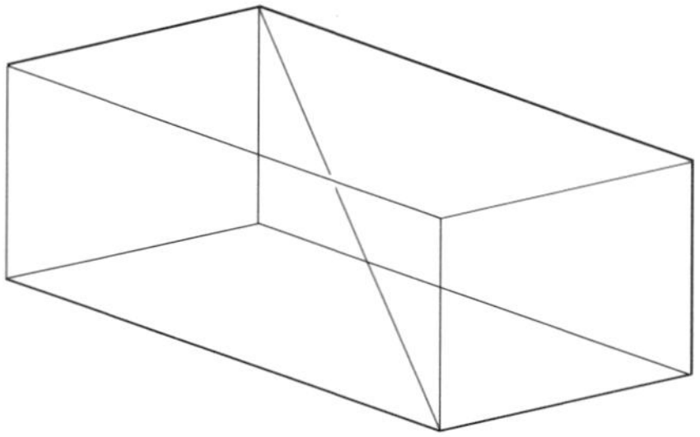

Slant height

See **Cone**.

Solid

A solid is the mathematical term for a rigid three-dimensional shape.

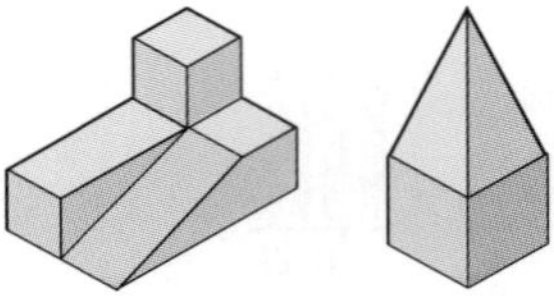

Solution

A solution is the line of reasoning which gives the answer to a mathematical problem. It is also used for the final answer if there is one. Consider, for example, the line of reasoning to find the value of x to satisfy the **equation**

$3(x - 4) = x - 6$

Multiplying out the bracket gives	$3x - 12 = x - 6$
Adding 12 and taking away x gives	$3x - x = 12 - 6$
Simplifying gives	$2x = 6$
Dividing by 2 gives	$x = 3$

Then $x = 3$ is the solution of the equation.

Solution set

Sometimes a problem has more than one answer. Then the set of different answers is called the solution set for the problem. For example, 2, –2 and 3 each satisfy the equation $(x^2 - 4)(x - 3) = 0$, so $\{2, -2, 3\}$ is its solution set.

Solve

To solve the equation $2x + 3 = 7$ means to find the number which makes the **equation** true. In general it is the process of finding a **solution** to a problem.

Speed

The speed of an object is a measure of how fast it is moving. It is given as the distance the object would travel in a unit of time. So, for example, a car which covers 18 **miles** at a constant speed on a motorway in 15 **minutes**, has a speed of 72 miles per hour (72 mph).

If an Intercity train is travelling at a speed of 120 mph then in $1\frac{1}{2}$ hours it will cover a distance of $120 \times 1\frac{1}{2} = 180$ miles.

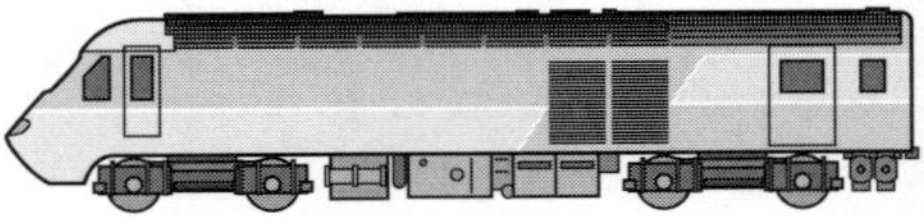

If an athlete averages a speed of 6.4 metres a second (6.4 ms^{-1}) in a race of 800 metres, she will have taken $800 \div 6.4 = 125$ seconds.

When the distance an object has travelled is plotted against the time it has taken, the slope or **gradient** of the **graph** at any point on it gives the speed of the object at that time.

For example, when a stone is thrown straight up with a speed of 20 ms^{-1}, its height, h metres, above the point of projection after t seconds is given by the **formula** $h = 5t(4 - t)$ and is shown on the graph. The speed of the stone after 1.5 seconds is given by the gradient of the **tangent** to the graph, shown in red, and is 5 ms^{-1}.

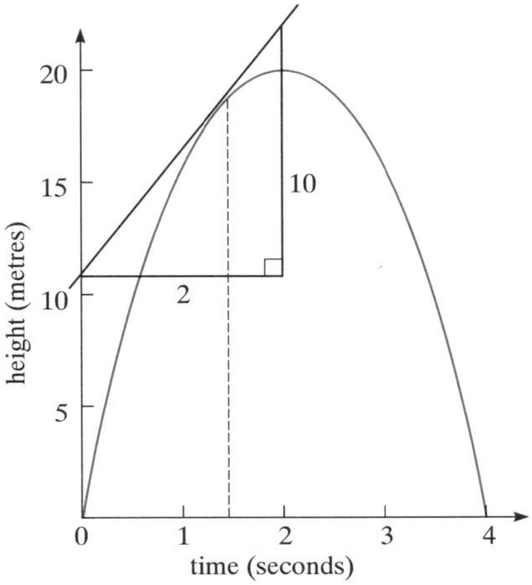

Sphere

A sphere is a perfectly round shape. Objects which are in the shape of a sphere are called *spherical*. Balls, balloons and soap bubbles are often spherical.

A sphere is defined as the set of points P in space which are all the same distance r from a fixed point O. O is the centre of the sphere and r is its **radius**.

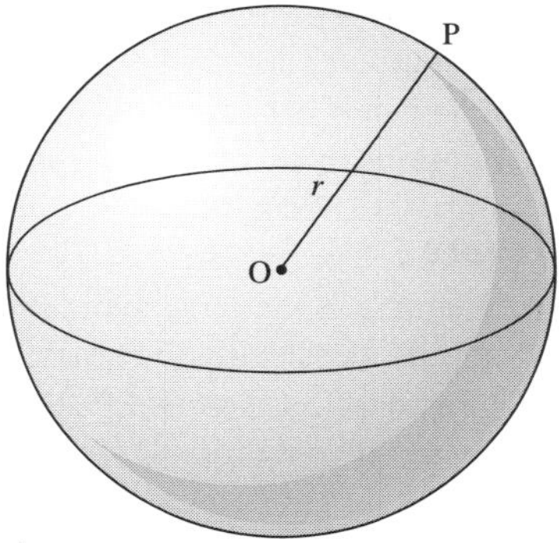

The **area** of the surface of the sphere is $4\pi r^2$.
The **volume** enclosed by the sphere is $\frac{4}{3}\pi r^3$.

Spiral

The spring in a clockwork toy, clock or watch is in the shape of a spiral. Spirals are to be found in nature in the arrangement of seeds in a sunflower head.

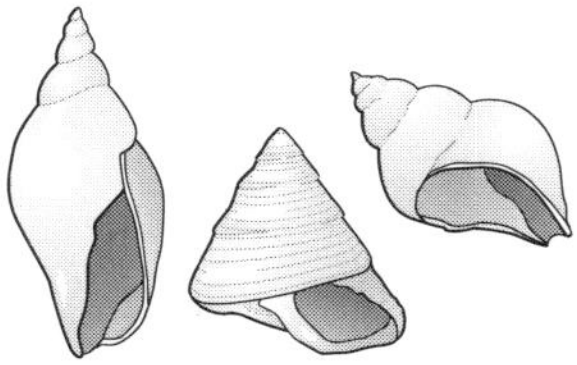

A three-dimensional spiral (known as a helix) can be seen as the thread on a screw, the path of a spiral staircase in a lighthouse, or in nature on a sea shell or as the pattern of seeds on a fir cone.

A spiral can be drawn by winding a piece of string around a pencil, attaching the free end to a drawing pin in the centre of a piece of paper and then drawing round and round with the string taut, letting it unwind.

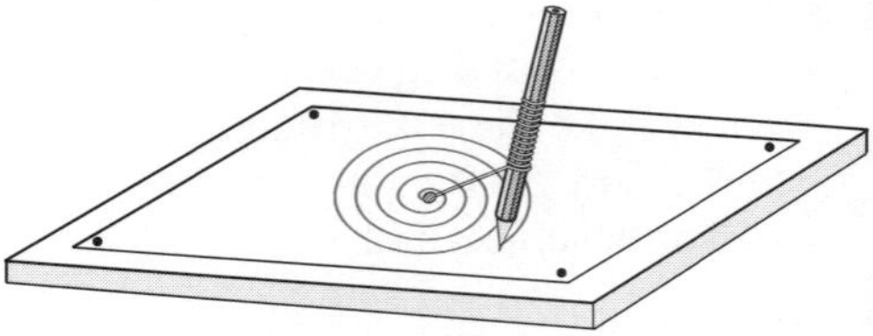

Spread

Spread is the name given in statistics to describe how the **data** lies. Is it close together or is it widely dispersed? It is measured in a variety of ways such as the **range**, the **interquartile range** and the **standard deviation**. For example, the spread of marks in a mathematics exam is often much wider than in English.

See **Quartile** and **Semi-interquartile range**.

Spreadsheet

A computer spreadsheet is a table of **data** arranged in rows and columns. The data can be manipulated easily by, for example, adding the numbers in two columns or by rewriting a list of names in alphabetical order.

Square

A square is the most symmetric **quadrilateral**. All its sides are of equal length and its **angles** are all **right angles**. Its **diagonals** are equal in length, **bisect** each other, and cross at **right angles**. It has 4 **lines of symmetry** and **rotational symmetry** of order 4. Its opposite sides are **parallel**.

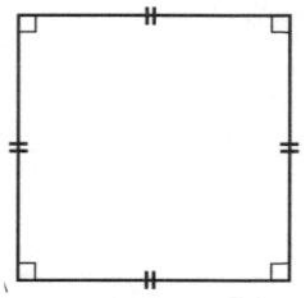

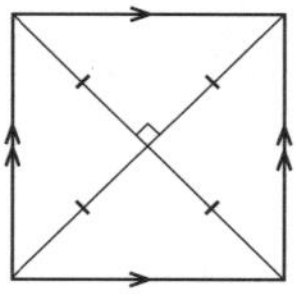

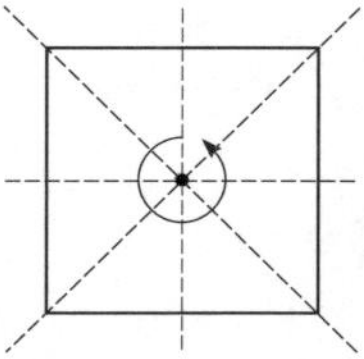

The square shape is commonly seen as a wall tile, or paving slab, or as the basic shape in a patchwork quilt, because it easily **tessellates**.

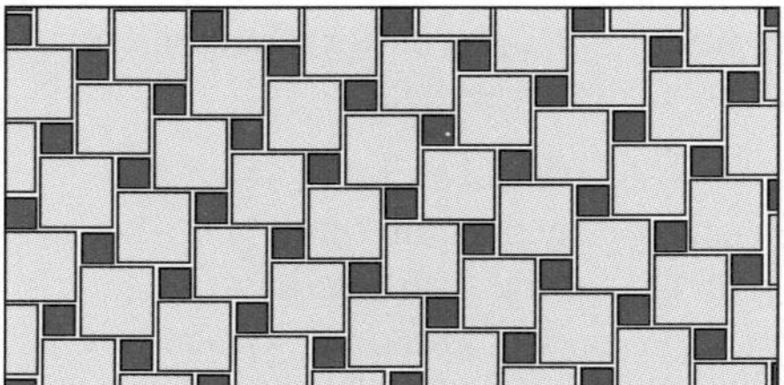

Square centimetre, square metre

See **Area** and **Metric units**.

Square numbers

1, 4, 9, 16, 25, 49, 64, …

are called square numbers. They are all equal to the **product** of a **whole number** with itself:

1 = 1 x 1 4 = 2 x 2 9 = 3 x 3 16 = 4 x 4 25 = 5 x 5

49 = 7 x 7 64 = 8 x 8 etc.

Any number which can be expressed in this way is called a square number. For example, 56169 is square as it is equal to 237 x 237. The name **square** comes from the fact that a square number of dots can be arranged in a square pattern.

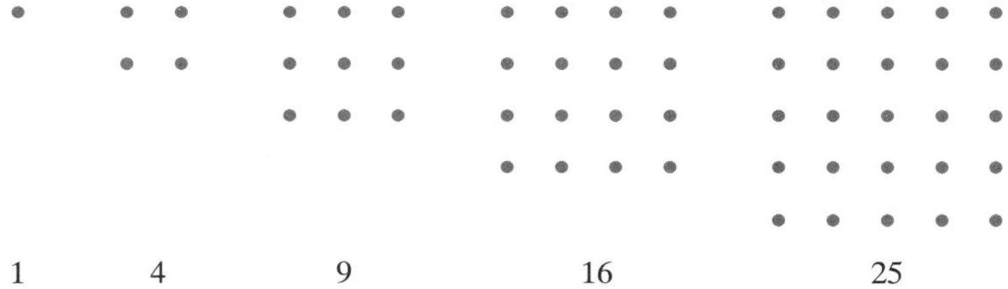

Square root

8 is called a square root of 64 because 8 x 8 = 64. But –8 is also a square root of 64 as –8 x –8 = 64. Every positive number has two square roots, one **positive** and one **negative**. 841, for example, has 29 and –29 as its square roots because 29 x 29 = 841 and –29 x –29 = 841.

In general, m is called a square root of a number N if $m \times m = N$, and then it will always be true that $-m$ is also a square root.

The notation $\sqrt{N}$ is used for the positive square root of a number, and can be found on a calculator by using the $\boxed{\sqrt{}}$ key.

For example, to find $\sqrt{3158.44}$, enter 3158.44 then press the $\boxed{\sqrt{}}$ key to get 56.2.

$\sqrt{N}$ can be interpreted as the length of the side of a **square** with **area** N. So, for example, a square of area 1369 cm^2 has edges of length $\sqrt{1369}$ = 37 cm.

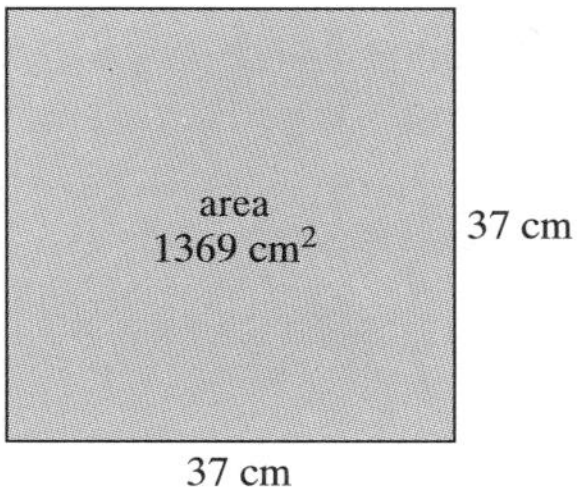

Note that the positive square root of a number between 0 and 1 is always bigger than that number. $\sqrt{0.1681}$, for example, equals 0.41 which is bigger than 0.1681.

Standard deviation

The standard deviation of a set of numbers, such as heights of people, is a measure of how spread out the numbers are from the **mean**.

A natural way to measure **spread** is as follows:

- find how each number deviates from the mean;
- since the signs of the deviations, positive or negative, are not of importance (for example, 2 above the mean is the same deviation as 2 below the mean) it is sensible to make the deviations positive by squaring them;
- find the total of the squared deviations;
- average out this total by dividing it by the number of items (in order to make fair comparison with other sets of data);
- take the square root to return to the original units (centimetres, rather than square centimetres in the case of heights).

The resulting number is called the *standard deviation*.

The process above can be written in one sentence as

$$\text{standard deviation} = \sqrt{\frac{\text{sum of squared deviations from the mean}}{\text{number of items}}}$$

For example, for the heights 159 cm, 172 cm, 158 cm and 167 cm, the mean is 164 cm and so the standard deviation is

$$\sqrt{\frac{(159-164)^2 + (172-164)^2 + (158-164)^2 + (167-164)^2}{4}}\ \text{cm} = 5.788\ \text{cm}\ (\text{to 3 d.p.})$$

Standard deviations are useful when comparing data. For example, if the standard deviation of the heights of another set of people was 3.214 cm then those in the first set are more spread out.

Standard (index) form

6.4721463 ^{08}

When the result of a calculation with a calculator goes beyond the size of the calculator's display it is presented in standard form. For example, the above result was recorded from a calculator's display after calculating 865^3. This has to be interpreted as

$6.472\ 146\ 3 \times 10^8$ which equals 647 214 630

A number is expressed in standard form when it is given as a number with one non-zero digit to the left of the **decimal** point multiplied by a **power** of 10. All numbers can be expressed in this way. For example,

$$329 = 3.29 \times 10^{2}$$
$$46\,700 = 4.67 \times 10^{4}$$
$$0.0071 = 7.1 \times 10^{-3}$$

The power of 10 required can be found by noting how many places the decimal point has to be moved to the left or right to obtain a number with one non-zero digit to its left. For example

$$870\,235.0 = 8.702\,35 \times 10^{5}$$

5 places

$$0.000\,276 = 2.76 \times 10^{-4}$$

4 places

Standard form is particularly useful in dealing with very large or very small numbers as needed in science and astronomy. For example:

- a molecule of water has a mass of 2.99×10^{-26} kg;
- the mass of the moon is 7.37×10^{22} kg.

Statistics

This is the branch of mathematics concerned with the collection, interpretation and analysis of **data**.

See **Average**, **Probability** and **Spread**.

Stretch

A stretch is a **transformation** of the **plane** in which all points move at **right angles** to a fixed line, a distance proportional to their distance from the line to start with. The example shows the effect of a stretch from the y-axis on a variety of shapes where the **scale factor** of the stretch is 2. All the x-coordinates are doubled but the y-coordinates are unchanged. This transformation is represented in **matrix** form as

$$\begin{pmatrix} x \\ y \end{pmatrix} \rightarrow \begin{pmatrix} 2 & 0 \\ 0 & 1 \end{pmatrix} \begin{pmatrix} x \\ y \end{pmatrix}$$

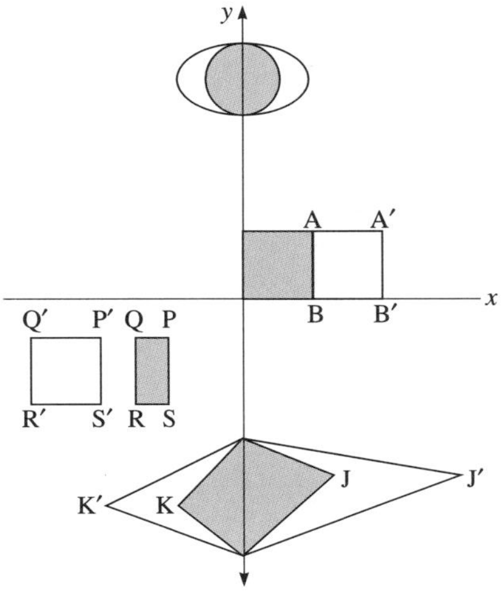

Subject of a formula

The **formula**

$$T = 2\pi \sqrt{\frac{L}{g}}$$

where g is the **acceleration** due to gravity, gives the time T for a pendulum of length L to complete one swing. Written in this form it is used to calculate T given the values of L and g, so T is said to be the subject of the formula. But it can be rearranged as

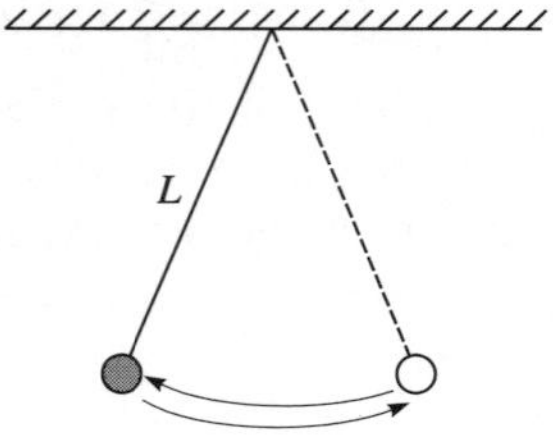

$$L = \frac{T^2 g}{4\pi^2}$$

to calculate the length of pendulum for a given time T, or as

$$g = \frac{4\pi^2 L}{T^2}$$

to calculate the acceleration of gravity. In these cases L and g are the subjects of the respective formulae.

The process of rearranging the original formula to have a different letter as its subject is called *changing the subject* of a formula

Subset

When the **elements** of a **set** A are all members of a set B, then A is a subset of B, written $A \subset B$.

Substitution

To *substitute* means to replace one thing by another. Substitution is the process of replacing the letters in a **formula** by numbers. For example, the surface area A cm² of a **cylinder** of **radius** 5 cm and height 12 cm can be calculated by substituting 5 for r and 12 for h in the formula

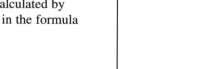

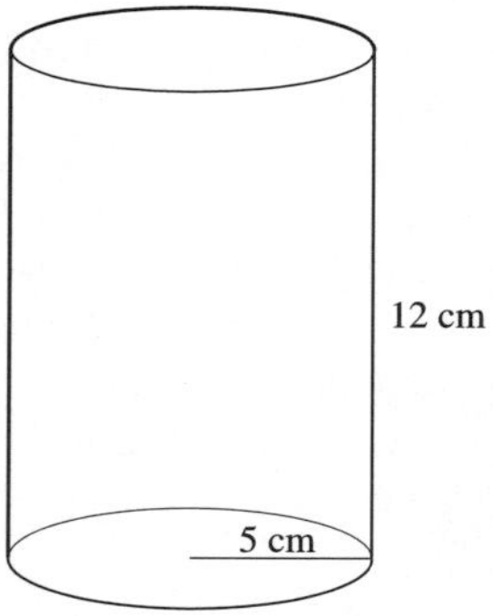

$$A = 2\pi r(r + h)$$

giving

$$A = 2\pi \times 5 \times (5 + 12)$$
$$= 170\pi$$

But substitution can also involve substituting one algebraic **expression** for another. For example, if a shoe box has dimensions a, b and c and it is required to find the length of the diagonal PQ, then by **Pythagoras' theorem**

$$PQ^2 = PR^2 + RQ^2$$

but

$$PR^2 = a^2 + b^2 \text{ and } RQ = c$$

so substituting for PR and RQ

$$PQ^2 = a^2 + b^2 + c^2$$

from which

$$PQ = \sqrt{a^2 + b^2 + c^2}$$

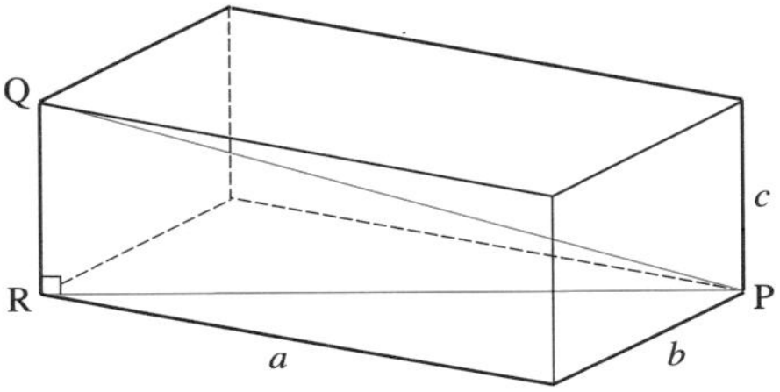

Subtend an angle

To subtend an **angle** is to form an angle at a point. When you look at an object such as a tree, the angle subtended at your eye is that formed by imagining two lines drawn from the top and bottom of the object to your eye.

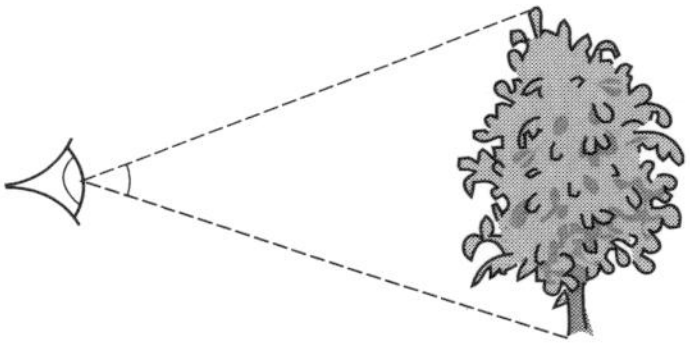

When two lines AP and BP are drawn joining the three points A, B and P on a **circle**, then the angle APB is said to be subtended by the chord AB or by the **arc** AB. All the angles formed on one side of a chord of a circle in this way are equal to each other. The angles subtended by a **diameter** at its circumference are all 90°.

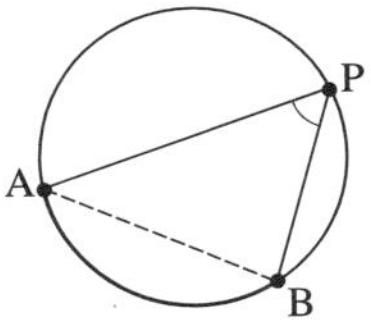

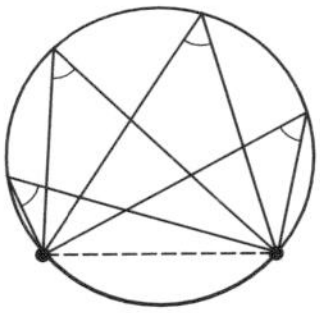

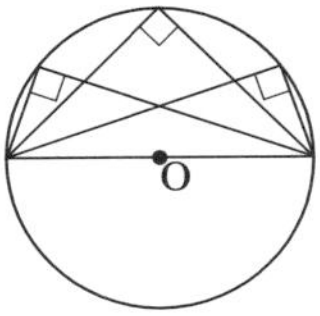

Sum

A sum is the total result from adding two or more numbers together. However, it is sometimes used more generally to describe any arithmetic calculation.

$$\begin{array}{r} 39 \\ +\ 28 \\ 46 \\ \hline 113 \\ \hline \end{array}$$

Supplementary angles

Two **angles** are called supplementary when their sum is 180°. Two angles formed on a straight line are supplementary, as are the two angles inside a pair of **parallel lines** on one side of a **transversal**. The opposite angles of a **cyclic quadrilateral** are also supplementary.

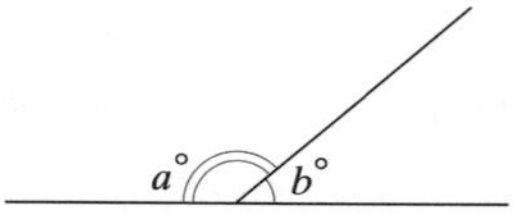

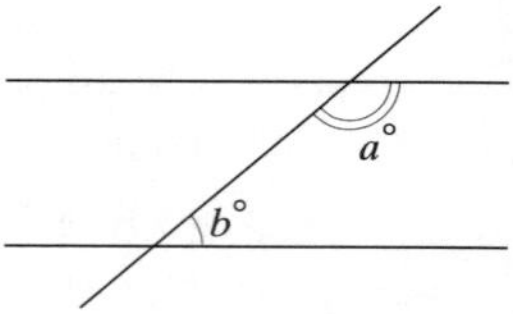

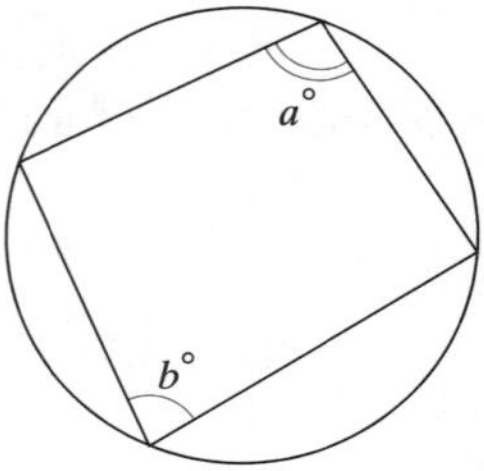

■ See **Complementary angles**.

Surd

Roots such as $\sqrt[3]{2}$ and $\sqrt[5]{3}$ which cannot be expressed exactly as a decimal with a finite number of **decimal places** are called surds. They are **irrational numbers**.

■ See **Cube root** and **Square root**.

Symmetry

The more ways a shape can be reflected and turned to fit onto itself, the more symmetry it has.

Plane shapes have two kinds of symmetry:

- when a shape can be reflected onto itself about a line it has **line symmetry**;
- when a shape can be rotated about a point through an angle of less than 360° to coincide with itself it has **rotational symmetry**.

The butterfly has one line of symmetry, while the flower has 3 lines of symmetry and rotational symmetry about its centre of order 3, because $\frac{1}{3}$ of a turn will fit it onto itself.

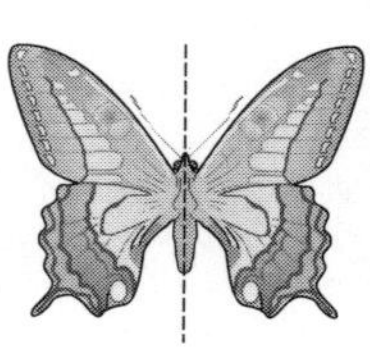

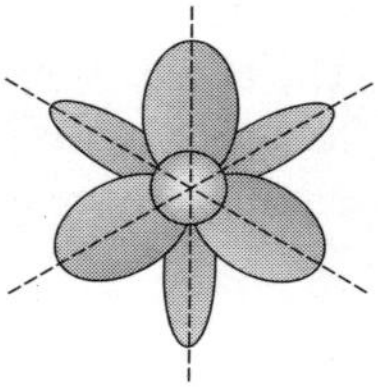

A **solid** shape similarly may have one or more planes of symmetry in which it can be reflected onto itself, and one or more axes about which it can be rotated to coincide with itself.

A Toblerone box, for example, has 4 planes of symmetry: 3 like the one shown along the length of the box, and 1 halfway along at right angles to the box, containing the red triangle.

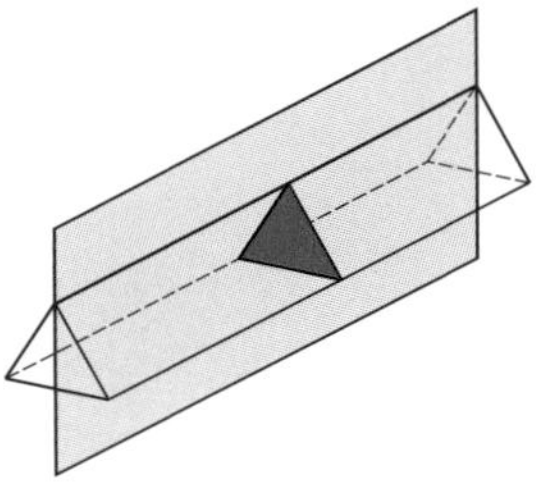

It also has 4 axes of rotational symmetry. One of these is the line through the mid-point of both its ends, about which it has rotational symmetry of order 3. The other 3 are like the one drawn with a red dashed line. The box fits onto itself after a half-turn about each of these axes, so has rotational symmetry of order 2 about them.

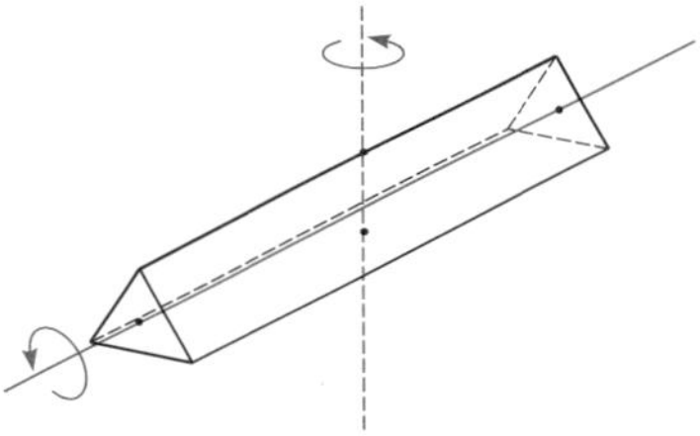

Tally

A tally is a means of checking off a number of items by making an appropriate mark for each item. The tally of the colours of cars travelling along a road is shown in the table. This is usually done in groups of five. A line is drawn for each item counted with every fifth item recorded by a line drawn across the previous four lines. This makes it easy to add up the number of items checked.

colour of car	tally	frequency
red	~~||||~~ ~~||||~~ ~~||||~~ ||	17
blue	~~||||~~ ~~||||~~ |||	13
white	~~||||~~ ~~||||~~ |	11

Tangent (tan) of an acute angle

The tangent of an **angle** θ, usually written tan θ, can be defined using a **right-angled triangle**, in which one of the angles is θ, by

$$\tan\theta = \frac{BC}{AB} = \frac{\text{length of side opposite to } \theta}{\text{length of side adjacent to } \theta}$$

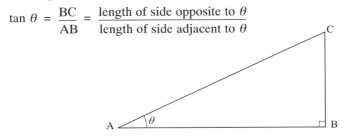

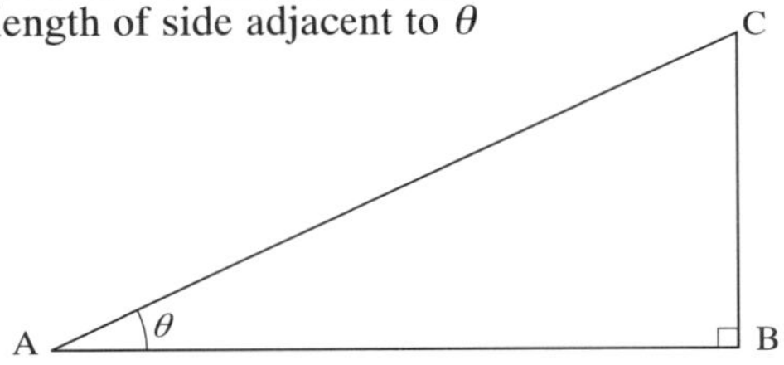

When AB = 1 then BC = $\tan\theta$, so by **enlargement**, if $A'B' = r$, then $B'C' = r\tan\theta$.

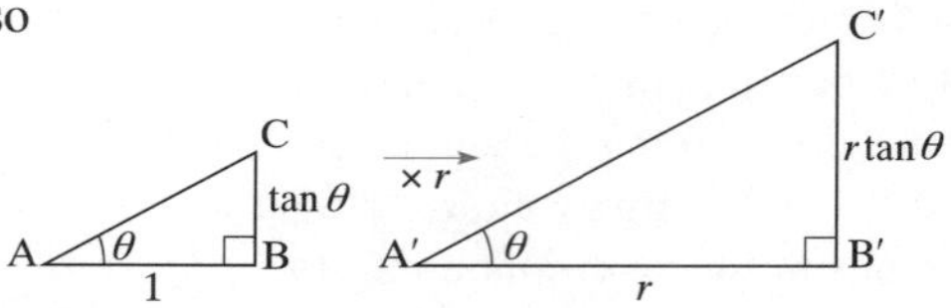

For example, if the **angle of elevation** of the top of a television mast from a point 600 m from its base is 25°, the height h of the mast is given by

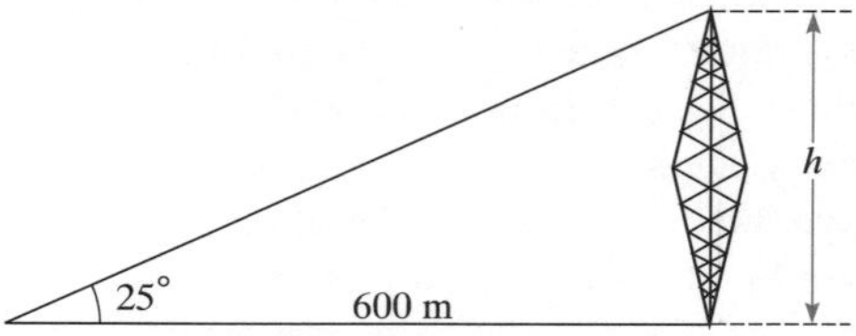

$$\frac{h}{600} = \tan 25°$$

so

$$h = 600 \tan 25°$$
$$= 600 \times 0.466\,307\,7$$

(by using the [tan] key on a calculator)

$$= 280 \text{ (to the nearest whole number)}$$

The height is therefore 280 metres.

If the height of the **apex** of a symmetrical roof is 3 m above the tops of the walls, which are 14 m apart, then the angle θ of the roof to the horizontal is given by

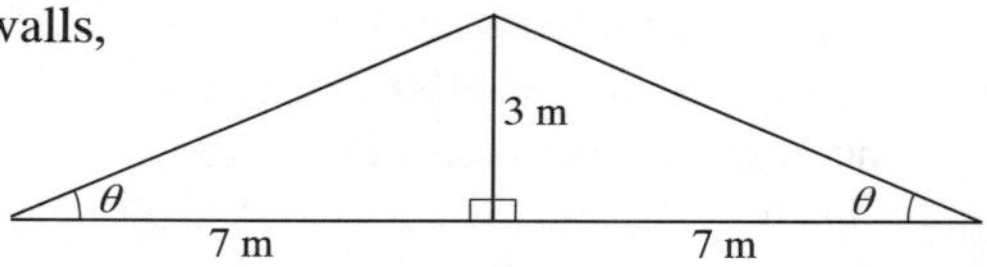

$$\tan\theta = \frac{3}{7} = 0.428\,571\,4$$

from which $\theta = 23.2°$ to 1 d.p. (using the [INV] and [tan] keys on a calculator).

Tangent to a curve

A straight line which touches a curve at a point P, as shown in the diagram, is called a tangent to the curve.

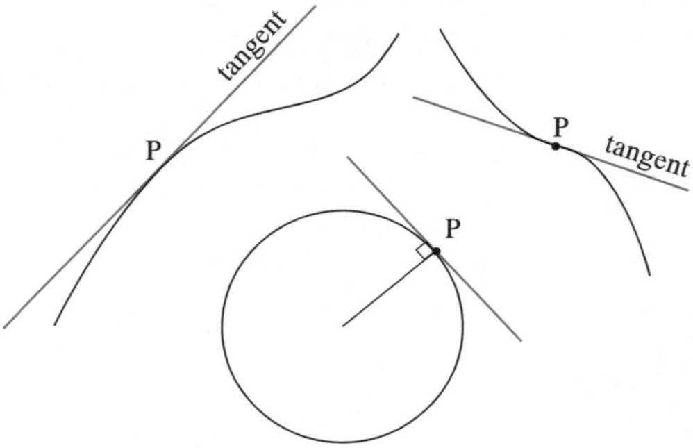

A tangent to a **circle** is at **right angles** to the **radius** of the circle at its point of contact.

Term

1 In a sequence of numbers such as 5, 8, 11, 14, 17, …, $3n + 2$, … where n is any integer, 5 is called the first term, 8 the second term, 11 the third term and so on.
The general term is the algebraic **expression** $3n + 2$ for the nth term.

2 The various parts of a **polynomial** such as $2x^2 + 6x + 7$ are called terms. $2x^2$ is called the x^2 term, $6x$ is called the x term and 7 the **constant** term.

Terminating decimal

When a number can be written as a **decimal** with only a **finite** number of places, it is called a terminating decimal. For example,

$$\frac{3}{5} = 0.6 \qquad \frac{7}{8} = 0.875 \qquad \frac{17}{625} = 0.0272$$

Such decimals when expressed as **fractions** always have **denominators** which consist of a **power** of 2 and/or a power of 5. In contrast, the decimal forms of **irrational numbers** such as $\sqrt{2}$ and π do not terminate. A **recurring decimal** such as 0.428571428571428571428571…, which is equal to the fraction $\frac{3}{7}$ also does not terminate.

Tessellation

When a set of shapes can be fitted together in a repeating pattern without leaving any gaps, it is said to *tessellate* and to form a *tessellation*. Tiles and bricks and paving slabs can often be seen forming such patterns.

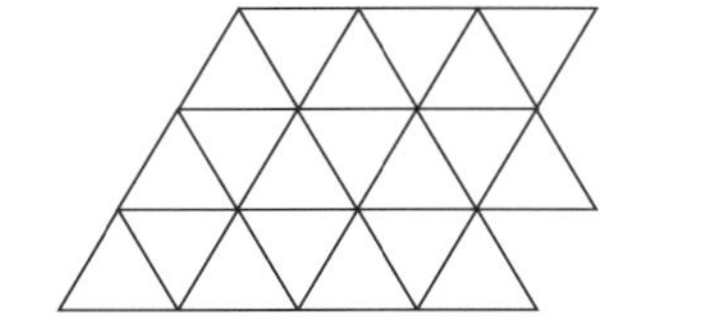

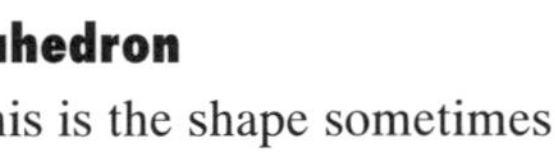

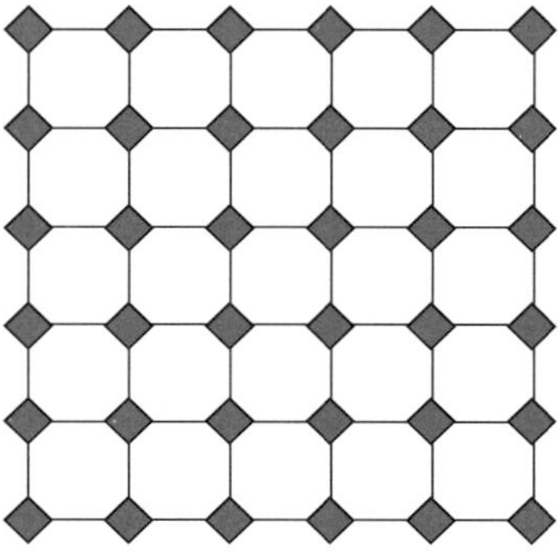

Tetrahedron

This is the shape sometimes called a triangular-based **pyramid**. It has four (*tetra*) triangular **faces** with three of them meeting at a point. The Tetrapak carton is an example of a tetrahedron.

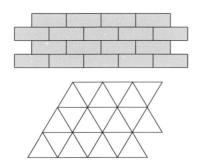

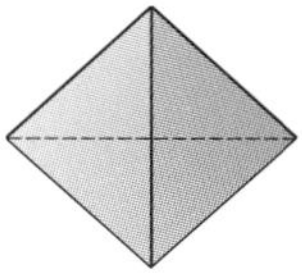

Theorem

A theorem is an important mathematical result which is found to be useful, such as **Pythagoras' theorem** for **right-angled triangles**.

Tiling

This is another name for a **tessellation**.

Ton, tonne

The ton is the **imperial unit** of **mass** equivalent to 2240 **pounds**. Its metric equivalent is the *tonne*, equal to 1000 **kilograms**. A metric tonne is almost equivalent to an imperial ton and for most purposes they can be considered to be the same.

A medium size family car has a mass of about 1 ton(ne), while a full grown African elephant has a mass of about 6 ton(ne)s, and a Jumbo Jet a mass of 375 ton(ne)s.

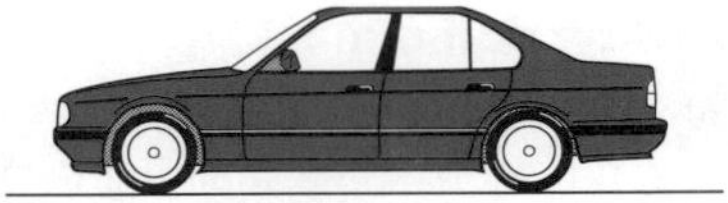

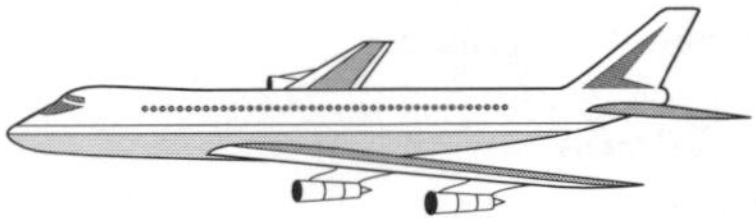

Topologically equivalent

Two shapes are said to be topologically equivalent if one can be transformed into the other by stretching without tearing. The number of the **nodes** and the order of each node is identical, as is the way in which the **arcs** are connected to the nodes. The example shows three **networks** which are topologically equivalent to each other.

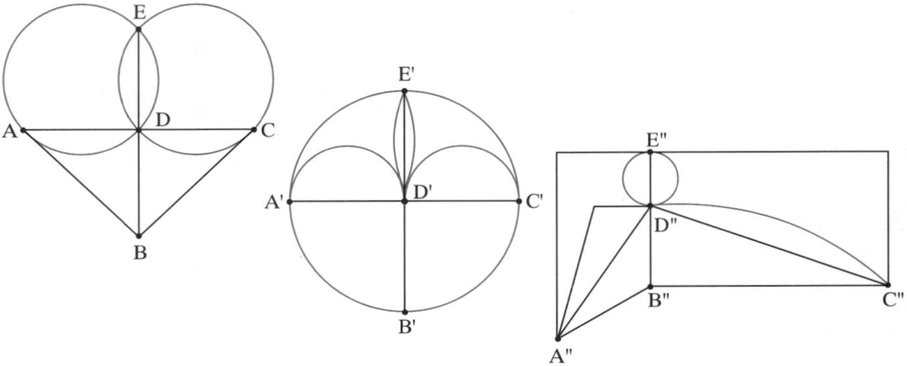

Topology

Topology is a branch of mathematics which has often been described as rubber-sheet geometry. Imagine a drawing on a sheet of rubber like a balloon, then no matter how much or in what direction the sheet is stretched, many aspects of the drawing will still remain true.

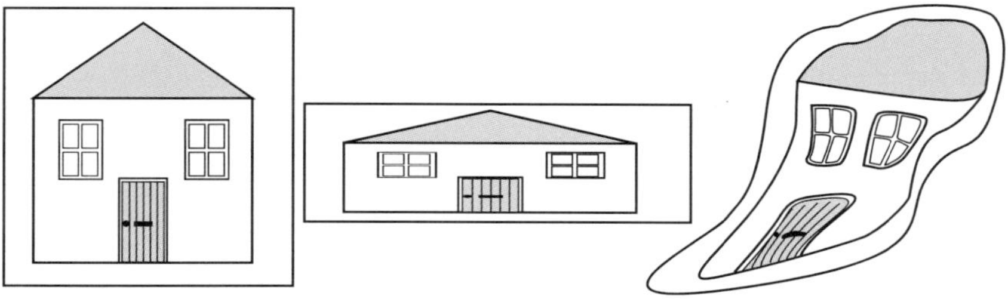

Transformations of this kind are called topological and the things which remain unchanged by them are called the topological **invariants**. Typical invariants are

- the number of **nodes** and their orders;
- the number of **arcs** and the **regions** they surround;
- the order of points along a line.

So much is changed, for example, length, **area**, **angle**, that it is difficult at first to see what point such a study has. However, many maps to help railway or airline travellers are drawn to emphasise the connections between places rather than the distances involved, and are typical of the way in which a topological distortion is helpful.

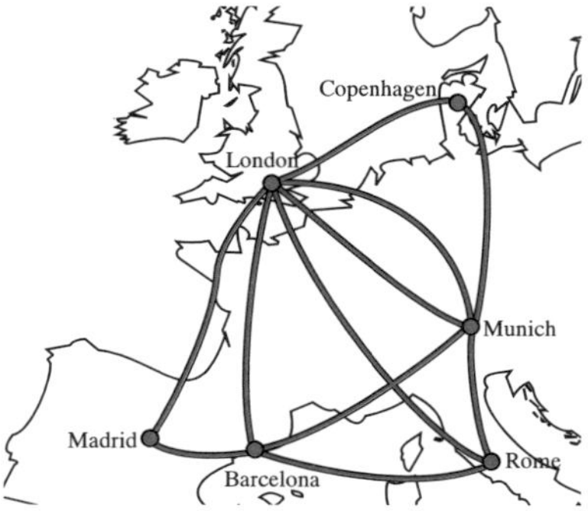

Torus

A torus is the mathematical name for a shape like a beach ring, a life belt, or a ring doughnut.

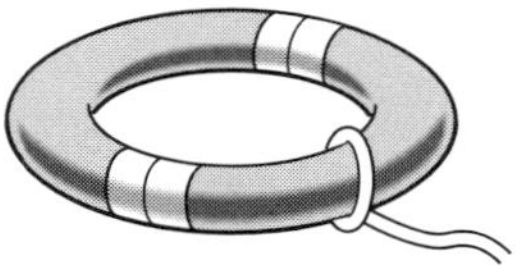

Transformation

To transform something is to change it in some way. A transformation is what brings about the change. It may transform a set of numbers or a set of points. The transformation $n \mapsto 7 - n$, for example, will transform a 'magic triangle' containing the numbers 1 to 6 into a different magic triangle with the same numbers.

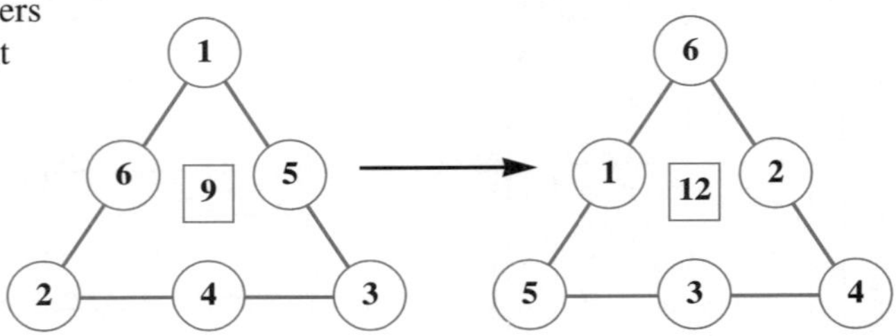

There are many kinds of geometric transformations, ranging from **translations** which move an object to a new position without changing its shape, size or direction, to topological transformations which can considerably distort a shape. In between these there are the **rotations**, **reflections**, **enlargements**, **stretches** and **shears**. Geometrical transformations can be represented by **matrices**.

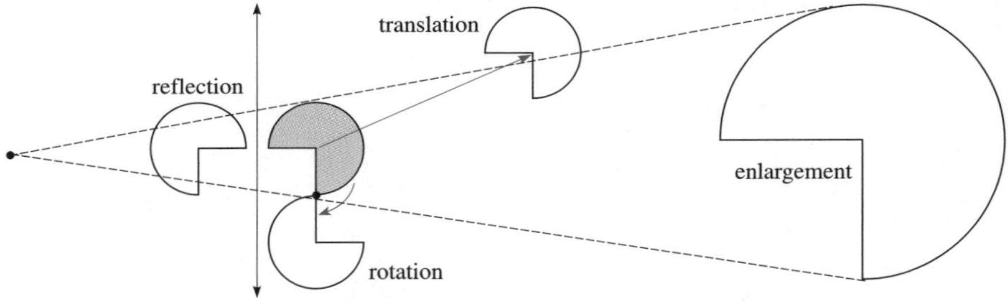

■ See **Isometry** and **Topology**.

Translation

When a shape is transformed by sliding it to a new position, without turning, it is said to have been *translated*. Every point of the shape will have undergone an identical **displacement**, which can be described by a **vector**. In the example shown, the **quadrant** has been displaced by $\begin{pmatrix}3\\1\end{pmatrix}$ so the translation can be described by $\begin{pmatrix}x\\y\end{pmatrix} \rightarrow \begin{pmatrix}x+3\\y+1\end{pmatrix}$

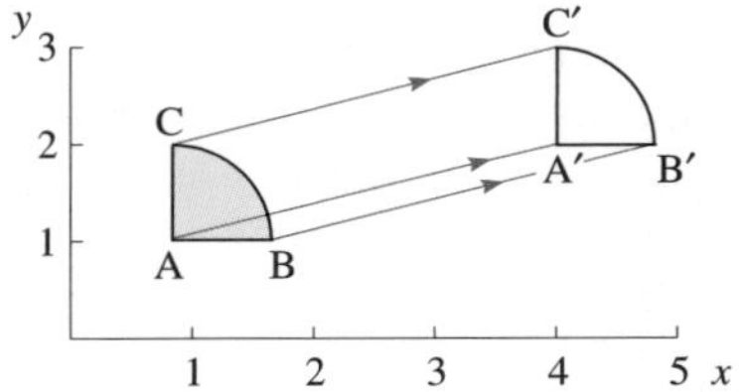

Transpose

To *transpose* means to cause two things to change places. The transpose of a **matrix** A, denoted by A′ or A^T, is the matrix formed from A by interchanging its **rows and columns**. For example,

$$A = \begin{pmatrix} 1 & 2 \\ 3 & 4 \end{pmatrix} \qquad A^T = \begin{pmatrix} 1 & 3 \\ 2 & 4 \end{pmatrix}$$

$$B = \begin{pmatrix} 1 & 2 & 3 \\ 4 & 5 & 6 \end{pmatrix} \qquad B^T = \begin{pmatrix} 1 & 4 \\ 2 & 5 \\ 3 & 6 \end{pmatrix}$$

Transversal

A line drawn across two or more **parallel lines** is called a transversal. A transversal forms equal **angles** with the parallel lines such as

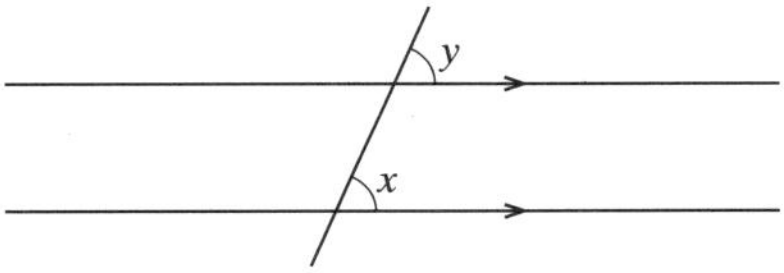

- *x* and *y*, called **corresponding angles**,
- *p* and *q*, called **alternate angles**, or Z angles.

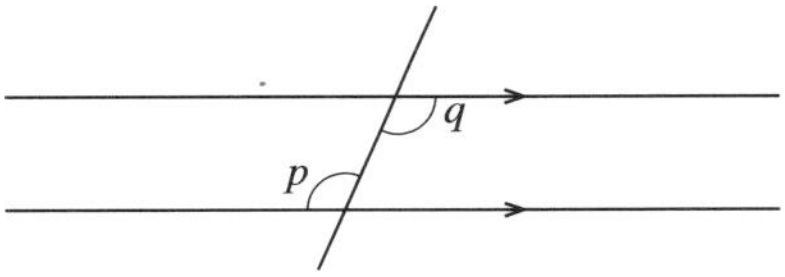

Trapezium (*pl.* trapezia)

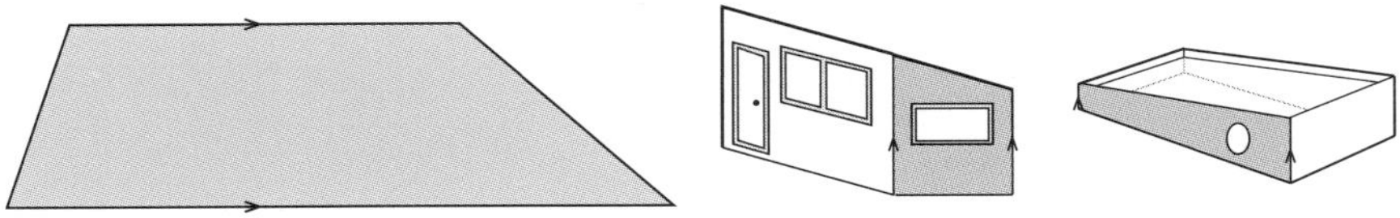

A trapezium is a **quadrilateral** with one pair of opposite sides **parallel**. The ends of a garden shed or the sides of a swimming pool are often trapezia.

The **area** of a trapezium is given by $\frac{1}{2}(a + b)h$, where the parallel sides are of lengths a and b, and h is the distance between them. It can be found by dividing the trapezium into two **triangles** by a **diagonal** as shown whose areas are $\frac{1}{2}ah$ and $\frac{1}{2}bh$.

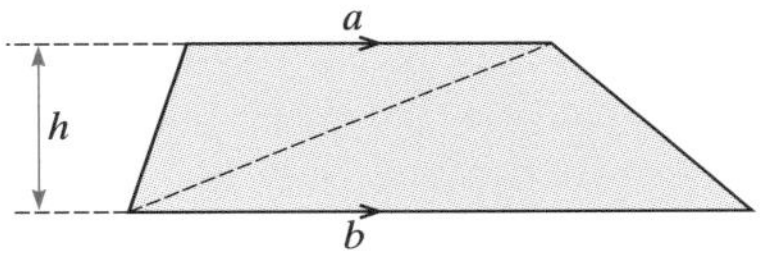

Traversable

A **network** is said to be traversable when it is possible to start at a **node** and trace out the whole network without having to retrace any **arc**.

It is only possible to traverse a network if either (a) all its nodes are of even order, in which case it can be traversed from any point, finishing the traverse at the same point, or (b) just two of its nodes are of odd order, in which case the traverse must start at one and end at the other. The examples show one of each kind.

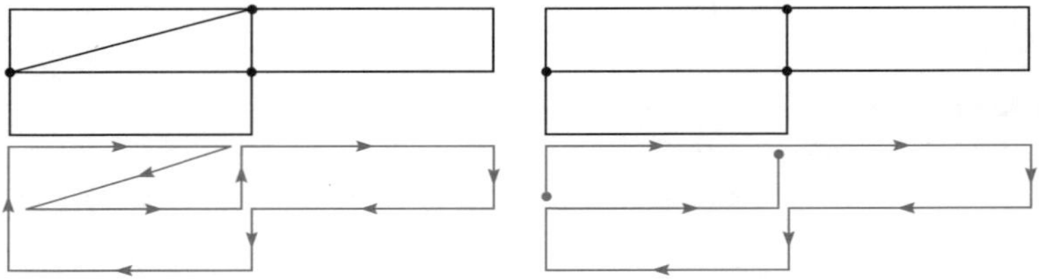

Tree diagram

A tree diagram is a diagram used to represent **probabilities** when two or more **events** are combined. Suppose, for example, a bag contains 3 red balls and 2 black balls. If two balls are drawn from the bag, one after the other, then there are four possible **outcomes**, RR, RB, BR, BB. These can be represented by a tree diagram, as shown, with the probabilities of drawing each ball along the branches.

■ See **Conditional probability**.

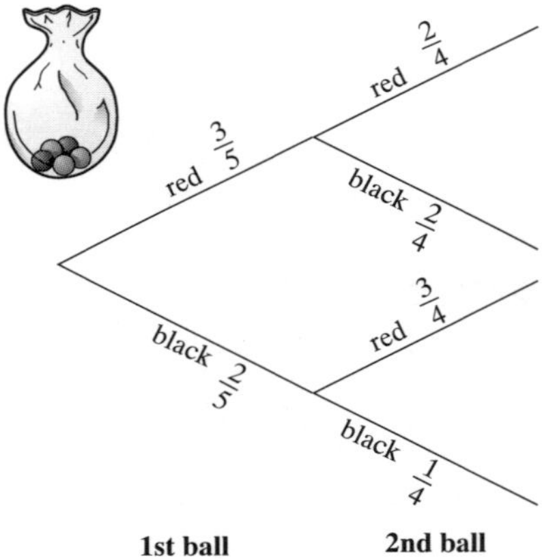

Trial and improvement

This is a method for obtaining a solution to a problem by making a succession of trials based on the results of the previous trials to get nearer to the required result. Suppose, for example, we want to find a number x so that x^2 lies between 29.5 and 30. We know that $5^2 = 25$ and that $6^2 = 36$, so we make a first trial guess of 5.5 and find that $5.5^2 = 30.25$. So 5.5 is too large, suggesting a next trial of 5.4, giving $5.4^2 = 29.16$, which is too small. The third trial is now made between the other two with 5.45, giving $5.45^2 = 29.7025$. This lies between 29.5 and 30 as required so no further trials are needed. If the gap had been 29.5 to 29.6 then further trials would be needed.

Triangle

Tri means three. A triangle is a shape formed from three straight lines, and has three **interior angles**. It is the simplest **polygon**. The sum of the interior angles of a triangle is 180°, $p + q + r = 180$. The **exterior angle** of a triangle is equal to the sum of the two opposite interior angles, $x = p + r$.

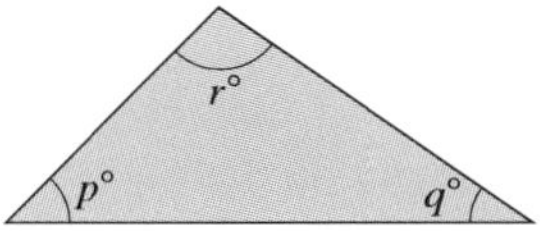

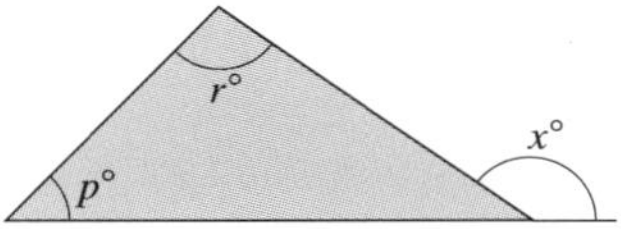

The **area** of a triangle is given by

$$\frac{1}{2} \times \text{length of base} \times \text{height} = \frac{1}{2}bh$$

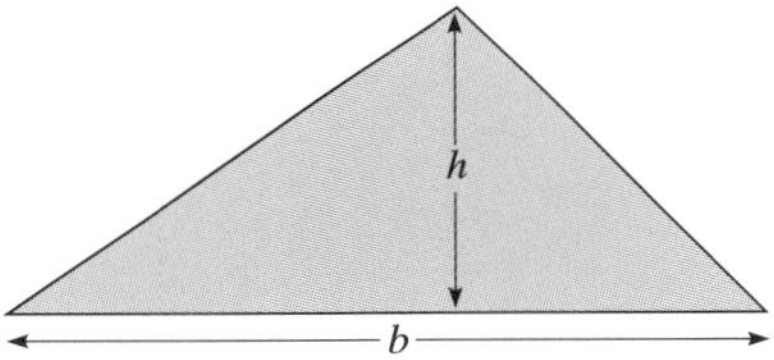

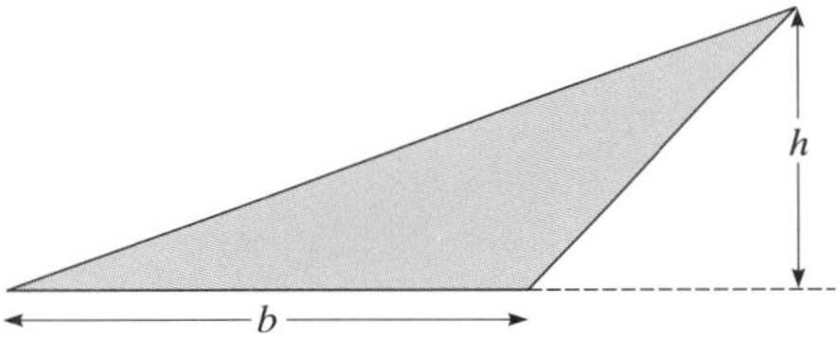

See **Equilateral triangle**, **Isosceles triangle**, **Right-angled triangle** and **Scalene triangle**.

Triangle number

The triangle numbers are the numbers in the **sequence**

$$1,\ 3,\ 6,\ 10,\ 15,\ 21,\ 28,\ 36,\ \ldots,\ \frac{1}{2}n(n+1),\ \ldots$$

where n is any whole number, and are so called because they correspond to the numbers of dots required to build shapes as shown.

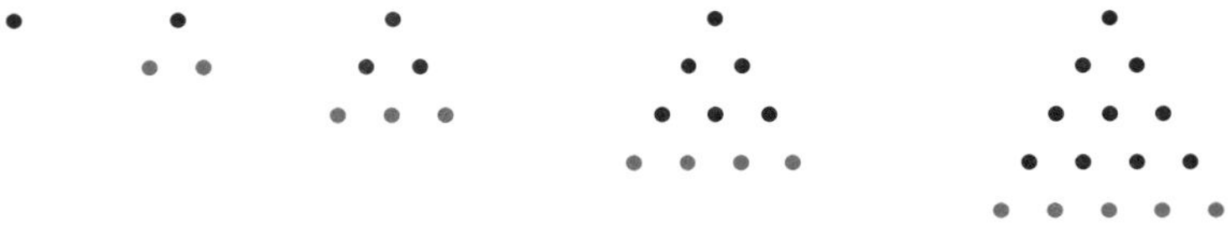

It can be seen that each new triangle is formed from the previous triangle by adding a new base with one more dot than the previous base. Each triangle number is the sum of consecutive whole numbers; for example, the fifth number is

$$1 + 2 + 3 + 4 + 5 = 15$$

Trigonometry

This is the branch of mathematics used in surveying and navigation, and in all applications of mathematics concerned with the relationships between the lengths of the sides of **triangles** and their **angles**, and in the analysis of wave motion. It makes use of **sines**, **cosines** and **tangents** and of **Pythagoras' theorem**.

Truncate (in calculation)

Electronic calculators carry out the calculations asked of them to a higher degree of **accuracy** than they give in their display. Some calculators round their answer to the number of places available in the display, while others just ignore the **digits** at the end when the display is full without **rounding**. This process of cutting off the tail is called *truncating*.

Try dividing 2 by 3 using your calculator. If the last figure in the display is 7 then it is rounding the answer, if it is 6 then it is truncating.

Truncated shape

A solid shape such as a **cone** or a **pyramid** which has had its top cut off is said to be truncated. For example, lampshades and fireworks are often to be seen in the shape of truncated cones.

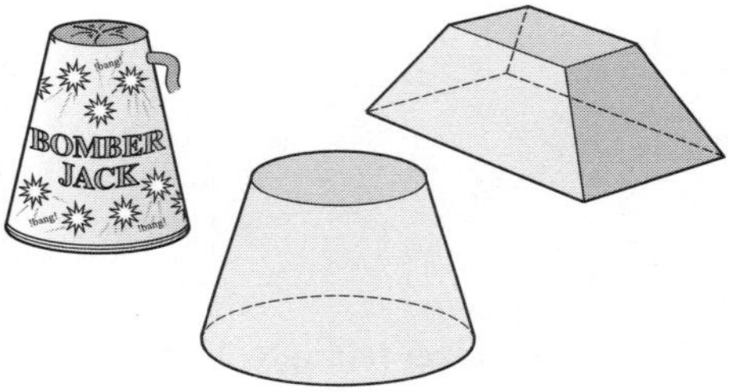

Two-way tables (networks)

The distances between towns on a road **network** can be put into a tabular form as shown. Such tables are known as two-way tables and can be stored in a computer to be used in solving problems about journeys around the network.

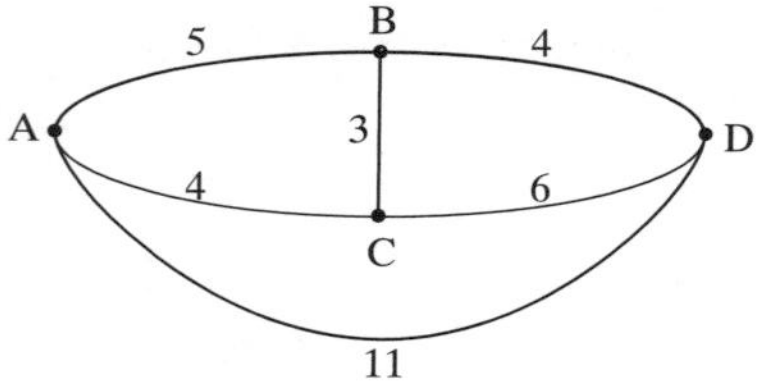

from \ to	A	B	C	D
A	0	5	4	11
B	5	0	3	4
C	4	3	0	6
D	11	4	6	0

Unicursal

A curve that can be traced out without removing a pencil from the paper, and which ends where it starts, is called unicursal. It must not retrace any part of itself but it can cross over itself. Such curves are always **traversable**.

It is always possible to colour the **regions** formed by a unicursal curve using two colours so that no two regions have the same colour if they have the same boundary.

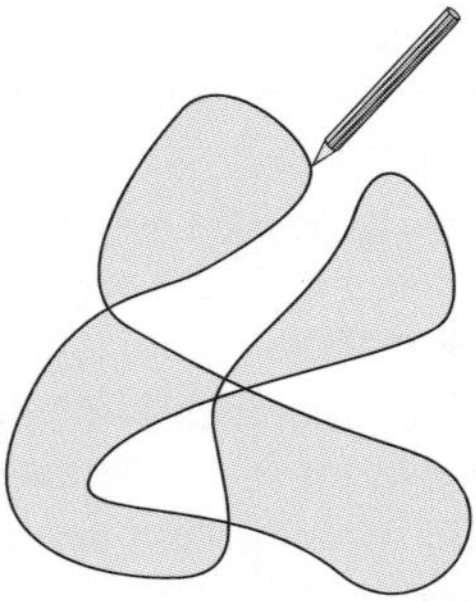

Union of sets

The union of two **sets** A and B, written A∪B, is the set consisting of the elements in A or in B or in both A and B. For example, if

A = {2, 3, 5, 7, 11} and B = {2, 5, 8, 11, 14}

then

A∪B = {2, 3, 5, 7, 8, 11, 14}

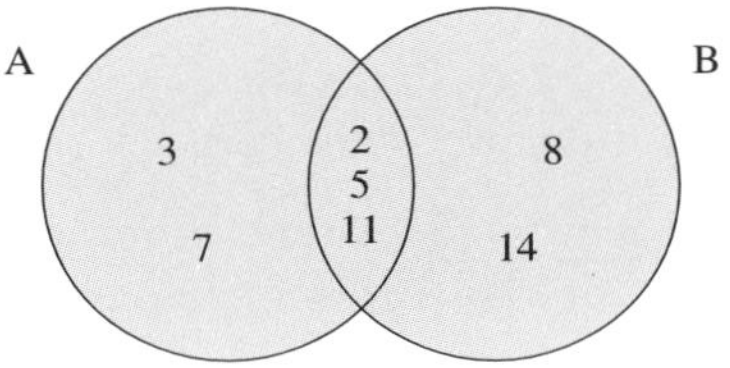

■ See **Intersection of sets**.

Unitary method

This is a method of carrying out a calculation to find the value of a number of items by first finding the cost of one of them. For example, suppose that 3 tennis balls cost £5.52 and we need to find the cost of 5 tennis balls. We can first find the cost of 1 ball as £5.52 ÷ 3 = £1.84, then of the 5 balls by £1.84 x 5 = £9.20.

The same approach can be used to find how far a train will travel in 25 minutes if in 8 minutes it covers 11.2 miles, assuming it travels at the same speed. In 1 minute the train travels 11.2 ÷ 8 = 1.4 miles, so in 25 minutes it will travel 1.4 x 25 = 35 miles.

Unitary ratio

Any **ratio** of the form $m : n$ can be put in the form $1 : k$ by dividing through by m. For example,

3 : 15 on division by 3 equals 1 : 5,

2 : 7 on division by 2 equals 1 : 3.5.

Ratios in the form $1 : k$ are called unitary.

Units of measurement

Each system of measures is based on a basic unit from which the others are formed as simple fractions or multiples. For example, the basic unit of length in the metric system is the **metre**, and this is divided into 100 equal parts to give a **centimetre** or 1000 equal parts to give a **millimetre**, while 1000 metres forms the large unit of a **kilometre**. Mass is measured in multiples of a **gram** and time in multiples of a **second**.

■ See **Imperial units** and **Metric units**.

Universal set

In a given situation the set of all the elements being considered is called the universal set and given the symbol ℰ. For example, various subsets of the pupils in a class may be looked at, such as
A = {pupils who play chess},
B = {pupils who cycle to school}.
In this case the universal set is the set of pupils in the class.

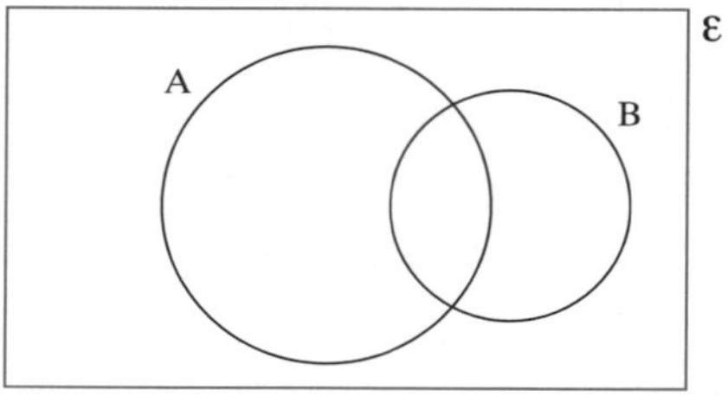

In a **Venn diagram** the universal set is usually drawn as a rectangle.

Variable

Algebraic **expressions** and **formulae**, such as $y = x^2$, $a^2 + b^2 = c^2$ and $v = u + at$, contain letters which can stand for many different numbers. These letters are the variables.

■ See **Constant**, **Dependent variable**, and **Independent variable**.

Varies directly as

When two **variables** such as x and y are related by an **equation** of the form $y = kx$, where k is a **constant**, then y varies directly as x.

For example, when a golf ball is dropped from a height x onto a hard surface it will bounce to a height y where $y = kx$. This shows on a **graph** as a straight line through the origin.

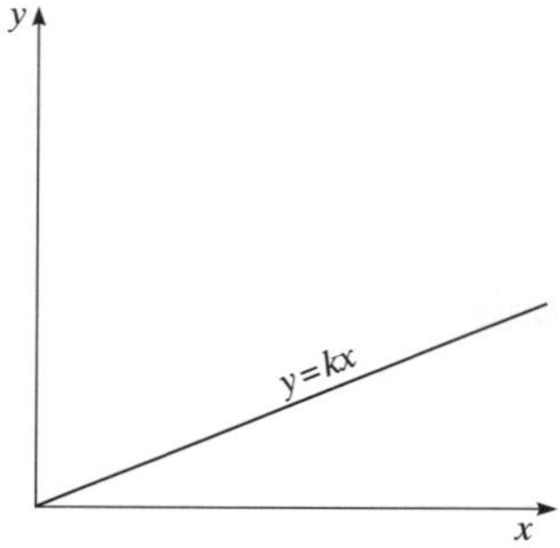

■ See **Direct proportion** and **Linear relation**.

Varies inversely as

When two **variables** x and y are related by an **equation** of the form $y = \frac{k}{x}$, where k is a **constant**,
then y varies inversely as x.

For example, the pressure P of a gas at constant temperature varies inversely as its volume V.

$$P = \frac{k}{V}$$

The **graph** of P plotted against V will be a **hyperbola**.

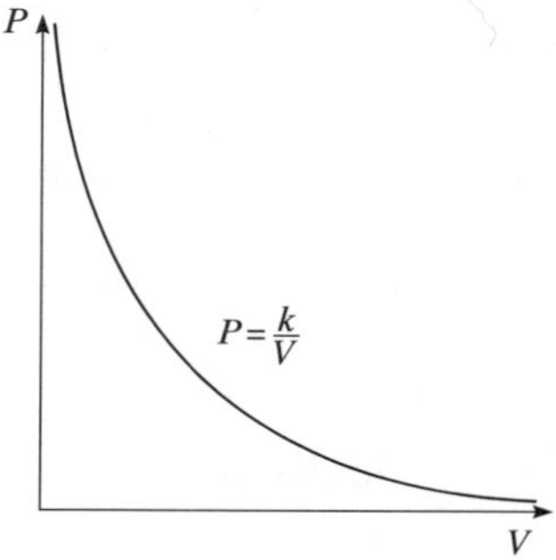

■ See **Inverse proportion**.

Vector

Ordered sets of numbers which can be added by adding the numbers in corresponding positions, and which can be multiplied by a **constant**, are known as vectors. For example, if

$$\mathbf{a} = \begin{pmatrix} 1 \\ 3 \\ 5 \end{pmatrix} \quad \text{and} \quad \mathbf{b} = \begin{pmatrix} 2 \\ -1 \\ 4 \end{pmatrix} \quad \text{then} \quad \mathbf{a} + \mathbf{b} = \begin{pmatrix} 3 \\ 2 \\ 9 \end{pmatrix} \quad \text{and} \quad 4\mathbf{a} = \begin{pmatrix} 4 \\ 12 \\ 20 \end{pmatrix}$$

In print, vectors are usually labelled with letters in **bold** type as shown, but when writing it is usual to put a squiggle under any letter representing a vector, such as $\underset{\sim}{a}$ and $\underset{\sim}{b}$. The number of elements in a vector corresponds to the dimension of its space, so the examples shown are 3-dimensional.

Vectors can be used to represent changes of position and **translations**. In the diagram, the **triangle** ABC has been translated to triangle A′B′C′. Each point of the triangle has been displaced 3 units to the right and 1 unit up, so its **displacement** is given by the vector $\begin{pmatrix} 3 \\ 1 \end{pmatrix}$. An arrow such as PP′ is often used on a diagram to represent the displacement vector.

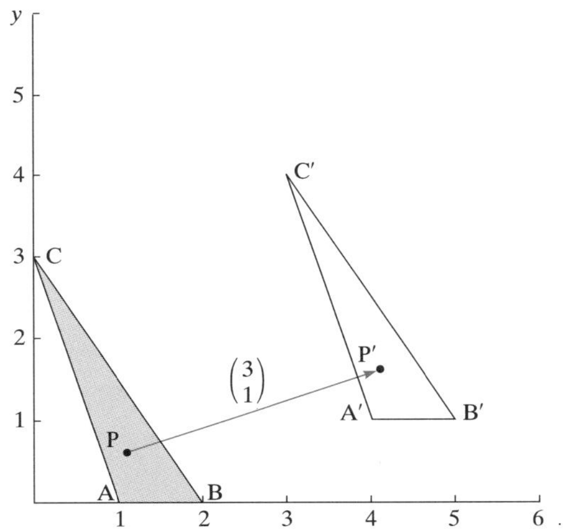

If two displacement vectors **u** and **v** are connected by a relation $\mathbf{v} = k\mathbf{u}$ where k is a constant, then **v** and **u** represent parallel vectors. For example,

$$\mathbf{u} = \begin{pmatrix} 1 \\ 2 \end{pmatrix} \quad \text{and} \quad \mathbf{v} = \begin{pmatrix} 3 \\ 6 \end{pmatrix} = 3\begin{pmatrix} 1 \\ 2 \end{pmatrix}$$

Quantities such as **acceleration**, **velocity**, force, displacement and momentum, which have direction as well as **magnitude** and can be combined by **vector addition**, are called vector quantities. In contrast, quantities such as distance, energy and speed, which have magnitude but no direction, are called **scalar** quantities.

■ See **Acceleration**, **Displacement**, **Distance**, **Speed**, **Velocity**, and **Scalar**.

Vector addition

Two **vectors** are added by adding their corresponding components. For example,

$$\begin{pmatrix}1\\2\end{pmatrix} + \begin{pmatrix}4\\1\end{pmatrix} = \begin{pmatrix}5\\3\end{pmatrix}$$

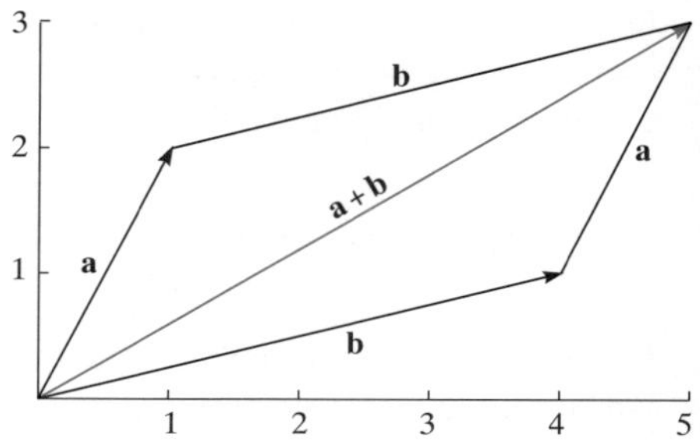

When these vectors are represented geometrically as the **displacements** **a** and **b** (see the diagram), their addition is equivalent to following one displacement by the other, and can be represented by arrows as shown. The diagram also shows that the **operation** of vector addition is **commutative**, since **a** + **b** = **b** + **a**

Velocity

The velocity of an object is the rate at which it changes its position with time. It is a **vector** quantity and defined by an object's direction of travel as well as its **speed**. For example, the velocity of a plane may be given as 560 mph on a **bearing** of 068°.

Venn diagram

A Venn diagram is a diagram where **regions** are used to represent the relation between two or more **sets**. In the example shown, the region inside the rectangle represents the letters of the alphabet, the region inside the red circle contains the vowels, and the region inside the black circle contains the letters with two lines of symmetry. The region common to the two circles then contains the vowels with two lines of symmetry.

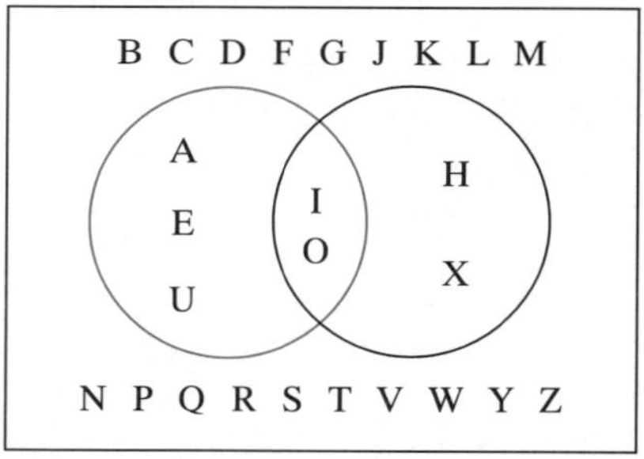

Venn diagrams are named after John Venn (1834 -1923), a Cambridge mathematician.

See **Intersection of sets** and **Union of sets**.

Vertex (*pl.* vertices)

A vertex of a shape is one of its corners. In a **polygon** a vertex is the point where two sides meet, while in a **polyhedron** it is a point where three or more **faces** or **edges** meet. The pointed end of a **cone** is also called its vertex.

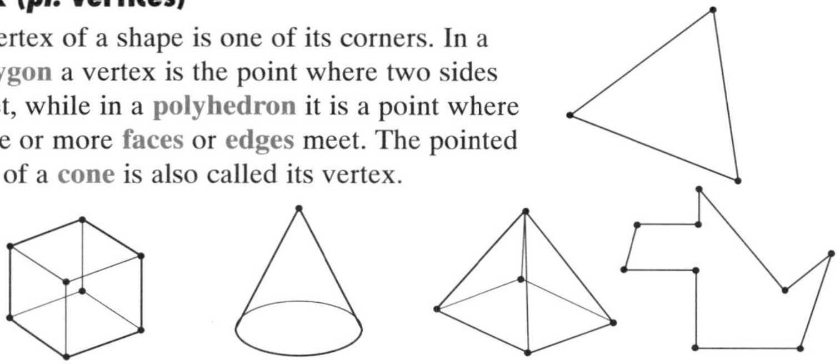

Vertical

The vertical direction is the direction in which an object would fall if dropped. It corresponds to the direction of gravity. When putting up wallpaper decorators use a ball of lead on the end of a string, known as a plumb line, to make sure the wallpaper is hung vertically.

■ See **Horizontal**.

Vertically opposite angles

When two lines cross, the pairs of **angles** which are opposite to each other are called vertically opposite and are equal. It has nothing to do with being **vertical**!

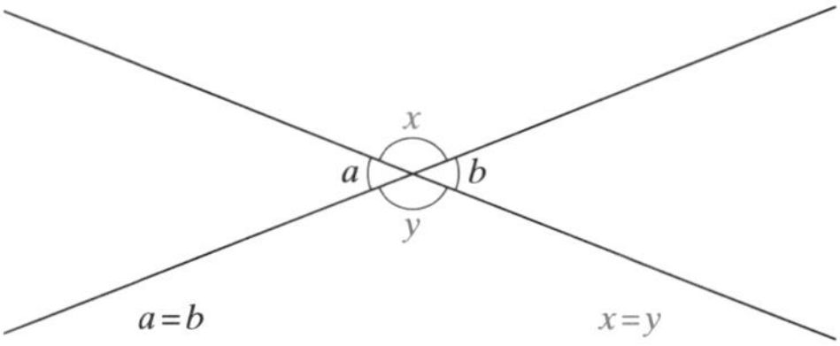

Volume

The volume of a solid shape is the amount of space that it occupies. It is measured by the number of unit **cubes** needed to fill the space. For example, a **cuboid** measuring 5 cm by 3 cm by 3 cm can be filled by 45 unit cubes (there are 3 layers each with 5 x 3 = 15 cubes). Each unit cube has a volume of one **cubic centimetre** so the cuboid has a volume of 45 cm^3.

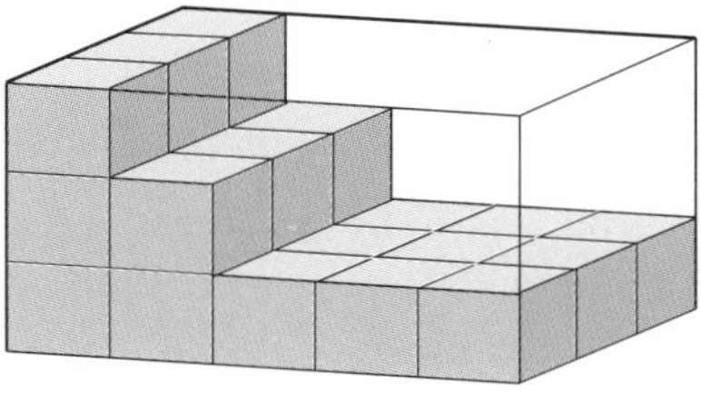

→

In general, the volume V of a cuboid is given by

$$V = l \times b \times h$$

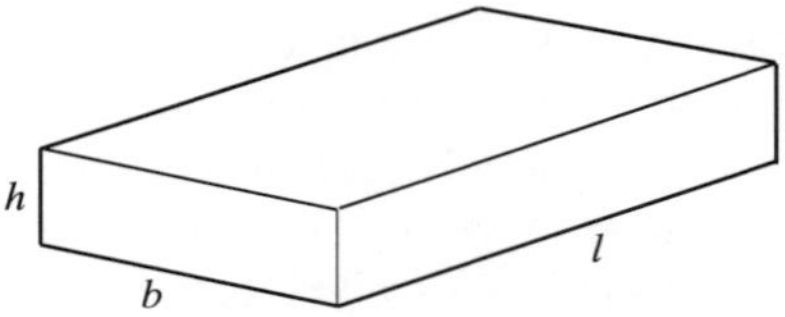

For example, a matchbox measuring 5 cm by 3.5 cm by 1.7 cm has a volume of

$$5 \times 3.5 \times 1.7 = 29.75 \text{ cm}^3$$

Larger volumes are measured using cubes with an edge of one **metre** and a volume of one cubic metre (1 m^3). A garage for a car, for example, might measure 6 m by 3 m by 2.5 m, and have a volume of 45 m^3, while the pyramid of Cheops is estimated to have a volume of 2 500 000 m^3.

The volume V of a **prism** is given by the formula

$$V = A \times h$$

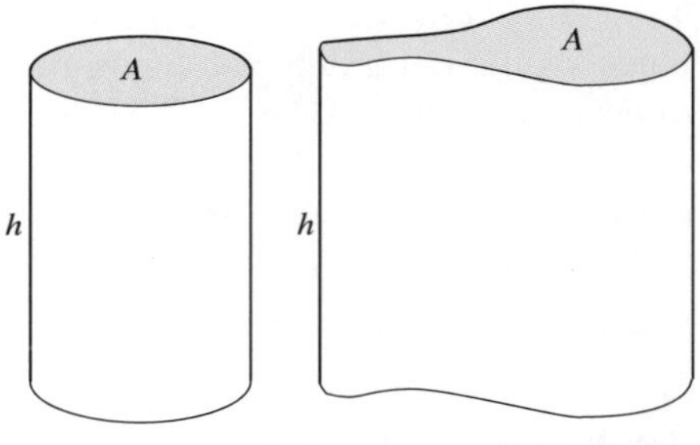

where A is the area of its **cross-section** and h is its height. In particular, for a **cylinder** of **radius** r,

$$V = \pi r^2 \times h$$

The volume of a **pyramid** or a **cone** is given by

$$V = \tfrac{1}{3} \times A \times h$$

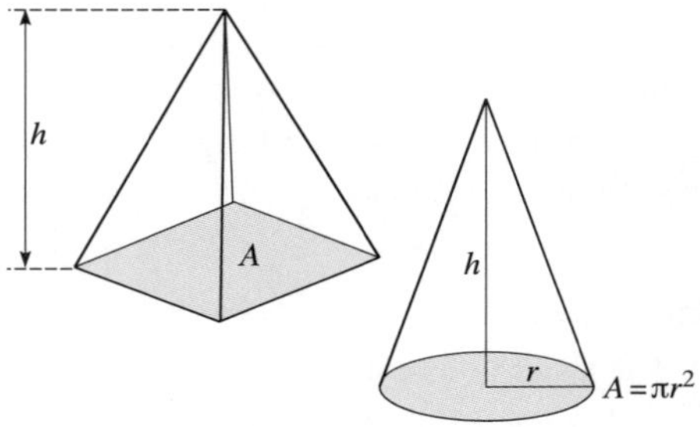

where A is the area of the **base** and h is its height. So for a cone whose base radius is r

$$V = \tfrac{1}{3} \times \pi r^2 \times h$$

The volume of a **sphere** of radius r is given by

$$V = \tfrac{4}{3} \times \pi \times r^3$$

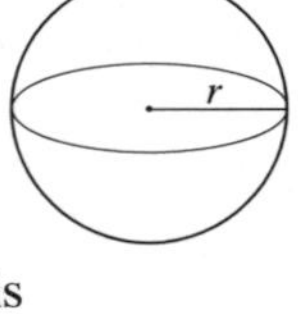

For example, the volume of a ball of radius 12 cm is

$$\tfrac{4}{3} \times \pi \times 12^3 \approx 7238 \text{ cm}^3$$

Volume scale factor

When the linear dimensions of a three-dimensional shape are all changed by a **scale factor** k (i.e. multiplied by k), its **volume** is changed by a scale factor of k^3 (i.e. multiplied by k^3). For example, the effect of doubling or trebling the edges of a **cube** is to increase its volume by factors of $2^3 = 8$ or $3^3 = 27$.

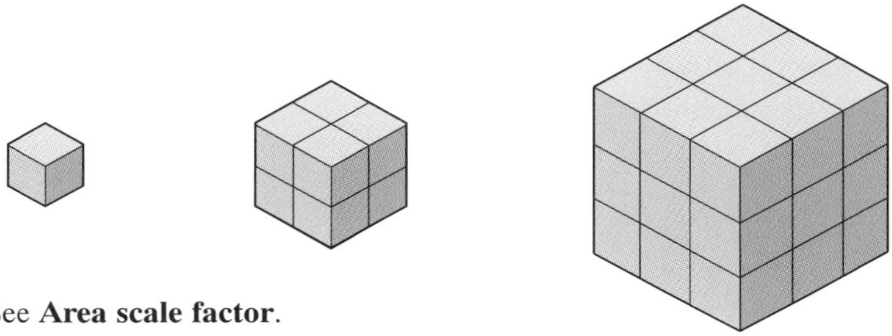

See **Area scale factor**.

Weight

The weight of an object is the force of gravity on the object. This can differ from place to place. The same object on the moon's surface would weigh only one-sixth of its weight on the Earth, while in an orbiting satellite it would be 'weightless'.

See **Mass**.

Whole number

The set of whole numbers is the set of **counting numbers**:

1, 2, 3, 4, 5, 6, …

Yard (*abbreviation* yd)

This is an **imperial unit** of length which approximates to the length of a walking pace. It is also approximately the distance from the tip of your nose to the tip of your fingers when your arm is stretched out to the side. The distance between the wickets of a cricket pitch is 22 yards, which corresponds to the length of the chain traditionally used by surveyors.

1 yard = 3 **feet** = 36 **inches** ≈ 0.9144 **metres**

1 **mile** = 1760 yards

Zero

Zero is symbolised by 0 and has several meanings:

- It is the starting point for many scales, such as temperature in **degrees** Celsius, where it corresponds to the freezing point of water.
- It is a place holder in our number system enabling us, for example, to distinguish between 4, 40, and 0.0004.
- It is the name given to the **identity element** under addition for numbers, **vectors** and **matrices**, for example:

$$5 + 0 = 5$$

$$\begin{pmatrix} 3 \\ 1 \end{pmatrix} + \begin{pmatrix} 0 \\ 0 \end{pmatrix} = \begin{pmatrix} 3 \\ 1 \end{pmatrix}$$

zero vector

$$\begin{pmatrix} 1 & 3 \\ 5 & 2 \end{pmatrix} + \begin{pmatrix} 0 & 0 \\ 0 & 0 \end{pmatrix} = \begin{pmatrix} 1 & 3 \\ 5 & 2 \end{pmatrix}$$

zero matrix